Vergil

Aeneid Book 2

The Focus Vergil Aeneid Commentaries

For intermediate students
>   *Aeneid 1* • *Randall Ganiban, general editor • Available now*
>   *Aeneid 2* • *Randall Ganiban, general editor • Available now*
>   *Aeneid 3* • *Christine Perkell, editor • Available now*
>   *Aeneid 4* • *James O'Hara, editor • Available now*
>   *Aeneid 5* • *Joseph Farrell, editor • Available now*
>   *Aeneid 6* • *Patricia Johnston, editor • Available now*

For advanced students
>   *Aeneid 1–6* • *Randall Ganiban, general editor; Christine Perkell, James O'Hara, Joseph Farrell, Patricia A. Johnston, editors • Available now*
>   *Aeneid 7–12* • *In preparation*
>   *Contributors:*
>   *Randall Ganiban, co-general editor • Aeneid 7*
>   *James O'Hara, co-general editor • Aeneid 8*
>   *Joseph Farrell, editor • Aeneid 9*
>   *Andreola Rossi, editor • Aeneid 10*
>   *Charles McNelis, editor • Aeneid 11*
>   *Christine Perkell, editor • Aeneid 12*

VERGIL

Aeneid Book 2

Randall T. Ganiban
Middlebury College

focus an imprint of
Hackett Publishing Company, Inc.
Indianapolis/Cambridge

Vergil Aeneid 2
© 2008 Randall T. Ganiban

Previously published by Focus Publishing / R. Pullins Company

Focus an imprint of
Hackett Publishing Company, Inc.
P.O. Box 44937
Indianapolis, Indiana 46244-0937

www.hackettpublishing.com

Interior illustration by Sam Kimball
ISBN: 978-1-58510-226-6

The paper used in this publication meets the minimum requirements of American National Standard for Information Sciences—Permanence of Paper for Printed Library Materials, ANSI Z39.48–1984.

Table of Contents

For Claire

Preface

Aeneid 2 tells the tragic story of Troy's fall and is one of the most powerful books of the entire epic. This volume is an introductory commentary on *Aeneid* 2 for use at the intermediate level or higher. It provides a generous amount of basic information about grammar and syntax so that students of varying experience will have what they need to translate the Latin. At the same time, it addresses issues of interpretation and style so that students at all levels will have a richer experience of the poem. Finally, it includes extensive bibliographic notes that will help readers pursue areas of special interest.

This commentary takes as its starting point the valuable school edition of *Aeneid* 2 by T. E. Page (1889), reprinted without vocabulary in his *Virgil: Aeneid* 1-6 (1894). Page's commentary notes have been pared down, and new and updated material has been included throughout. In addition, the general introduction, appendices on meter and style, and an index of grammatical, stylistic, and metrical items are all new. In adapting Page's vocabulary, I have altered some definitions, and have made various changes in formatting and the presentation of word listings. I have also consulted a wide range of commentaries on the *Aeneid*; those by Conington, Austin, and Williams have been particularly helpful.

The Latin text of *Aeneid* 2 used here is that of F. A. Hirtzel (Oxford, 1900) with several changes in punctuation and with the following differences in readings: 69 *nunc* for *me*, 349 *audentem* for *audendi*, 392 *Androgei* for *Androgeo*, 503 *tanta* for *ampla*, 616 *nimbo* for *limbo*, and 771 *furenti* for *ruenti*.

It is with pleasure that I offer thanks to a number of people who have read various portions of this edition and have given insightful advice: Antony Augoustakis and Elaine Fantham; the anonymous readers from Focus Publishing; my colleagues in the Classics Department at Middlebury College (Jane Chaplin, Pavlos Sfyroeras, Chris Star, and Marc Witkin); my collaborators on a larger *Aeneid* 1-6 commentary project for Focus (Joe Farrell, Pat Johnston, Jim O'Hara, and Christine Perkell); my intermediate Latin students in 2003 and 2007, who tested the commentary and gave me valuable feedback; several student research assistants (Matt Friend, Caroline Gersh, Sarah Miller, and Rebecca Scholtz), who helped in various ways with this project and others and whose work was generously funded by Middlebury College; and Elizabeth Ennen, who has provided helpful counsel and constant support. Whatever flaws or errors remain are mine alone.

Finally, I would like to thank all the people at Focus Publishing. It was Ron Pullins' idea to create new *Aeneid* commentaries by using Page's editions, and he was kind enough to give me the opportunity to contribute this volume. Throughout the process he has been unceasingly generous, supportive, and patient.

Randall T. Ganiban
Middlebury College

Introduction

Vergil's lifetime and poetry

Publius Vergilius Maro (i.e. Vergil)[1] was born on October 15, 70 BCE near the town of Mantua (modern Mantova) in what was then still Cisalpine Gaul.[2] Little else about his life can be stated with certainty, because our main source, the ancient biography by the grammarian Donatus (fourth century CE),[3] is of questionable value.[4] The historical and political background to Vergil's life, by contrast, is amply documented and provides a useful framework for understanding his career. Indeed, his poetic development displays an increasing engagement with the politics of contemporary Rome, an engagement that culminates in the *Aeneid*.

Vergil lived and wrote in a time of political strife and uncertainty. In his early twenties the Roman Republic was torn apart by the civil wars of 49-45 BCE, when Julius Caesar fought and defeated Pompey and his supporters. Caesar was declared *dictator perpetuo* ("Dictator for Life") early in 44 BCE but was assassinated by a group of senators led by Brutus[5] and Cassius on the Ides of March in the same year. They sought to restore the Republic, which, they believed, was being destroyed by Caesar's domination and intimations of monarchy.[6]

---

1   The spelling "Virgil" (*Virgilius*) is also used by convention. It developed early and has been explained by its similarity to two words: *virgo* ("maiden") and *virga* ("wand"). For discussion of the origins and potential meanings of these connections, see Jackson Knight (1944): 36-7 and Putnam (1993): 127-8 with notes.

2   Cisalpine Gaul, the northern part of what we now think of as Italy, was incorporated into Roman Italy in 42 BCE. Mantua is located ca. 520 kilometers north of Rome.

3   This biography drew heavily from the *De poetis* of Suetonius (born ca. 70 CE).

4   Horsfall (1995: 1-25; 2006: xxii-xxiv) argues that nearly every detail is unreliable.

5   Kingship was hateful to the Romans ever since Brutus' own ancestor, Lucius Junius Brutus, led the expulsion of Rome's last king, Tarquin the Proud, in ca. 509 BCE, an act that ended the regal period of Rome and initiated the Republic (cf. *Aeneid* 6.817-18). In killing Caesar, Brutus claimed that he was following the example of his great ancestor—an important concept for the Romans.

6   For the reasons behind Caesar's assassination and the fall of the Republic, see the brief accounts in Scullard (1982): 126-53 and Shotter (2005): 4-19.

The assassination initiated a new round of turmoil and altered the course of Roman history. In his will, Caesar adopted and named as his primary heir his great-nephew Octavian (63 BCE-14 CE), the man who would later be called "Augustus."[7] Only eighteen years old, Octavian boldly accepted and used this inheritance. Through a combination of shrewd calculation and luck, he managed to attain the consulship in 43 BCE, though he was merely nineteen years of age.[8] He then joined forces with Marc Antony and Lepidus, two of Caesar's lieutenants; together they demanded recognition as a Board of Three (*triumviri* or "triumvirs"). They sought to reconstitute the state and were granted extraordinary powers to do so by the Roman senate and people. In 42 BCE they avenged Caesar's murder by defeating his assassins led by Brutus and Cassius at the battle of Philippi in Macedonia, but their alliance gradually began to deteriorate as a result of further civil strife and interpersonal rivalries.

Vergil composed the *Eclogues*, his first major work, during this tumultuous period.[9] Published ca. 39 (or ca. 35) BCE,[10] the *Eclogues* comprise a sophisticated collection of ten pastoral poems that treat the experiences of shepherds.[11] The poems were modeled on the *Idylls* of Theocritus, a Hellenistic Greek poet of the third century BCE (see below). But whereas Theocritus' poetry created a world that was largely timeless, Vergil sets his pastoral world against the backdrop of contemporary Rome and of the disruption caused by the civil wars. *Eclogues* 1 and 9, for example, deal with the differing fortunes of shepherds during a time of land confiscations that resonate with historical events in 41-40 BCE.[12] *Eclogue* 4 describes the birth

---

7   See below.

8   By the *lex Villia annalis* of 180 BCE, a consul had to be at least forty-two years of age.

9   Other works have been attributed to Vergil: *Aetna, Catalepton, Ciris, Copa, Culex, Dirae, Elegiae in Maecenatem, Moretum,* and *Priapea.* They are collected in what is called the *Appendix Vergiliana* and are generally believed to be spurious.

10   The traditional dating is ca. 39 BCE, but it has been called into question through re-evaluation of *Eclogue* 8, which may very well refer to events in 35 BCE. See Clausen (1994): 232-7.

11   Coleman (1977) and Clausen (1994) are excellent commentaries on the *Eclogues.* For a discussion of the pastoral genre at Rome, see Heyworth (2005). For general interpretation of the *Eclogues,* see Hardie (1998): 5-27 with extensive bibliography in the notes.

12   Octavian rewarded veterans with land that was already occupied.

of a child during the consulship of Asinius Pollio (40 BCE) who will bring a
new golden age to Rome.[13] By interjecting the Roman world into his poetic
landscape,[14] Vergil creates an important, though ultimately unresolved tension whereby political developments both threaten and give promise to the
very possibility of pastoral existence.

The *Eclogues* established Vergil as a new and important poetic voice, and
led him to the cultural circle of the great literary patron Maecenas, an influential supporter and confidant of Octavian. Their association grew throughout
the 30s.[15] The political situation, however, remained precarious. Lepidus was
ousted from the triumvirate in 36 BCE because of his treacherous behavior.
Tensions between Octavian and Antony that were simmering over Antony's
collaboration and affair with the Egyptian queen Cleopatra eventually ex-
ploded.[16] In 32 BCE war was declared against Cleopatra, and Octavian had
Antony's powers revoked. In September of 31 BCE, the two men met in a na-
val confrontation off Actium on the coast of western Greece. Octavian's fleet
decisively routed the forces of Marc Antony and Cleopatra, who fled to Egypt
and committed suicide in the following year.[17] From Octavian's perspective,

---

13   This is sometimes called the "Messianic Eclogue" because later ages read it as
      foreseeing the birth of Christ, who came nearly four decades later. The identity
      of the child is debated, but the poem may celebrate the marriage between Marc
      Antony and Octavian's sister Octavia that resulted from the Treaty of Brundisium
      in 40 BCE; this union staved off the immediate outbreak of war between the two
      triumvirs. For more on this poem, see Van Sickle (1992) and Petrini (1997): 111-21,
      as well as the commentaries by Coleman (1977) and Clausen (1994).

14   In addition to the contemporary themes that Vergil treats, he also mentions or
      dedicates individual poems to a number of his contemporaries, including Asinius
      Pollio, Alfenus Varus, Cornelius Gallus, and probably Octavian, who is likely the
      iuvenis ("young man") mentioned at 1.42 and perhaps also the patron addressed at
      8.6-13.

15   For the relationship between Augustus and the poets, see White (2005). White
      (1993) is a book-length study of this topic. For an overview of literature of the
      Augustan period from 40 BCE-14 CE, see Farrell (2005).

16   In addition to the political conflicts, there were also familial tensions: Antony
      conducted a nearly decade-long affair with Cleopatra, even though he had married
      Octavia, Octavian's (Augustus') sister, as a result of the treaty of Brundisium in 40
      BCE (see n. 13 above). Antony divorced Octavia in 32 BCE.

17   For the history of the triumviral period, see the brief accounts in Scullard (1982):
      154-71 and Shotter (2005): 20-7; for more detailed treatments, see Syme (1939): 187-
      312 and Pelling (1996). For discussion of the contemporary artistic representations
      of Actium, see Gurval (1995).

this victory marked him as the protector of traditional Roman values against the detrimental influence of Antony, Cleopatra, and the East. [18]

Vergil began his next work sometime in the 30s and completed it in the aftermath of Actium. Published ca. 29 BCE and dedicated to Maecenas, the *Georgics* is a rich and allusive poem. On the surface, it purports to be a poetic farming guide.[19] Each of its four books examines a different aspect or sphere of agricultural life: crops and weather signs (book 1), trees and vines (book 2), livestock (book 3), and bees (book 4). Its actual scope, however, is much more ambitious. The poem explores the nature of humankind's struggle with the beauty and difficulties of the agricultural world, but it does so within the context of contemporary war-torn Italy. It bears witness to the strife following Caesar's assassination, and sets the chaos and disorder inherent in nature against the upheaval caused by civil war (1.461-514). Moreover, Octavian's success and victories are commemorated both in the introduction (1.24-42) and conclusion (4.559-62) of the poem, as well as in the introduction to the third book (3.1-39). Thus once again, the political world impinges upon Vergil's poetic landscape, but the relationship between the two is not fully addressed.[20]

Octavian's victory at Actium represented a turning point for Rome's development. Over the next decade, he centralized political and military control in his hands. He claimed to have returned the state (*res publica*) to the senate and Roman people in 27 BCE.[21] His powers were redefined, and he was granted the name "Augustus" ("Revered One") by the senate. It is true that he maintained many traditional Republican institutions, but in reality he was transforming the state into a monarchy. So successful was his stabilization and control of Rome after decades of civil war that he reigned

---

18   This ideological interpretation is suggested in Vergil's depiction of the battle on Aeneas' shield (8.671-713).

19   Recent commentaries on the *Georgics* include Thomas (1988) and Mynors (1990). For interpretation, see the introduction to the *Georgics* in Hardie (1998): 28-52 with extensive bibliography in the notes. Individual studies include Wilkinson (1969), Putnam (1979), Johnston (1980), Ross (1987), Perkell (1989), and Nappa (2005). For allusion in the *Georgics*, see Thomas (1986), Farrell (1991), and Gale (2000).

20   The overall meaning of the *Georgics* is contested. Interpretation of the *Georgics*, like that of the *Aeneid* (see below), has optimistic and pessimistic poles. Otis (1964) is an example of the former; Ross (1987) the latter. Other scholars, such as Perkell (1989), fall in between by discerning inherent ambivalence. For discussion of these interpretive trends, see Hardie (1998): 50-2.

21   Augustus, *Res Gestae* 34.

as *Princeps* ("First Citizen") from 27 BCE to 14 CE, and founded a political framework (the Principate) that served the Roman state for centuries.[22]

Vergil wrote his final poem, the *Aeneid*, largely in the 20s, during the beginning of Augustus' reign, when the Roman people presumably both hoped that the civil wars were behind them and feared that the Augustan peace would not last. The *Aeneid* tells the story of the Trojan hero Aeneas. He fought the Greeks at Troy and saw his city destroyed, but with the guidance of the gods and fate he led his people across the Mediterranean to establish a new homeland in Italy.[23] As in the *Eclogues* and *Georgics*, Vergil interjects his contemporary world into his poetic world. In the *Aeneid*, however, the thematic connections between these two realms are developed still more explicitly, with Aeneas' actions shown to be necessary for and to lead ultimately to the reign of Augustus.

Vergil was still finishing the *Aeneid* when he was stricken by a fatal illness in 19 BCE. The ancient biographical tradition claims that he traveled to Greece, intending to spend three years editing his epic there and in Asia, but that he fell ill in Greece, returned to Italy, and died in Brundisium (in southern Italy) in September of 19 BCE. The *Aeneid* was largely complete but had not yet received its final polish. We are told that Vergil asked that it be burned, but that Augustus ultimately had it published. While such details regarding Vergil's death are doubted, it is clear that the poem still needed final revision.[24] However, its present shape, including its controversial ending, is generally accepted to be as Vergil had planned.

---

22   For general political and historical narratives of Augustus' reign, see the relatively brief account in Shotter (2005); longer more detailed treatments can be found in A. H. M. Jones (1970), Crook (1996), and Southern (1998). A classic and influential book by Syme (1939) paints Augustus in dark colors. For broader considerations of the Augustan age, see the short but interesting volume by Wallace-Hadrill (1993) and the more comprehensive treatments by Galinsky (1996, 2005). For the interaction of art and ideology in the Augustan Age, see Zanker (1988).

23   For general interpretation of the *Aeneid*, see Hardie (1998): 53–101, Perkell (1999), Anderson (2005), and Ross (2007). For the literary and cultural backgrounds, see Martindale (1997), Farrell (2005), and Galinsky (2005).

24   We can be sure that the poem had not received its final revision for a number of reasons, including the presence of roughly fifty-eight incomplete or "half" lines. See commentary note on 2.66.

Vergil and his predecessors

By writing an epic about the Trojan war, Vergil was rivaling Homer, the greatest of all the Greek poets. The *Aeneid* was therefore a bold undertaking, but its success makes it arguably the quintessential Roman work because it accomplishes in an exemplary way what Latin poetry had always striven to do: to appropriate the Greek tradition and transform it into something that was both equally impressive and distinctly "Roman."

Homer's *Iliad* tells the story of the Trojan war by focusing on Achilles' strife with the Greek leader Agamemnon and consequent rage, while the *Odyssey* treats the war's aftermath by relating Odysseus' struggle to return home. These were the earliest and most revered works of Greek literature,[25] and they exerted a defining influence on both the overall framework of the *Aeneid* and the close details of its poetry. In general terms, *Aeneid* 1-6, like the *Odyssey*, describes a hero's return (to a new) home after the Trojan war, while *Aeneid* 7-12, like the *Iliad*, tells the story of a war. But throughout the *Aeneid*, Vergil reworks ideas, language, characters, and scenes from both poems. Some ancient critics faulted Vergil for his use of Homer, calling his appropriations "thefts," but Vergil is said to have responded that it is "easier to steal his club from Hercules than a line from Homer."[26] Indeed, Vergil does much more than simply quote material from Homer. His creative use and transformation of Homeric language and theme are central not only to his artistry but also to the meaning of the *Aeneid*. (See *Structure and major themes of Aeneid 2* below.)

Though Homer is the primary model, Vergil was also greatly influenced by the Hellensitic Greek tradition of poetry that originated in Alexandria, Egypt in the third century BCE. There scholar-poets such as Apollonius, Callimachus, and Theocritus reacted against the earlier literary tradition (particularly epic), and developed a poetic aesthetic that valued sophistication in meter and word order, small-scale treatments over large, the unusual and recherché over the conventional. Hellenistic poetry was introduced into the mainstream of Latin poetry a generation before Vergil by

---

25   These poems were culminations of a centuries-old oral tradition and were written down probably in the eighth century BCE.

26   *...facilius esse Herculi clavam quam Homeri versum subripere* (Donatus/Suetonius, *Life of Vergil* 46).

the so-called "neoterics" or "new poets," of whom Catullus (c. 84-c. 54 BCE) was the most influential for Vergil and for the later literary tradition.[27]

Vergil's earlier works, the *Eclogues* and *Georgics*, had been modeled to a significant extent on Hellenistic poems,[28] so it was perhaps a surprise that Vergil would then have turned to a large-scale epic concerning the Trojan war.[29] However, one of his great feats was the incorporation of Hellenistic and neoteric sensibilities into the *Aeneid*. Two models were particularly important in this regard: the *Argonautica* by Apollonius of Rhodes, an epic retelling the hero Jason's quest for the Golden Fleece,[30] and Catullus 64 on the wedding of Peleus and Thetis. Both poems brought the great and elevated heroes of the past down to the human level, thereby offering new insights into their strengths, passions and flaws, and both greatly influenced Vergil's presentation of Aeneas.

Vergil looked back to many other predecessors in both Greek and Latin literature. In Latin epic, the most important was Ennius (239-169 BCE), often called the father of Roman poetry.[31] His *Annales*, which survives only in fragments, was an historical epic about Rome that traced the city's origins back to Aeneas and Troy. It remained the most influential Latin poem until the *Aeneid* was composed, and provided a model not only for Vergil's poetic language and themes, but also for his integration of Homer and Roman history. In addition, the *De Rerum Natura* of Lucretius (ca. 94-55/51 BCE), a hexameter poem on Epicurean philosophy, was also a crucial model. Though not a narrative poet, Lucretius, through his refinement of

---

27   Cf. Clausen (1987, 2002), George (1974), Briggs (1981), and Thomas (1988, 1999) display these influences, while O'Hara (1996) provides a thorough examination of wordplay (important to the Alexandrian poets) in Vergil.

28   The *Eclogues* were modeled on Theocritus' *Idylls* (see above); the *Georgics* had numerous models, though the Hellenistic poets Callimachus, Nicander, and Aratus were particularly important influences.

29   For example, at *Eclogue* 6.3-5, Vergil explains in highly programmatic language his decision to compose poetry in the refined Callimachean or Hellenistic manner rather than traditional epic. See Clausen (1994): 174-5.

30   On the influence of Apollonius on Vergil, see the important book by Nelis (2001).

31   Ennius introduced the dactylic hexameter as the meter of Latin epic. Two earlier epic writers were Livius Andronicus who composed a translation of Homer's *Odyssey* into Latin, and Naevius who composed the *Bellum Punicum*, an epic on the First Punic War. Both Naevius and Livius wrote their epics in a meter called Saturnian that is not fully understood. For the influence of the early Latin poets on the *Aeneid*, see Wigodsky (1972).

the Latin hexameter and of Latin poetic style, had a significant impact on Vergil, who engages Lucretian ideas at various points in the *Aeneid*.[32]

Finally, Vergil drew much from Greek and Roman[33] tragedy. Many episodes in the *Aeneid* share tragedy's well-known dramatic patterns (such as reversal of fortune), and explore the suffering that befalls mortals often as a result of the immense and incomprehensible power of the gods and fate.[34] As a recent critic has written, "The influence of tragedy on the *Aeneid* is pervasive, and arguably the single most important factor in Vergil's successful revitalization of the genre of epic."[35]

The *Aeneid* is thus a highly literary work. By considering its interactions with these and other models, or, to put it another way, by examining Vergil's use of "allusion" or "intertextuality,"[36] we can enrich both our experience of his artistry and our interpretation of his epic.

---

32   See Hardie (1986): 157-240 and Adler (2003). The influence of the Epicurean Philodemus on Vergil (and the Augustans more generally) can be found in the collection by Armstrong, Fish, Johnston, and Skinner (2004). For Lucretius' influence on Vergil's *Georgics*, see especially Farrell (1991) and Gale (2000).

33   The earliest epic writers (Livius, Naevius and Ennius; see above) also wrote tragedy, and so it is not surprising that epic and tragedy would influence one another. Latin tragic writing continued into the first century through the work of, e.g., Pacuvius (220-ca. 130 BCE) and Accius (170-ca. 86 BCE). Their tragedies, which included Homeric and Trojan War themes, were important for Vergil. However, since only meager fragments of them have survived, their precise influence is difficult to gauge.

34   Cf., e.g., Heinze (1993): 251-8. Wlosok (1976, trans. 1999) offers a reading of the Dido episode as tragedy, and Pavlock (1985) examines Euripidean influence in the Nisus and Euryalus episode. Hardie (1991, 1997), Panoussi (2002), and Galinsky (2003) examine the influence of tragedy, particularly in light of French theories of Greek tragedy (e.g. Vernant and Vidal-Naquet (1988)), and draw important parallels between the political and cultural milieus of fifth-century Athens and Augustan Rome. On tragedy and conflicting viewpoints, see Conte (1999) and Galinsky (2003).

35   Hardie (1998): 62.

36   See Farrell (1997) for a full and insightful introduction to the interpretive possibilities that the study of intertextuality in Vergil can offer readers. For a general introduction to intertextuality, see Allen (2000). For the study of intertextuality in Latin literature, see Conte (1986), Farrell (1991): 1-25, Fowler (1997), Hinds (1998), and Edmunds (2001). For Vergil's use of Homer, see Knauer (1964a, 1964b) and Barchiesi (1984).

The *Aeneid*, Rome, and Augustus

While Aeneas' story takes place in the distant, mythological past of the Trojan war era, it had a special relevance for Vergil's contemporaries. Not only did the Romans draw their descent from the Trojans, but the emperor Augustus believed that Aeneas was his own ancestor.[37] Vergil makes these national and familial connections major thematic concerns of his epic.

As a result, the *Aeneid* is about more than the Trojan war and its aftermath. It is also about the foundation of Rome and its flourishing under Augustus. To incorporate these themes into his epic, Vergil connects mythological and historical time by associating three leaders and city foundations: the founding of Lavinium by Aeneas, the actual founding of Rome by Romulus, and the "re-founding" of Rome by Augustus. These events are prominent in the most important prophecies of the epic: Jupiter's speech to Venus (1.257-96) and Anchises' revelation to his son Aeneas (6.756-853). Together these passages provide what may be called an Augustan reading of Roman history, one that is shaped by the deeds of these three men and that views Augustus as the culmination of the processes of fate and history.[38]

This is not to say that the associations among Aeneas, Romulus, and Augustus are always positive or unproblematic, particularly given the ways that Aeneas is portrayed and can be interpreted.[39] To some, Vergil's Aeneas represents an idealized Roman hero, who thus reflects positively on Augustus by association. [40] In general this type of reading sees a positive imperial ideology in the epic and is referred to as "optimistic" or "Augustan." Others are more troubled by Vergil's Aeneas, and advocate interpretations that challenge the moral and spiritual value of his actions, as well as of the role of the

---

37   Augustus' clan, the Julian *gens*, claimed its descent from Iulus (another name for Aeneas' son Ascanius) and thus also from Aeneas and Venus. Julius Caesar in particular emphasized this ancestry; Augustus made these connections central to his political self-presentation as well. See, e.g., Zanker (1988): 193-210 and Galinsky (1996): 141-224.

38   See O'Hara (1990), however, for the deceptiveness of prophecies in the *Aeneid*.

39   For general interpretation of the *Aeneid*, see n. 23 (above).

40   This type of reading is represented especially by Heinze (1915, trans. 1993), Pöschl (1950, trans. 1962), and Otis (1964). More recent and complex Augustan interpretations can be found in Hardie (1986) and Cairns (1989).

gods and fate. Such readings perceive a much darker poetic world[41] and have been called "pessimistic" or "ambivalent."[42] Vergil's portrayal of Aeneas is thus a major element in debates over the epic's meaning,[43] and Book 2 plays an important role in them.

Book 2 within the context of the *Aeneid*

The *Aeneid* begins as Aeneas and the Trojans are sailing to Italy, about to reach the land that fate has promised them, when their nemesis Juno intervenes by sending a storm that shipwrecks them at Carthage. There, with some divine assistance, they are welcomed by Dido, the Carthaginian queen. At a feast at the end of book 1, she asks Aeneas to tell his story about the end of the Trojan war and its aftermath.

Aeneas agrees, and the next two books are flashback narratives related in his own voice. In book 2, he provides an eyewitness account of the fall of Troy (see below, *Structure and major themes of* Aeneid 2). In book 3, he describes his often confused wanderings from Troy in search of Italy, and ends his narration with his arrival at Dido's city.

Book 4 then treats the tragic love affair that develops between Dido and Aeneas, whose desire to linger with the queen in Carthage is set against his duty to lead his people to Italy. Aeneas ultimately leaves Dido and, after a stop in Sicily (book 5) and a heroic journey through the Underworld (book 6), he reaches Latium in Italy (book 7). Upon his arrival there, however, he

---

41   See, e.g., Putnam (1965), Johnson (1976), Lyne (1987), and Thomas (2001). Putnam's reading of the *Aeneid* has been particularly influential. Of the ending of the poem he writes: "By giving himself over with such suddenness to the private wrath which the sight of the belt of Pallas arouses, Aeneas becomes himself *impius Furor*, as rage wins the day over moderation, disintegration defeats order, and the achievements of history through heroism fall victim to the human frailty of one man" (1965: 193-4).

42   For a general treatment of the optimism/pessimism debate, see Kennedy (1992). For a critique of the "pessimistic" view, see Martindale (1993); for critique of the "optimistic" stance and its rejection of "pessimism," see Thomas (2001). For the continuing debate over the politics of the *Aeneid* and over the Augustan age more generally, see the collections of Powell (1992) and Stahl (1998).

43   Indeed some readers also question whether it is even possible to resolve this interpretive debate because of Vergil's inherent ambiguity. See Johnson (1976), Perkell (1994), and O'Hara (2007): 77-103. Martindale (1993) offers a critique of ambiguous readings.

is immediately entangled in a troubling war that occupies the remainder of the poem.

Throughout the epic Aeneas appears as a complicated figure, whose strengths and weaknesses are always on display. Book 2 provides a key entry point into his portrayal. In it, we see Aeneas at a defining moment, as he witnesses the fall of Troy. His account of his experiences involves many of the epic's central themes.

Structure and major themes of *Aeneid* 2

Book 2 opens with the Greek camps deserted and the Trojans cautiously believing that the war is over; it ends with Troy's utter destruction and Aeneas' flight from it. In between we hear Aeneas' account of the city's capture, a tale imbued with tragic motifs of reversed fortune, disastrous misinterpretation, and human suffering at the hands of the gods and fate. The book can be divided into three large sections: the ruse of the wooden (i.e. "Trojan") horse (1-267), the sack of Troy (268-558), and Aeneas' flight from the city with his family and people (559-804).

Though Aeneas' narration bears the influence of earlier tragic and epic accounts of Troy's fall (see 1-267 n.), Homer's *Odyssey* remains a defining model, as it had been in the previous book. *Aeneid* 1, which describes the shipwreck of Aeneas at Carthage, is modeled on *Odyssey* 5-8, in which Odysseus is shipwrecked at Scheria. Likewise, Aeneas' inset narrative to the Carthaginians in *Aeneid* 2-3 recalls *Odyssey* 9-12, in which the Greek hero relates his wanderings after the Trojan war to king Alcinous and his palace court. Odysseus and Aeneas are thus both internal narrators, who have survived Troy, nearly died at sea, and now seek assistance from those people to whom they direct their tales.[44]

It is therefore important here, as elsewhere, to consider the *Aeneid*'s interaction with Homeric epic as a creative medium through which Virgil defines his characters and their struggles. For example, Aeneas in book 2 turns the Homeric Odysseus into a symbol of treachery (see e.g. 90 n.). At the same time, he recasts the Trojans' loss of their city as an opportunity for them to achieve a still greater achievement, the eventual foundation of Rome. Such reinterpretations of Homer, in turn, set in relief several issues

---

44   On Aeneas as narrator, see commentary note on 1-267.

and themes important for our understanding of book 2 and of Vergil's epic more generally.

First, the derogatory depiction of Ulysses (i.e. Odysseus) is central to the portrayal of the Greeks as a whole, for throughout book 2 they will act with characteristic treachery and impiety (cf. Sinon and Pyrrhus). Aeneas and the Trojans, however, will suffer because of their lack of deception, their guilelessness, as they painfully come to accept their fate and the will of their gods. Aeneas, in fact, will embody the ideal of *pietas* (duty and respect for one's family, state, and the gods), and this virtue will also be the defining trait of the future Romans.

Second, we witness in Aeneas' actions a gradual transformation of Homeric heroism (one that privileges the individual's glory) into a heroism based in *pietas* (one that strives for the good of the community). By leading his people from their fallen city to pursue the land fate has promised them, Aeneas in *Aeneid* 2-3 differs significantly from his Homeric counterpart in Odysseus, who gradually loses all his companions in the course of his inset narrative.

Finally, these differing modes of heroism are implicated in the conflict between *pietas* and *furor* that operates throughout book 2. Aeneas will ultimately act to save his family and people (i.e. *pietas*-based heroism), but along the way he will be distracted by *furor* and *ira* to attempt acts for his own glory (i.e. Homeric heroism). It will be Aeneas' challenge to control his passions so that he may fulfill the mandates of the gods and fate.

Central to this transformation in Aeneas' heroism are actions on the divine level. The plan of fate and the gods' machinations are largely unknown to mortal characters, but they place significant pressure on Aeneas. At important moments in book 2 (289-95, 594-620, 776-89), he is given special access to the divine dimension behind Troy's fall. But for the mandates of fate to be fulfilled, Aeneas endures many misfortunes — in book two and throughout the entire epic. He loses his city, his king, and his wife (book 2), his father (book 3), his lover Dido (book 4). He becomes a refugee settler (book 7), and must fight another war (books 7-12). One of Aeneas' defining struggles is to come to understand and to accept fate, the role of the gods (sometimes incomprehensibly violent) in overseeing it, and the requirements placed upon him as a result.

Because book 2 involves themes that matter for the entire poem, it figures in a number of debates that have defined interpretation of the *Aeneid*. It is clear that Aeneas in book 2 is not a perfect being. He is constantly tested by emotions that threaten to distract him from what fate requires of him. In what ways does his yielding to *furor* in book 2 shed light on his actions later in the poem, particularly his slaying of Turnus at the poem's conclusion? And what does book 2 tell us about the nature and moral quality of fate and of the gods?

Bibliography. For more on the general themes and shape of book 2, see commentary notes on 1-267, 268-558 and 559-804. For general interpretations of book 2, see Heinze (1915, 1993: 3-49), Putnam (1965) 3-63, Anderson (2005), Gransden (1990), Johnson (1999), Adler (2003) 253-79. On the literary tradition of Troy's fall, see Heinze (1915; 1993: 49) and Gantz (1993) 646-57, 713-17. For the influence of tragedy in particular, see 1-267 n.

On the imagery of book 2, see Knox (1950) and Putnam (1965) 3-63. On Greek treachery, see R. M. Smith (1999) and Syed (2005) 199-204. For the differing conceptions of heroism, see Johnson (1999) 50-4 and Adler (2003) 252-79. On wrath and fury in book 2 and beyond, contrast the "pessimistic" view of Putnam (1995) 172-200 with the "optimistic" and philosophical arguments of Galinsky (1988) and Wright (1997). On the gods in book 2 (and beyond), see Coleman (1982), G. W. Williams (1983) 3-39, Cairns (1989) 1-28, E. L. Harrison (1990), Feeney (1991) 129-87, and Johnson (1999).

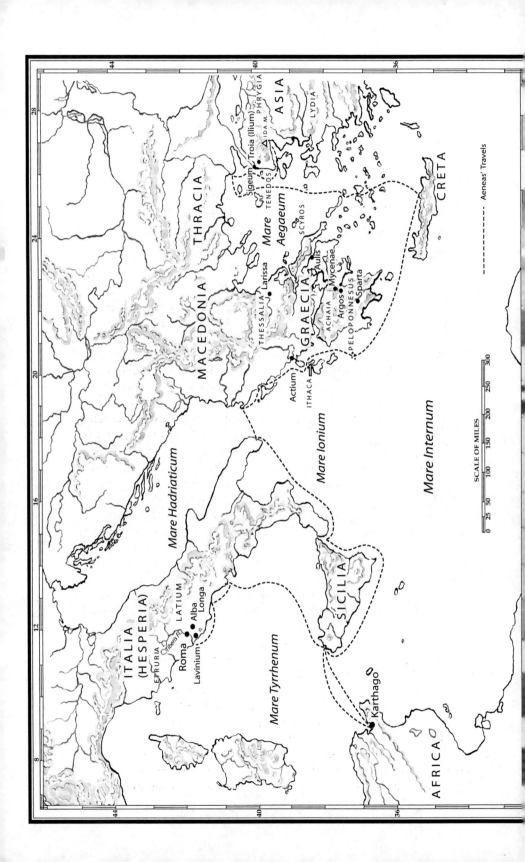

Liber Secundus

Sinon and the Trojan Horse (lines 1-267)

In the midst of a banquet at Carthage at the end of book 1, Queen Dido asked Aeneas to tell the story of Troy's fall, his subsequent wanderings, and the misfortunes of his people (1.753-6). Aeneas reluctantly (3-8) begins his narrative at the opening of book 2 by recounting the ruse of the Trojan Horse, the most widely known myth of the classical tradition. The tale goes back to the earliest of Greek literature. In *Odyssey* 8.499-520, the bard Demodocus, at Odysseus' request, sings a brief account of it at a banquet. Other poets, both Greek and Roman, treated the theme, but their versions exist now only in meager fragments, making their direct influence on Vergil difficult to gauge: e.g. the *Little Iliad* of Lesches and the *Sack of Troy* of Arctinus (Greek epics, ca. seventh/sixth century BCE), the Greek tragedies *Laocoon* and *Sinon* of Sophocles (fifth century BCE), and the early Latin tragedies (mid third-early first century BCE) of Livius Andronicus and Naevius (*Equus Troianus*) and of Accius (*Deiphobus*).

Like so much of classical myth, the tale of the Trojan Horse was not a monolithic story but one that varied from poet to poet. There are several aspects of Vergil's presentation that seem significant. First, though some versions place Aeneas already away from Troy when the Greeks pour out of the horse, Vergil has Aeneas remain in the city to assume the lead role in the Trojans' escape. Second, Vergil elevates Laocoon, the priest who forcefully counsels the Trojans to distrust and destroy the horse, to the position of primary critic of the horse, though for most of the tradition that role is played by Cassandra (or both Cassandra and Laocoon). The forcefulness and relative credibility of Vergil's Laocoon makes the Trojans' failure to heed his warnings all the more tragic. And finally Sinon, the Greek captive who in Vergil contrives to be caught by the Trojans to convince them to accept the horse, is not mentioned in Homer, though he appears in the *Sack of Troy* and the *Little Iliad*, where he lights a fire signaling to the Greeks to sail from Tenedos against Troy. In Vergil, Sinon becomes a key symbol of Greek treachery, whose masterful speeches convince the Trojans to show compassion to him and thus bring on their own destruction.

Aeneas plays a background role in his account of the decisions and events involved in this section. It is not until the second segment of book 2 (see 268-558 n.) that he begins to take the lead — first by attempting to resist the Greek invasion, and then by shepherding his family and people from their ravaged city (559-804). The use of Aeneas as narrator is crucial: by allowing us to hear Aeneas' visceral responses to the sack of his city, the first-person narrative contributes significantly to the tragic tone of the book, to the subversion of traditional Homeric values, and to the redefinition of heroism. See Johnson (1999) for more on these themes and on the complex relationship between

Vergil the narrator, Aeneas the inset narrator, and Aeneas the narrated (i.e. as character in the narrative).

Bibliography. The fragmentary works mentioned above are available with translations in the relevant Loeb Classical library editions: West (2003) on Greek epic, Lloyd-Jones (1994-96, vol. 3) on Sophocles, and Warmington (1935-40, vols. 1-2) on early Latin tragedy. Comprehensive lists of possible allusions in Vergil to Greek and Latin tragedy can be found in the articles on "Eschilo," "Euripide," "Sofocle," and "tragici latini" in Della Corte (1984-91).

For general readings of this section of book 2, see Putnam (1965) 5-28, Hexter (1990), R. M. Smith (1999), and Adler (2003) 252-63. On the theme of sacrifice in book 2 (and the *Aeneid* more generally), see Bandera (1981), Hardie (1984) and (1993) 19-56 (especially 27-8), and R. M. Smith (1999). For the Trojan horse myth and Vergil's adaptation of it, see Heinze (1915, 1993: 5-14), Austin (1964) 34-6, Gransden (1990), Gantz (1993) 646-54, and Clausen (2002) 61-74.

Please note: when reference is made to a line in *Aeneid* 2, the number of the line is given (e.g. "cf. 229"); when the reference is to another book of the *Aeneid*, the number of the book is added (e.g. "cf. 4.229"). References to *Allen and Greenough's New Latin Grammar* ("AG"; see Mahoney (2001) in Works Cited) are provided by section number (e.g. "AG §290"). An asterisk (*) indicates a term discussed in Appendix B.

CONTICVERE omnes intentique ora tenebant.
inde toro pater Aeneas sic orsus ab alto:

1-13: *The Carthaginians fall silent, as Aeneas agrees to tell the story of Troy's fall.* By the time Aeneas begins his narrative, Dido has already been inflamed with love for Aeneas by Venus and Cupid (1.657-722), a love that will be stoked by Aeneas' tale (4.1-5) and ultimately reciprocated (e.g. 4.395).

1. **CONTICVERE:** = *conticuerunt*. The alternative ending *–ere* of the third person plural perfect indicative active is used often in Vergil. **ora tenebant:** *ora* (*os, oris, n.*), probably means "faces" or "gazes," though "voices" is also possible. Note that the verb tense switches from perfect (*conticuere*), emphasizing the quiet that has fallen, to imperfect (*tenebant*), perhaps underscoring the continuing nature of the audience's rapt attention. **intenti:** translate adverbially. Adjectives that refer to a subject or object of a verb sometimes qualify that verb and can thus be construed adverbially (AG §290). Cf. *primusque* at 32.

2. **inde:** indicates the ordered stateliness of the action. First silence, then (*inde*) Aeneas rises to speak. **pater:** as their leader, Aeneas is *pater* of the Trojans, but perhaps this word also looks forward to Aeneas as forefather of the Romans. **toro...ab alto:** suggests his special seating at Dido's banquet. **orsus:** from the deponent verb *ordior*, "begin"; supply *est*. The omission of *esse*-forms from compound passives and deponents in the third person is common; such omissions also occur in the first and second person, though much less frequently, and usually when a deponent verb is involved.

"infandum, regina, iubes renovare dolorem,
Troianas ut opes et lamentabile regnum
eruerint Danai, quaeque ipse miserrima vidi   5
et quorum pars magna fui. quis talia fando
Myrmidonum Dolopumve aut duri miles Vlixi
temperet a lacrimis? et iam nox umida caelo

---

3. **infandum:** modifies *dolorem*; it is derived from *fari* ("speak") and means "not to be spoken." Aeneas is thus asked to recount the "unspeakable." The etymological paradox is implied both by the emphatic position of *infandum* with its three long syllables at the beginning of the line, and by its proximity to *fando* (6), the gerund of *fari*. **regina:** Dido, the queen of Carthage. She had requested Aeneas' tale at 1.753-6 (cf. 1-267 n.). **iubes:** supply *me* as the object.

4-6. **Troianas...fui:** these lines offer a brief overview of the narrative Aeneas will tell in book 2. No mention is made here of Aeneas' wanderings after Troy's fall, also requested by Dido at 1.755 (see 3 n.), but they will be the subject of Aeneas' continued narration in book 3.

4. **Troianas...Danai:** indirect question, dependent on the general sense of "telling" in *infandum renovare dolorem*; *ut* = "how." Since *iubes* (3) indicates primary sequence, *eruerint* is in the perfect subjunctive and expresses prior time. For the sequence of tenses, see AG §482-5.

5-6. **quaeque...miserrima vidi...quorum...fui:** construe *miserrima* substantively (i.e. as a noun, here neuter plural), referring generally to the actions described in 4-5. The relative pronouns *quae* (5) and *quorum* (6) refer to *miserrima*, and are connected by the archaic construction *–que...et*. **fando:** gerund of *fari* in the ablative. Cf. 3 n.

7. **Myrmidonum Dolopumve:** partitive genitives with *quis* (6), the nominative interrogative pronoun (AG §148). These were two tribes from Thessaly. The *Myrmidones* (Myrmidons) were led by Achilles, the greatest Greek warrior; the Dolopians (*Dolopes, -um*, m. pl.) by Achilles' son Pyrrhus, who will play an important role at 469-558. Moskalew (1990) sees a wordplay in the phrase *MyrmiDONUM DOLOpumve* that would involve the double nature of the wooden horse as a *donum* (to Minerva) and as a *dolus*. This potential wordplay appears again at 252 (*MyrmiDONUMque DOLOS*), and at other points may involve (and therefore explain) Vergil's more frequent use in book 2 of *Danai* for "Greeks," because of the similarity of its first syllable *DANai* to *DONum* (cf. 36, 44, and 49). **miles:** supply *quis* (6); though technically the interrogative pronoun, *quis* is sometimes used as the interrogative adjective *qui*. **Vlixi:** Ulysses, called Odysseus in Homer. The Latin *Vlixes* is based on a Greek variant of the hero's name and is here in the genitive case. Vergil forms genitives of Greek nouns variously. Greek nouns ending in *–eus* have their Latin genitive in *–eos* (as in Greek), or are treated like Latin nouns ending in *-eus*, and have genitives in *–ei* or *–i*, as here.

8. **temperet:** present tense, potential subjunctive (AG §445-7). **caelo:** *(de) caelo*. Note that Odysseus had indeed cried upon upon hearing Demodocus sing of the Trojan horse (*Od.* 8.521-31), though perhaps not solely for the reasons Aeneas here suggests.

praecipitat suadentque cadentia sidera somnos. *poetic plural.*
sed si tantus amor casus cognoscere nostros   10
et breviter Troiae supremum audire laborem,
quamquam animus meminisse horret luctuque refugit,
incipiam.
        Fracti bello fatisque repulsi *chiasmus*
ductores Danaum tot iam labentibus annis
instar montis equum divina Palladis arte   15

---

9. **praecipitat:** intransitive. Night is conceptualized as sinking or setting, like the sun and day. This is a line of remarkable artistry. Its use of dactyls and its lack of a strong third foot caesura combine to suggest the falling stars, while alliteration (*suadent…sidera somnos*) and an almost "chiastic" consonance (*suadent-que ca-dentia*) help achieve an overall aural and rhythmic relaxation in *somnos*.

10-11. **tantus amor…cognoscere…et…audire:** supply *tibi est.* The infinitives depend on the sense of "desire" contained in *amor.* Cf. *ira…ulcisci* (575-6). **supremum:** "last," "final." Cf. the expression *dies supremus* (i.e. "day of death").

12. **luctu:** ablative of cause (AG §404). **refugit:** "recoiled," perfect tense ("u" is long). This verb may suggest Aeneas' sudden and initial reaction to Dido's request, while *horret* describes his present state.

13-20: *Aeneas explains the Greek ruse of the wooden horse.* Note that the Greeks, though exemplary warriors in the *Iliad*, are characterized by their skill at deception (13-20), which is juxtaposed against the Trojans' naiveté (21-39). This contrast between the Greeks and Trojans is central to Aeneas' description of how his people were persuaded to bring the horse into the city.

13. **Fracti bello fatisque repulsi:** an example of *chiasmus**, a rhetorical figure whereby parallel constructions are expressed in reverse word order: here *fracti* (A) *bello* (B) *fatisque* (b) *repulsi* (a). The phrase provides both human (*bello*) and divine (*fatis*) explanations for the construction of the horse.

14. **ductores Danaum:** *Danaum* is a contracted genitive plural. Vergil often uses the contracted form in *-um* with proper names (e.g. *Teucrum, Danaum, Argivum*) and names describing a class of persons (e.g. *virum, superum, caelicolum*). See AG §49d. The phrase *ductores Danaum* is used by Lucretius at 1.86 (cf. 18 n.) of the Greek leaders as they perform the horrifying sacrifice of Iphigenia, Agamemnon's daughter, due to their mistaken trust in *religio.* Here, Vergil uses the phrase where the Greek leaders manipulate *religio* (through the ruse of the horse) to their advantage in order to sack Troy. For more on Iphigenia's sacrifice, see 116 n. **tot iam labentibus annis:** an ablative absolute construction; the present participle emphasizes the ongoing nature of the ten-year war.

15. **instar montis:** "huge as a mountain" (lit. "the image of a mountain"), in apposition to *equum.* **divina Palladis arte:** Pallas not only favored the Greeks but was also the patroness of all handicrafts. As we learn at line 264, Epeus built the horse (*doli fabricator*). For more on the tradition of the Trojan Horse, see 1-267 n.

aedificant, sectaque intexunt abiete costas;
votum pro reditu simulant; ea fama vagatur.
huc delecta virum sortiti corpora furtim
includunt caeco lateri penitusque cavernas
ingentis uterumque armato milite complent.   20
    Est in conspectu Tenedos, notissima fama
insula, dives opum Priami dum regna manebant,

equivalent to acc. pl. (margin note)

poetic pl. (margin note)

16. **sectaque...abiete:** ablative of means, "with cut pine" (i.e. "with planks of pine"). For the varieties of wood Vergil uses to describe the horse, see 112 n. **intexunt:** a verb often used of weaving. The process of placing the planks horizontally across the ribs (*costas*) is metaphorically compared to the passing of the horizontal threads (of the woof) across the vertical threads (of the warp). Cf. also 112 *contextus* and 186 *textis*. The metaphor* is especially appropriate here since Pallas was renowned for this craft (cf. 15 n.), as can be seen in the tale of Pallas and Arachne told by Ovid at *Metamorphoses* 6.1-145. *Intexunt* and *aedificant* could also be used of building ships (Conington), and they thus provide another metaphor for imagining the horse. **abiete:** the "i" is consonantal (i.e. construe as a "j"), and thus the word is scanned as a dactyl.

17. **votum...simulant:** *simulant (equum esse) votum pro (suo) reditu.* **ea fama:** *ea* is a demonstrative adjective.

18. **huc:** i.e. in the horse. **sortiti:** modifies *Danai* (or *ductores Danaum* from line 14), as the understood subject of the sentence. *Sortior* originally meant "choose by lot" but also came to encompass the more general sense of "choose," as here. **delecta virum...corpora:** *virum* = *virorum* (cf. 14 n.). *Delecta* is the past participle of *deligo* ("pick out," "choose") and means "select" or "choice"; the entire phrase is a lofty periphrasis (compound phrase) for "select (i.e. outstanding) heroes." The phrase may recall Lucretius' *ductores Danaum delecti, prima virorum*, on which see 14 n.

19. **caeco lateri:** dative with the compound verb *includunt* (AG §370). The phrase explains *huc* (18).

20. **uterum:** the horse's "womb," as if it is pregnant with all the Greek warriors it hides. Cf. line 238, where the horse (*machina*) is *feta armis* (this metaphor also appears at Euripides, *Trojan Women* 11). For other metaphors involved in the horse, see 16 n., Knox (1950), and Putnam (1965) 5-28. **milite:** here a collective noun, "soldiers." They are described further at 261-4 as they come out of the horse.

21-39: *The Trojans' initial debate over the horse.* The Trojans leave their city with an almost reckless abandon, exposing themselves to the dangers lying in wait. Note that the matter-of-fact style of 21-30 underscores the untroubled certainty of the Trojans' naive (and fatal) interpretation of events.

21. **in conspectu Tenedos:** *Tenedos* (nominative feminine) is an island not far off the coast of Troy and is thus *in conspectu* from the Trojan vantage point. **fama:** final "a" is long (i.e. ablative). Note that Aeneas begins with fairly straightforward language. This will be in striking contrast to what follows, particularly in Sinon's speeches.

22. **dives opum:** *opum* is genitive plural with *dives* (adjectives indicating want or fullness often take the genitive). Vergil also uses this phrase to describe Carthage at 1.14.

nunc tantum sinus et statio male fida carinis:
huc se provecti deserto in litore condunt.
nos abiisse rati et vento petiisse Mycenas.   25
ergo omnis longo solvit se Teucria luctu:
panduntur portae, iuvat ire et Dorica castra
desertosque videre locos litusque relictum:
hic Dolopum manus, hic saevus tendebat Achilles;
classibus hic locus, hic acie certare solebant.   30
pars stupet innuptae donum exitiale Minervae

---

23. **male fida:** *fidus, -a, -um,* used of things or places, can mean "safe," "reliable" (cf. *litora… fida,* 399-400). When *male* qualifies an adjective that has a good sense, it negates that good sense, as here (*male fida = infida*); when, however, it qualifies an adjective that has a bad sense, it intensifies the bad sense, cf. Horace, *Odes* 1.17.25 *male dispari* "very ill-matched."

24. **huc:** i.e. to Tenedos. **provecti:** modifies *Danai,* the understood subject of *condunt.*

25. **nos…rati:** with *rati* (from *reor,* "think") understand *sumus.* The inclusion of the nominative pronoun *nos* is emphatic. **abiisse…petiisse:** infinitives in indirect discourse with accusative subject *eos* (i.e. the Greeks) understood. **vento:** ablative of means, "by wind" here means "by sailing." **Mycenas:** *Mycenae* (feminine plural) was the city Agamemnon ruled and here stands for Greece in general.

26. **Teucria:** another name for Troy. Teucer was a forefather of the Trojans, who were also called *Teucri* (Teucrians). **longo…luctu:** ablative of separation (AG §400) with *solvit.* On the length of the war, see 14 n. This line, heavy with spondees and disyllabic words, perhaps suggests the weariness and suffering caused by the decade-long war (*longo…luctu*) from which the Trojans think they are experiencing a release.

27-8. **Dorica:** "belonging to the Dorians"; here = "Greek" (cf. 83 n.). **iuvat:** begins an impersonal construction (AG §388c), *iuvat (eos) ire…et videre.*

29. **hic…:** note the repetition of *hic* (adverb), conveying the drama of the Trojans pointing out the former locations of the Greek troops, which they can now freely visit. **Dolopum… Achilles:** the Trojans display a special interest in the areas Achilles and his people, the Thessalians, occupied (see 7 n.). **tendebat:** here, "encamped." The implied construction is *tendo* ("stretch") + e.g. *tentorium*: "pitch one's tent"; the direct object, however, can be omitted, as here.

30. **hic locus:** supply *erat.* **acie:** supply *in*; prepositions are often omitted in poetry. Here *acies* means "battle."

31. **pars:** supply the partitive genitive *Troianorum. Pars* (nominative singular) is subject of both *stupet* and *mirantur,* though with the latter (a plural), it is taken as a collective noun (AG §317d). **innuptae donum…Minervae:** *Minervae* is objective genitive with *donum,* "gift for Minerva." Minerva (also called Pallas) was known for her chastity (hence *innuptae*). **exitiale:** "fatal," is proleptic, since it looks forward to the destruction the gift will eventually cause Troy.

et molem mirantur equi; primusque Thymoetes
duci intra muros hortatur et arce locari,
sive dolo seu iam Troiae sic fata ferebant.
at Capys, et quorum melior sententia menti,   35
aut pelago Danaum insidias suspectaque dona

dative of direction

---

32. **primusque:** adjective, but it can be translated adverbially (cf. 1 n.). **Thymoetes:** a Trojan who plays no further role in the poem, but see 34 n. for possible motives behind his actions here.

33. **duci...locari:** present passive infinitives; the horse (*equum* or *donum*) is understood as their accusative subject in indirect command after *hortatur*. In prose *hortor* would usually take an *ut*-clause. **arce:** for *in arce* (cf. 30 n.). In addition to being a defensive position, the citadel of Troy (*arx*) housed temples and other sacred objects. As we shall see, Thymoetes' suggested course of action will eventually be taken (244-5) and prove to be fatal, as Aeneas has already indicated with *exitiale* in line 31. This scene differs from the brief version in Homer, where the Trojans first bring the horse inside the citadel and then discuss what to do with it (*Odyssey* 8.504-10).

34. **sive dolo seu...fata:** Aeneas provides two possible explanations for Thymoetes' advice: 1.) he is playing a trick (*dolo*, ablative of cause, AG §404) or 2.) fate (*fata*) required that this happen. On the former, the fourth century commentator Servius (on line 32) notes that an oracle had claimed that a child born on a certain day would bring destruction on Troy. King Priam's son Paris and Thymoetes' son (unnamed) were born on that very day, but Priam only had the latter killed along with his mother (i.e. Thymoetes' wife). These murders could therefore have provided Thymoetes with a powerful motive for treachery (*dolo*) against Priam's kingdom. **sic fata ferebant:** the verb *fero* can be used without an object after words like *ut, ita, sic* to indicate a direction of events, and so here means "tend" or "incline."

35. **at Capys, et quorum melior sententia menti:** supply *ei* (nominative masculine plural) as antecedent of *quorum*, and *erat* as verb for which *sententia* is subject in the relative clause; *menti* is dative of possessor. Thus: *At Capys, et (ei) quorum melior sententia menti (erat)*. This entire line then forms the subject of *iubent* (37). **sententia:** seems to have originally meant "opinion" or "judgment" (as here), and only later took on the additional meanings "aphorism" and "sentence." Aeneas claims that this *sententia* was *melior* because, in the narrative present of the poem, he realizes through hindsight that if this counsel had been followed, Troy would not have fallen (cf. his use of *exitiale* at 31). Throughout the episode Aeneas gives little clear indication of his role in the debate about the horse or what he was thinking at the time.

36. **aut...latebras (38):** three courses of action are suggested: 1.) to hurl the horse into the sea, 2.) to burn it, 3.) to examine it. Of these the first two are similar (both involve the horse's destruction), and Vergil therefore joins them with *-que*. The real alternative between either 1 or 2 and 3 is indicated by *aut...aut* (36, 38). (Cf. *Odyssey* 8.506-10 and 33 n.) **pelago:** dative of direction. **Danaum:** for the form, cf. 14 n.

praecipitare iubent subiectisque urere flammis,
aut terebrare cavas uteri et temptare latebras.
scinditur incertum studia in contraria vulgus.
　　Primus ibi ante omnis magna comitante caterva   40
Laocoon ardens summa decurrit ab arce,
et procul 'o miseri, quae tanta insania, cives?
creditis avectos hostis? aut ulla putatis

---

37. **iubent…:** indirect command construction. For the subject of *iubent*, see 35 n. Supply *nos* as accusative subject of the infinitives *praecipitare* and *urere* (AG §563a). **suspectaque:** the enclitic *-que* here has the force of *–ve* ("or"), since *urere* offers an action alternative to *praecipitare*.

38. **terebrare…temptare…:** the *(nos) iubent* indirect command structure continues here. **terebrare:** "bore a hole through" to see if there is anything inside.

39. **studia in contraria:** *studia* has the sense of "factions" or "sides"; the phrase thus refers to the opposing advice of Thymoetes (32-4) and Capys (35-8).

40-56: *Laocoon urges the Trojans to distrust the Greeks and the wooden horse.* In contrast to the wavering Trojans, the older yet powerful (50) Laocoon voices certainty about the horse's treachery, but he will be tragically ignored. His speech is impassioned (42 n.) yet rational, split between rhetorical questions (42-4) and practical analysis (45-9). At this point, he appears simply as a man of importance (40 n.), though his role as priest of Neptune will be revealed at 201. Lynch (1980) interprets Laocoon as representative of traditional republican Roman virtue (in contrast to Sinon's problematic Greek eloquence), while Adler (2003) 259-60 discerns a strong Lucretian aspect in Laocoon because he privileges rational explanation over *religio* – this is what Lucretius' poem on Epicurean philosophy (*De Rerum Natura*) advocates. For more on Laocoon, see 199-233 n., Austin (1964) 40-56 n. and 199-227 n., Lynch (1980), Tracy (1987), E. L. Harrison (1990) 52-4, R. M. Smith (1999), and Adler (2003) 252-63.

40. **magna comitante caterva:** ablative absolute. This detail suggests Laocoon's importance. **primus…ante omnis:** an example of pleonasm*, since *ante omnis* is redundant after *primus*. The combination, however, underscores Laocoon's stature.

41. **Laocoon:** the delay of his name by a line adds drama to the scene. Laocoon's frenzied entrance and deep distrust of the horse contrast with the ambivalent feelings of the Trojans (39). **summa ab arce:** "from the top of the citadel"; some kind of watchtower is implied. At 226, we learn that a temple of Pallas stood on the citadel (*Tritonidis arcem*).

42. **et procul:** understand *clamat*. Verbs of speaking are sometimes omitted (cf. 287, 547). Note also the omission of forms of *sum* in 43-4 and the clipped nature of the questions. **quae:** interrogative adjective modifying *tanta insania*; supply something like *est ista*.

43. **avectos:** supply *esse*. **hostis:** accusative plural.

dona carere dolis Danaum? sic notus Vlixes?
aut hoc inclusi ligno occultantur Achivi,   45
aut haec in nostros fabricata est machina muros,
inspectura domos venturaque desuper urbi,
aut aliquis latet error; equo ne credite, Teucri.
quidquid id est, timeo Danaos et dona ferentis.'
sic fatus validis ingentem viribus hastam   50
in latus inque feri curvam compagibus alvum

---

44. **dona...dolis Danaum:** *dolis* is ablative of separation with *carere* (AG §401). Note the alliteration*, assonance*, and consonance* in this phrase; for the potential wordplay, cf. 7 n. **sic notus Vlixes?:** supply *est nobis*. "Is Ulysses known to us in this way" (i.e. do you think that the Greeks, with Ulysses as their leader, would send us a horse without some trick involved?). Laocoon echoes Capys' skepticism about the horse (36). Ulysses epitomizes duplicity for the Trojans, and is taken as representative of Greek character (cf. Syed (2005) 207-8). The ambiguous nature of Ulysses and of his trickery was also part of the Greek tradition. In the *Odyssey*, Odysseus himself describes the wooden horse as a trick (Gr. *dolos*, *Od.* 8.494) and proudly connects his fame to his Gr. *doloisin* (*Od.* 9.19-20). However, in the *Iliad* and especially in later Greek writing (cf. 82 n.), Odysseus' trickery was also portrayed as somewhat troubling. Aeneas/Vergil expands on this latter strain of the tradition.

45. **ligno:** "wood" (of the horse).

46. **in nostros...muros:** "to harm our walls (i.e. city)"; here *in* + accusative describes action taken against something.

47. **inspectura...ventura:** future active participles, modifying *machina* and expressing purpose. **desuper:** adverb. **urbi:** = *in urbem*.

48. **aliquis...error:** *aliquis* is the indefinite pronoun used as an adjective (cf. AG §151e); *error* here means "trick." **ne credite:** a poetic negative imperative. In prose, negative prohibitions are usually formed as follows: *nolite* + infinitive (i.e. *credere*), *cavete* + present subjunctive (i.e. *credatis*), or *ne* + present or perfect subjunctive (i.e. *credideritis*). See AG §450.

49. **id:** i.e. the horse. **et:** "even." **dona:** here "offerings" to Pallas, not simply "gifts," as the popular usage of this line usually implies. **ferentis:** accusative masculine plural participle modifying *Danaos*.

50. **sic fatus:** supply *est* or *erat*; this is a standard formula indicating the conclusion of a speech.

51. **feri:** genitive singular, referring to the wooden horse; it depends on both *latus* and *alvum*. Conington suggests that instead of construing *alvum* "externally" as defining the horse's *latus*, we should view "the spear piercing through the 'latus,' into the 'alvus,' as the spear e.g. of Turnus, 10.482, pierces through the various parts of Pallas' armour." **curvam compagibus alvum:** = *curvis compagibus alvum*, "the belly with its curved seams." The adjective *curvam* really describes *compagibus* but is transferred to *alvum*.

contorsit. stetit illa tremens, uteroque recusso
insonuere cavae gemitumque dedere cavernae.
et, si fata deum, si mens non laeva fuisset,
impulerat ferro Argolicas foedare latebras,   55
Troiaque nunc staret, Priamique arx alta maneres.
     Ecce, manus iuvenem interea post terga revinctum
pastores magno ad regem clamore trahebant
Dardanidae, qui se ignotum venientibus ultro,
hoc ipsum ut strueret Troiamque aperiret Achivis,   60

---

52. illa: sc. *hasta*. **utero recusso:** ablative absolute; the verb *recutio* ("strike so as to cause to vibrate").

53. insonuere...dedere: i.e. *insonuerunt...dederunt*. **cavae...cavernae:** the alliteration* and assonance* perhaps mimic the echo caused by the spear. **gemitum:** gives a human quality to the echo that resulted from the initial striking of the horse by the spear.

54. si...si...fuisset: past contrafactual protases. **non laeva fuisset:** must be understood with both *si fata...* and *si mens...*, though *laeva* has a different shade of meaning in these two clauses. With *fata*, it means "ill-disposed"; with *mens*, "deluded" (i.e. if our minds had not been deluded).

55. impulerat: understand Laocoon as subject and *nos* as object. The pluperfect of the indicative is used instead of the subjunctive (*impulisset*) for vividness in this past contrafactual apodosis (cf. AG §517b).

56. staret...maneres: an additional apodosis but this time present contrafactual with the imperfect subjunctive, making the entire conditional mixed (cf. 54 n.). Aeneas adds emotional effect by addressing the *Priamique arx alta* (vocative) directly in the second person (*maneres*). This is an example of apostrophe*.

57-76: Shepherds drag a Greek captive into the city.

57. manus...revinctum: *manus* is accusative of specification (A&G §397b) with the perfect passive participle *revinctum*. The convoluted syntax of 57-62 reflects the unexpectedness (cf. *ecce*) of Sinon's entrance and the confusion that results.

58. regem: i.e. Priam. His compassion here will result in Troy's destruction. Note the metrical suggestiveness of the line: "The stolid spondaic rhythm suggests the grim determination of the *pastores* as they pushed Sinon relentlessly along, and the strong clash of ictus and accent suggests the force that they used" (Austin).

59. Dardanidae: "Sons of Dardanus," "Trojans," used adjectivally with *pastores*. Dardanus was an ancestor of the kings of Troy. **qui:** the subject of *obtulerat* (61), which takes *se* as its object. **venientibus:** (i.e. Trojans), dative of reference with *ignotum*. **ultro:** "willingly," modifying *obtulerat*; Sinon's intentions are explained in the following line.

60. ut strueret...aperiret: secondary sequence purpose clause with imperfect subjunctive. **hoc ipsum:** "this very thing" is ambiguous, since it can refer both to Sinon's scheme to get caught and to his plan described in the second half of the line (i.e. *Troiamque aperiret Achivis*). **strueret:** here not "construct" but "arrange" or "contrive."

obtulerat, fidens animi atque in utrumque paratus,
seu versare dolos seu certae occumbere morti.
undique visendi studio Troiana iuventus
circumfusa ruit certantque inludere capto.
accipe nunc Danaum insidias et crimine ab uno   65
disce omnis.
namque ut conspectu in medio turbatus, inermis,

---

61. **obtulerat:** see 59 n. **fidens animi:** "trusting in his courage" or "boldness"; the genitive *animi* with locative sense is used with several verbs and adjectives that express feeling (AG §358). Cf. *infelix animi* (4.529) and *furens animi* (5.202). **in utrumque paratus:** "prepared for either (outcome)," as explained in the *seu...seu...* construction of the next line.

62. **versare dolos:** "to perform his deceptions" (lit. "spin out his tricks"). Cf. *illa dolos dirumque nefas in pectore versat* (4.563). **certae occumbere morti:** i.e. because he had fallen into enemy hands. *Morti* is dative with the compound verb *occumbere* ("meet" or "face"). The phrase adds an almost heroic nuance to Sinon's scheming.

63. **visendi studio:** gerund construction expressing purpose; *studio* is ablative.

64. **circumfusa:** "crowded around" (lit. "poured around"). **certantque inludere:** *certare* takes an infinitive, as if it were a verb expressing a desire (cf. 10 n.). The infinitive is so convenient a form, and the final dactyl or trochee which it provides so useful metrically, that the poets extend its use, and introduce it after verbs where a subordinate clause would be more common. (Cf. 55 *impulerat foedare*, 105 *ardemus scitari*.) **ruit certantque inludere:** the change from singular (*ruit*) to plural verb (*certant*) is fitting: the crowd of youth (*iuventus* 63) "rushes in," and they (its separate members) "compete in mocking..." **capto:** describes Sinon and is dative with *inludere*.

65. **accipe nunc Danaum insidias:** Aeneas here responds to Dido's request at 1.753-4: *a prima dic, hospes, origine nobis/ insidias.*

66. **disce omnis:** understand *Danaos* (not *insidias*) with *omnis*. Notice the juxtaposition of *uno* (65) and *omnis*. On the Trojan stereotype of the Greeks, see 44 n. This is the first example in book 2 of a "half-line" – a line left unfinished at the time of Vergil's death. In his *Life of Vergil*, Donatus (fourth century CE) claims that on his deathbed Vergil wanted the *Aeneid* burnt but ultimately left it in the hands of Varius and Tucca to edit *ea conditione, ne quid adderent quod a se editum non esset, et versus etiam imperfectos, si qui erant, relinquerent.* There are approximately 58 incomplete verses in the entire *Aeneid* (the number is disputed because some half lines may have been completed by scribes and thus now seem complete). There are 10 in this book alone (66, 233, 346, 468, 614, 623, 640, 720, 767, and 787), a relatively high number that suggests this book needed perhaps more polish than many of the others.

67. **ut:** temporal, "as" or "when." **conspectu in medio:** "in the midst of our sight." **turbatus:** surely part of Sinon's act; he knows exactly why he is there and what he is about to do.

constitit atque oculis Phrygia agmina circumspexit:
'heu, quae nunc tellus' inquit 'quae me aequora possunt
accipere? aut quid iam misero mihi denique restat,   70
cui neque apud Danaos usquam locus, et super ipsi
Dardanidae infensi poenas cum sanguine poscunt?'

 quo gemitu conversi animi compressus et omnis
impetus. hortamur fari quo sanguine cretus, *ind.-question*
quidve ferat; memoret quae sit fiducia capto.   75

connect. rel.

---

68. **circumspexit:** a spondaic line (i.e. it has a spondee in the fifth foot), of which there are relatively few in Vergil. The word's heaviness perhaps suggests the way in which Sinon scans the hostile Trojans. **Phrygia:** "Trojan," with *agmina*.

69. **quae...quae:** interrogative adjectives. With *quae...tellus* understand *me accipere potest*. **nunc...iam...denique:** observe the temporal emphasis in 69-70.

70. **misero:** dative modifying *mihi*. **aut quid...:** this phrase ends a string of three rhetorical questions, increasing in length, that began in 69. Sinon establishes his wretched state in order to win over the sympathy of the Trojans by tantalizingly claiming that he is hated by both Trojans and Greeks.

71. **neque...locus:** supply *est*. The *-que* is correlative with *et* but translated as a simple negative: "...there is not a place (i.e. no place) anywhere..." **super:** adverb, "in addition." **et...poscunt:** construe as a second relative clause with an understood *a quo* that has *mihi* (70) as its antecedent.

72. **cum sanguine:** *cum* here = "by means of"; *sanguine* = "blood spilled in violence" (i.e. "death" or "slaying"). (In 366 *poenas dant sanguine*, *sanguine* is ablative of means, thus expressing a similar idea as *cum sanguine*.)

73. **quo gemitu:** "this groan," referring back to Sinon's questions in 69-72. Sinon's initial words have apparently been crucial in winning over the attention and sympathy of the Trojans. **compressus et:** *et compressus (est)*. The postponement of *et* is a stylistic device providing metrical flexibility that the neoteric poets of the mid-first century BCE (e.g. Catullus) took over from the Hellenistic poets (e.g. Callimachus and Theocritus, third century BCE). Note that Sinon's speeches at 69-72, 77-104, and 108-44 are each followed by three lines describing the Trojans' responses, which he has manipulated with rhetorical skill.

74. **impetus:** "violent urge." **hortamur fari:** understand *eum* (i.e. Sinon). **quo sanguine:** ablative of source or origin (AG §403); *quo* is an interrogative adjective. **cretus:** supply *sit*; the form is subjunctive (as is *ferat*) in a primary sequence indirect question. Note the disjointed nature of 74-5, perhaps mirroring the confusion and fear that Sinon both simulates and stimulates.

75. **quid:** "what (information or news)." **memoret...:** subjunctive in indirect command, still dependent on the idea in *hortamur*. The phrase is a difficult one but can be construed as follows: "(we urge him) to say what confidence there is for him, a prisoner" (i.e., what makes him believe the Trojans would trust him rather than kill him on the spot). **capto:** dative of possessor, referring to Sinon.

abl. abs.

[ille haec deposita tandem formidine fatur:]
 'Cuncta equidem tibi, rex, fuerit quodcumque, fatebor
vera,' inquit; 'neque me Argolica de gente negabo;
hoc primum; nec, si miserum fortuna Sinonem
finxit, vanum etiam mendacemque improba finget.   80
fando aliquod si forte tuas pervenit ad auris

---

76. **ille...fatur**: since *fatur* here is redundant because of *inquit* in 78, and since this sentence is repeated at 3.612 and not contained in the most important manuscripts, the line may very well not belong here and is thus bracketed.

77-198. *The Sinon Episode* Sinon, the captured Greek, has insinuated himself into Troy in order to convince the Trojans to bring the wooden horse into their city. His success results largely from his ability to interweave "truths" the Trojans would recognize (e.g. the treacherous nature of Ulysses, the departure of the Greeks from their camps, and the theft of the Palladium) with falsehoods (e.g. his near sacrifice by the Greeks and the meaning of the horse). See especially Gransden (1990) 124-6, Hexter (1990), and Adler (2003) 257-9. His rhetorical artistry helps explain how the Trojans are deceived and also embodies the treacherous nature of the Greeks that this episode epitomizes for Aeneas.

The episode breaks down into three large sections: 77-104 (Sinon explains his predicament and hatred of Ulysses); 105-44 (he explains the reason for his flight from the Greeks); and 144-98 (he explains the meaning of the wooden horse). For more on Sinon, see 1-267 n., J. W. Jones (1965, 1970), Lynch (1980), Manuwald (1985), Molyneux (1986), Frangoulidis (1992), and R. M. Smith (1999).

77-104. In this passage, Sinon skillfully wins over the good will of the Trojans in two ways: first, through ostentatious professions of his honesty (77-80), and second, by his self-proclaimed hatred of Ulysses (81-104). Throughout, Sinon strives to identify himself as a victim and enemy of Ulysses.

77. **fuerit quodcumque**: "whatever will happen" (i.e. no matter what will happen to me).

78. **vera:** emphatically placed; construe with *cuncta* (77). **Argolica de gente:** Sinon immediately admits he is Greek in an attempt to substantiate his claim of honesty.

79. **hoc primum:** "(I admit) this first"; cf. 78 n. More usually, this phrase would precede the thing to which it refers.

80. **vanum...finget:** construe with *nec* (79). *Vanum* implies gullibility, while *mendacem* suggests active deceitfulness. **improba:** modifies *fortuna*. Cf. 356 n. **finget:** future active indicative, takes the understood object *eum* (i.e. *Sinonem*).

81. **fando...:** "Perhaps (*si forte*) in conversation (*fando*; cf. 5-6 n.) some mention of the name (*aliquod nomen*, "any name") of Palamedes, son of Belus, has come to your ears..." Notice the artful diffidence of *si forte* and *aliquod*.

Belidae nomen Palamedis et incluta fama
gloria, quem falsa sub proditione Pelasgi
insontem infando indicio, quia bella vetabat,
demisere neci, nunc cassum lumine lugent: 85
illi me comitem et consanguinitate propinquum
pauper in arma pater primis huc misit ab annis.
dum stabat regno incolumis regumque vigebat

---

82. **Belidae...Palamedis:** genitives with *nomen*. The patronymic (*Belides, -ae*, m. "son/ descendant of Belus") should have a short "i," but Vergil lengthens this vowel, as if *Belus* were an *–eus* noun; cf. *Tydides* (long "i"), "son of *Tydeus*." In some versions of the myth, Belus was Palamedes' great-great-grandfather. Palamedes, who had discovered Ulysses' ruse to avoid the Trojan war, was falsely accused of treason by Ulysses, who forged a letter (cf. 83 *infando indicio*) implicating Palamedes in betraying the Greeks to the Trojans. Though this story does not appear in Homer, it was important in Greek tragedy; Aeschylus, Sophocles and Euripides all composed a *Palamedes*, though these plays do not survive, except for some fragments. On Ulysses' troublesome nature, cf. 44 n. **incluta fama/gloria:** *fama* is ablative of cause explaining *incluta...gloria*, another subject of *pervenit* (81). The adjective *incluta* goes back to early Roman epic, and thus suggests the high stylistic pitch of Sinon's speech.

83. **quem:** antecedent is *Palamedis*. **falsa sub proditione:** "on a false charge of treason" (*proditio*); see 82 n. **Pelasgi:** the Pelasgians were from the North Aegean and were thought to be among the oldest inhabitants of Greece. *Pelasgi* was often used as a synonym for "Greeks."

84. **insontem:** modifying *quem*. **infando indicio:** ablative of cause or means. Note the emphatic repetition of *in-*, the harsh double elision, and "the clash between word accent and verse accent (*ictus*)" (Austin). **quia bella vetabat:** Palamedes' opposition to the Trojan war seems a Vergilian contrivance that reflects well on Sinon (Servius).

85. **demisere:** *demiserunt*. **neci:** "to death," dative of direction. **nunc...:** the asyndeton* here suggests contrast, "but whom they now mourn." **cassum lumine:** a euphemism for "dead." *Lumine* is ablative of separation with *cassum* ("bereft"), which modifies *quem* (i.e. Palamedes) in line 83.

86. **illi:** dative, referring us back in thought to the convoluted introduction of Palamedes at line 81. **comitem...propinquum:** *comitem* is predicative, while *propinquum* is attributive. **consanguinitate:** ablative of cause. Vergil seems to be the first poet to use this word, which means "blood-relationship." The sense is of the line is: perhaps you have heard of Palamedes (81), "to *that man* (*illi*) my father sent me as a comrade and (being his) relative by blood..."

87. **pauper in arma:** Sinon suggests that his father's poverty (not his belief in the war's cause) compelled him to send Sinon to seek his fortune as a soldier in early youth. The alliteration* of "p" (*pauper...pater primis*) gives further emphasis to Sinon's pitiable past. **huc:** adverb, "here" (i.e. to Troy).

88. **stabat:** the subject is Palamedes, the focus of 81-7. **regno:** "power," ablative of specification with *incolumis*.

conciliis, et nos aliquod nomenque decusque
gessimus. invidia postquam pellacis Vlixi   90
(haud ignota loquor) superis concessit ab oris,
adflictus vitam in tenebris luctuque trahebam
et casum insontis mecum indignabar amici.
nec tacui demens et me, fors si qua tulisset, *if any*
si patrios umquam remeassem victor ad Argos,   95
promisi ultorem et verbis odia aspera movi.
hinc mihi prima mali labes, hinc semper Vlixes
criminibus terrere novis, hinc spargere voces

---

89. **conciliis:** ablative of place where. **et nos:** "even I." *Nos* is probably the singular for plural (AG §143a), emphasizing the respected place that Sinon held while Palamedes was alive. **aliquod nomenque decusque:** *aliquod* suggests understatement as in 81-2, but this time it is applied to Sinon himself.

90. **invidia:** ablative of cause or means. **postquam:** markedly differentiates Sinon's happy position with his life after Ulysses got involved. **pellacis:** "deceitful," first occurs here in Latin.

91. **haud ignota:** *ignota* is a neuter plural adjective used substantively; the phrase is an example of litotes*. **superis concessit ab oris:** another euphemism for "died" (cf. 85 *cassum lumine*). The subject of *concessit* is Palamedes.

92. **in tenebris:** i.e. in gloom.

93. **insontis...amici:** note the effective use of spondees. **mecum:** *cum me*, "to myself," "in my heart" (Goold).

94-5. **tacui...:** observe the change of tense from imperfect (*trahebam, indignabar*) to perfect (*tacui*). Cf. 1 n. **me:** *me...promisi ultorem (futurum esse)*, indirect statement. **si...tulisset... si...remeassem...:** future more vivid protases in secondary sequence (cf. *promisi*) indirect statement. The pluperfect subjunctives are used here to express action prior to that conveyed by the perfect indicative *promisi* (cf. AG §589a3), as the future perfect indicative can when this type of conditional is stated directly: *si fors tulerit, si remeavero, ero ultor*. **remeassem:** for *remeavissem*.

96. **odia aspera movi:** *odia* (i.e. Ulysses') is plural for singular. Note the elisions in this line that perhaps suggest Sinon's (feigned) anger.

97. **hinc:** either causal or temporal, "hence," "then." Note the repetition of *hinc* in describing Ulysses' wrath. **prima mali labes:** "the first slip of (i.e. toward) destruction." Supply *fuit*.

98. **terrere...spargere...quaerere (99):** historical infinitives, here adding vividness to the spite Sinon roused in Ulysses, who is the subject. Subjects of historical infinitives are nominative. **terrere:** here has sense of "kept terrifying." Supply *me* as object.

in vulgum ambiguas et quaerere conscius arma.
nec requievit enim, donec Calchante ministro—   100
sed quid ego haec autem nequiquam ingrata revolvo,
quidve moror? si omnis uno ordine habetis Achivos,
idque audire sat est, iamdudum sumite poenas:
hoc Ithacus velit et magno mercentur Atridae.'   *potenti-*
                                            subj.
Tum vero ardemus scitari et quaerere causas,   105

---

99. **in vulgum:** "among the general public," "publicly." *Vulgum* is masculine only here in
Vergil; it is usually neuter. **ambiguas:** perhaps so that Ulysses can deny his role, if necessary.
quaerere conscius arma: "conscious (of his guilt) sought weapons (to destroy me)." The
arma here refer to Ulysses' trickery and treachery in attaining his revenge.

100. **donec Calchante ministro — :** Sinon suddenly and artfully cuts off his speech (an
example of aposiopesis*), at the very moment that he has most aroused his audience to hear
the terrifying results of Ulysses' campaign to destroy him (cf. 105). **Calchante ministro:**
ablative absolute, "with Calchas as his minion." Calchas was the main seer among the Greeks
(see, for example, *Iliad* 1.68-100 for his role in revealing Apollo's anger at Agamemnon),
and was involved in the call for the human sacrifice of Iphigenia at Aulis (cf. 116 n.).

101. **sed...autem:** "but indeed..." This is a conversational phrase, common in the comic poets
Plautus and Terence. **quid:** interrogative adverb. **nequiquam:** here perhaps "idly." **ingrata:**
here, "disagreeable"; construe with *haec*.

102. **quidve moror:** supply *vos* as direct object. **uno ordine habetis:** "hold in one rank,"
"deem alike."

103. **idque:** *id* = "this" (i.e. the name "Greek"/*Achivos*). The connective –*que* continues the
si-clause from 102. **iamdudum sumite poenas:** *iamdudum* refers to past time, while the
imperative *sumite* refers to future. The sense is: "exact the punishment you should have
taken already!"

104. **Ithacus:** "Ithacan" (i.e. Ulysses, who was from Ithaca). Note Sinon's seeming inability
to utter Ulysses' name. **velit...mercentur:** potential subjunctives with *hoc* as object.
magno: understand *pretio*, ablative of price. **Atridae:** "sons of Atreus" (i.e. Agamemnon
and Menelaus).

105-44. *Sinon explains why and how he fled Ulysses and the Greeks.* As Sinon continues, he
says little about the horse: he only gestures to it at 112-13, vaguely suggesting that it is an
offering for their return home. Instead he concentrates his story on Ulysses' treacherous
treatment of him and calls for the Trojans' pity. Sinon's use of Ulysses' deceitfulness to
persuade the Trojans to trust him and to accept the horse is especially interesting, because
in Homer Odysseus claims to have (somehow) led the horse into the city (*Odyssey* 8.492-5).
Vergil's Sinon and Homer's Odysseus are thus intriguingly connected in their guile. See J.
W. Jones (1965) and (1970) 242-3.

105. **ardemus scitari:** *ardemus* strongly conveys the Trojans' desire to hear more. For the
infinitive, cf. 64 n.

ignari scelerum tantorum artisque Pelasgae.
prosequitur pavitans et ficto pectore fatur:
'Saepe fugam Danai Troia cupiere relicta
moliri et longo fessi discedere bello;
fecissentque utinam ! saepe illos aspera ponti   110
interclusit hiems et terruit Auster euntis.
praecipue cum iam hic trabibus contextus acernis
staret equus toto sonuerunt aethere nimbi.
suspensi Eurypylum scitatum oracula Phoebi   *supine/purpose*
mittimus, isque adytis haec tristia dicta reportat: 115

---

106. **ignari:** takes the genitive case. **artis Pelasgae:** the phrase essentially means "Greek deception." For *Pelasgae*, see 83 n.

107. **prosequitur:** "continues" (lit. "follows"). **pavitans:** certainly feigned fear is involved, but perhaps some may be authentic as well. **pectore:** here "heart," the seat of emotions.

108. **saepe...saepe:** two clauses are connected by this repeated word and thereby underscore the alleged eagerness of the Greeks to quit Troy. For this rhetorical method of joining clauses by repeating an important word, see 306, 325, 358 and n., 483-4, and 560-2. **cupiere:** for *cupierunt*. **Troia...relicta:** ablative absolute. The explanation Sinon provides here (i.e. the Greeks want to give up the war) rests uncomfortably with his later claim (176-82) that the Greeks have temporarily returned home to regain divine favor so that they could sack Troy. Lynch (1980) attempts a reconciliation of the two strands of Sinon's tales.

109. **moliri...discedere:** infinitives with *cupiere* (AG §563b); **fugam...moliri:** "to take flight." **longo...bello:** either ablative of cause explaining *fessi* or ablative of separation with *discedere*.

110. **fecissentque utinam!:** past unfulfillable wish. **ponti:** genitive, "at sea" (lit. "of the sea").

111. **Auster:** the South wind, which is often associated with harsh weather. **euntis:** accusative masculine plural of the present participle of *ire*, modifying *illos*. Here = "trying to go" (conative sense).

112. **hic...equus:** "this horse," as if Sinon is pointing to it; it must still have Laocoon's spear sticking from it (50-3). This is Sinon's first reference to the horse. The previous forty lines have skillfully separated him from the treachery of the Greeks. **contextus:** for the metaphor, cf. 16 n. **acernis:** "maple," though the horse is made of fir (*abiete*) at 16 and oak (*roboribus*) at 186. Vergil may be using particular names (*acernis, abiete, roboribus*) to indicate the general category of wood, though Hexter (1990) argues that uncertainty about the actual material of the horse is emblematic of the problem of interpretation in the *Aeneid*.

113. **staret:** imperfect subjunctive in a *cum*-circumstantial clause. **toto...aethere:** supply *in*.

114. **suspensi:** i.e. Sinon and the Greeks. **scitatum:** accusative supine with verb of motion (*mittimus*) expressing purpose (cf. AG §509).

115. **adytis:** supply *ex*.

hendiadys

"sanguine placastis ventos et virgine caesa,
cum primum Iliacas, Danai, venistis ad oras:
gerundive sanguine quaerendi reditus animaque litandum *gerundive*
Argolica." vulgi quae vox ut venit ad auris,
obstipuere animi gelidusque per ima cucurrit   120
ossa tremor, cui fata parent, quem poscat Apollo. *ind. quest.*
hic Ithacus vatem magno Calchanta tumultu
protrahit in medios; quae sint ea numina divum *ind. quest.*
flagitat. et mihi iam multi crudele canebant
artificis scelus, et taciti ventura videbant.   125

116. **placastis:** for *placavistis*. See Hardie (1984) 406-7 on the influence of the Lucretian passage here, and at 199-231 and 679-91. **sanguine...virgine caesa:** "with blood and slaughtered virgin," i.e. "with a slaughtered virgin's blood" (an instance of hendiadys*). Agamemnon's daughter Iphigenia was sacrificed at Aulis to appease Diana, who detained the expedition there with hostile winds. For the sacrifice, see Aeschylus, *Agamemnon* 183-247 and Lucretius 1.84-101.

117. **cum primum:** "when first..." **Iliacas:** adjectival form of *Ilium*; "Trojan."

118. **sanguine...:** note the parallelism with 116. **quaerendi reditus:** supply *sunt* in a passive periphrastic construction (AG §194-6); *reditus* is nominative masculine plural. **litandum:** supply *est* in an impersonal passive periphrastic construction: "an Argive life must be sacrificed" (lit. "sacrifice must be made by means of an Argive life").

119. **Argolica:** emphatic by position. **quae vox ut:** *quae vox* ("this response") refers to the oracular response retold in lines 116-19. *Ut* is temporal, "when."

120. **per ima...ossa:** "through their inmost marrow."

121. **parent...poscat:** understand a phrase like "as they wondered" governing these present subjunctives in indirect question. **cui fata parent:** supply *hoc* (i.e. death). *Cui* and *quem* are interrogative pronouns.

122. **hic:** temporal adverb. **Ithacus:** cf. 104 n. **Calchanta:** Greek accusative form (*Calchas, -antis,* m.).

123. **in medios:** "into the midst of the people," *medios* being an adjective used substantively. **sint:** present subjunctive in an indirect question, set off by *flagitat* ("demands"). **divum:** for *divorum*. The oracle expresses the "will of the gods" (*numina divum*), but the seer is needed to interpret it.

124. **canebant:** *canere* is commonly used of delivering an oracle (cf. 176 n.); here it conveys the prophetic foreboding which was felt but not uttered.

125. **artificis:** from *artifex* ("schemer") substitutes for the name Ulysses, as if it were a synonym. **taciti:** an adjective describing *multi* (124) that can be translated adverbially. **ventura:** neuter accusative plural of the future participle of *venio*.

bis quinos silet ille dies tectusque recusat
prodere voce sua quemquam aut opponere morti.
vix tandem, magnis Ithaci clamoribus actus,
composito rumpit vocem et me destinat arae.
adsensere omnes et, quae sibi quisque timebat,   130
unius in miseri exitium conversa tulere.   *not infin.*
iamque dies infanda aderat; mihi sacra parari
et salsae fruges et circum tempora vittae.
eripui, fateor, leto me et vincula rupi,
limosoque lacu per noctem obscurus in ulva   135
delitui dum vela darent, si forte dedissent.   *reported in discourse*
nec mihi iam patriam antiquam spes ulla videndi,   *gerund*

---

126. **bis:** "twice" (adverb). **quinos...dies:** accusative of duration, "for twice five (i.e. ten) days." **ille:** Calchas, the seer. **tectus:** modifying *ille*/Calchas, "shut up (in his tent)."

127. **voce sua:** ablative of means; *vox* here means "prophecy." **quemquam:** indefinite pronoun. **morti:** dative singular with compound verbs *prodere* and *opponere*.

128. **vix tandem:** emphasizes Calchas' apparent hesitation.

129. **composito:** "by their agreement." Calchas was acting according to Ulysses' plan. **rumpit vocem:** "breaks silence" (lit. "makes an utterance break forth"). **arae:** dative with *destinat*.

130-1. **adsensere:** for *adsenserunt*. **quae...tulere:** "(the things) which each feared for himself (*quae...timebat*) they tolerated (*tulere*), when they (i.e. the things, *quae*) were turned to one unhappy man's destruction." **conversa:** modifies understood *illa*, antecedent of *quae*.

132. **infanda:** note that the day of Sinon's sacrifice (and thus of Ulysses' treachery) is characterized in the same language as Aeneas' pain in recalling the fall of Troy and his consequent suffering (cf. 3 n.). **parari:** present passive infinitive, here an historical infinitive with *sacra, salsae fruges,* and *vittae* as subjects. Cf. 98 n.

133. **salsae fruges:** corn meal mixed with salt (*mola salsa*) was sprinkled on the head of the victim just before sacrifice. **tempora:** here "temples" (of the head).

134. **leto:** ablative of separation with *eripui*. **vincula:** Sinon was fettered as the sacrifical rite was being prepared.

135. **limoso...lacu:** supply *in*; perhaps recalling Marius taking refuge in the marshes of Miturnae in 88 BCE (cf. Lucan 2.70).

136. **dum vela...dedissent:** these words give in indirect discourse the thought in Sinon's mind at the time he hid himself: "I will lie hidden until they set sail (*dum vela dent*), if by chance they will have set sail (*si forte dederint*)." After the past tense *delitui* (i.e. secondary sequence), *dent* passes into *darent* and *dederint* into *dedissent*. This *dum*-clause with subjunctive expresses expectation.

137. **mihi:** dative of possessor; supply *erat* or *fuit*. **videndi:** objective genitive of gerund after *spes ulla*; it takes as objects *patriam antiquam, dulcis natos* (138), *exoptatum...parentem.*

nec dulcis natos exoptatumque parentem,
quos illi fors et poenas ob nostra reposcent
effugia, et culpam hanc miserorum morte piabunt.   140
quod te per superos et conscia numina veri,
per si qua est quae restet adhuc mortalibus usquam *dat vj*
intemerata fides, oro, miserere laborum   *ref.*
tantorum, miserere animi non digna ferentis.'
        His lacrimis vitam damus et miserescimus ultro.   145

---

138. **dulcis natos:** at 87 Sinon says that he was sent to Troy as a youth (*primis...ab annis*), a claim that may contradict his statement here.

139. **illi:** i.e. Ulysses and his partisans. **fors et:** *fors* is probably an archaism for *forsitan* ("perhaps"); the *et* is a delayed connective. **reposcent:** takes an accusative of the person of whom the demand is made (*quos*, whose antecedents are *natos* and *parentem*, 138) and an accusative of the thing demanded (*poenas*).

140. **culpam hanc:** "this guilt of mine" (i.e. from avoiding his own sacrifice). **morte:** ablative of means.

141. **quod:** "therefore," "as to which thing." This adverbial use of *quod* is common in oaths. **te:** direct object of *oro* (143). **conscia numina veri:** "the powers that know the truth" and therefore punish lies.

142. **per si qua est quae restet...:** the accusative after *per* is the whole clause *si qua...fides* (*qua* is an indefinite adjective modifying *fides*), which is thus parallel to the objects *superos* and *conscia numina*: "by whatever pledge that exists, which still remains inviolable anywhere among mortals." **restet:** subjunctive in a relative clause of characteristic.

143-4. **miserere:** present imperative of *misereor*, which here takes the objective genitives *laborum tantorum* and *animi...ferentis*. As with the first part of his speech, Sinon ends with an appeal to the Trojans that focuses on their pity for him.

145-98: *Sinon deceives the Greeks about the meaning of the wooden horse.* Sinon now turns to his second task: to convince the Trojans to bring the horse into their city. Their fatal compassion and acceptance of the suppliant Sinon here must be contrasted with their more successful and unproblematic display of compassion to the suppliant Achaemenides at the end of book 3.

145. **His lacrimis:** dative (indirect object) or ablative of cause. **ultro:** "willingly," "on our own initiative," emphasizing the Trojans' pity for Sinon. This word, which is connected to *ultra*, is used of acts that are purely voluntary, that go beyond what might be expected. Cf. 279, 372, 4.304 where *ultro compellare* is to address a person without waiting for him to speak first; 3.155 *ultro mittit* "he sends without waiting for you to come to him"; 5.55 *ultro adsumus* "we are here beyond what we could expect"; 5.446 *ultro concidit* of a boxer who misses his aim and so literally goes farther than he expected.

ipse viro primus manicas atque arta levari
vincla iubet Priamus dictisque ita fatur amicis:
'quisquis es (amissos hinc iam obliviscere Graios)
noster eris; mihique haec edissere vera roganti:
quo molem hanc immanis equi statuere? quis auctor?   150
quidve petunt? quae religio? aut quae machina belli?'
dixerat. ille dolis instructus et arte Pelasga
sustulit exutas vinclis ad sidera palmas:

146-7. **ipse...Priamus:** King Priam takes the lead in believing and showing compassion to Sinon. **viro:** i.e. Sinon, dative of reference. Taken in connection with *manicas*, *viro* essentially = "his." **primus:** construe adverbially (cf. 32 n.). **manicas:** just as Sinon's guile helped him escape his chains before his (alleged) sacrifice (134-6), so it here frees him from his Trojan *vincla*. **levari:** present passive infinitive in an accusative and infinitive construction after *iubet*. **amicis:** the adjective, not the noun; it emphasizes Priam's (misplaced) magnanimity.

148. **obliviscere:** present imperative of *obliviscor*, taking the accusative instead of the more usual genitive. **hinc:** temporal; construe with *obliviscere*. **iam:** construe with *amissos*. Sinon has escaped from the Greeks, who are now surely all hostile toward him. They are thus "lost" in that they will no longer welcome him back.

149. **noster:** directly contrasted with *Graios* at the end of 148. **edissere:** present imperative of *edissero* ("tell"), a verb appearing only here in Vergil. **vera:** a predicate accusative (AG §285 with n.), modifying *haec*; it can be translated adverbially ("truthfully"). **roganti:** modifies *mihi*.

150. **quo:** "for what purpose?," "why?" **molem hanc immanis equi:** *immanis* is masculine genitive singular with *equi*. Note the emphasis on the size of the horse; cf. 15. **auctor:** a predicate noun; supply *est*.

151. **petunt:** understand *Grai* (148) as subject. **quae religio:** here *religio* means "sacred offering"; supply *est ea*. "What sacred offering is it?" The first syllable of *religio* is short, but from Augustan poetry on, it is usually scanned long. **quae machina belli:** supply *est ea*. It is ironic that Priam suggests (but ultimately rejects) that the horse could be a machine of war, as it actually turns out to be. Note that Priam's question echoes Laocoon's words at 46.

152. **ille:** i.e. Sinon. **instructus:** *instruo* originally meant to "build" or "construct," but it could also be used of outfitting an animal, person, army, etc. with necessary equipment. Eventually that equipment could involve more abstract ideas, as here with *dolis* and *arte*, so that *instruo* could also mean "train" or "instruct." **dolis...arte Pelasga:** virtually synonymous here. The Trojans are shown falling victim to the *ars Pelasga* that Aeneas had said the Trojans were ignorant of, as he began his story of Sinon at 106.

153. **sustulit:** from *tollo* (3). **vinclis:** for *vinculis*, whose metrical rhythm cannot be used in dactylic hexameter. It is an ablative of separation with *exutas*. Observe the skill of Sinon's gesture: he treacherously lifts his "unbound" hands to heaven in order to deceive the man who had "unbound" them.

'vos aeterni ignes, et non violabile vestrum
testor numen,' ait, 'vos arae ensesque nefandi,   155
quos fugi, vittaeque deum, quas hostia gessi:
fas mihi Graiorum sacrata resolvere iura,
fas odisse viros atque omnia ferre sub auras,
si qua tegunt; teneor patriae nec legibus ullis.
tu modo promissis maneas servataque serves   160
Troia fidem, si vera feram, si magna rependam.
omnis spes Danaum et coepti fiducia belli

---

154. **aeterni ignes:** i.e. the sun and moon (if not the heavenly bodies more generally). The phrase is vocative and stands in apposition to *vos* (accusative). **non violabile:** litotes* for *inviolabile* (a word occurring only at 11.363 in Vergil). *Violabile* seems to have been created by Vergil in this passage and appears nowhere else in his poetry.

155. **numen:** "power," "majesty." **arae ensesque nefandi:** also vocative plural, in appostion to *vos*, accusative plural with *testor* understood.

156. **vittae:** vocative, also in apposition to *vos* from 155. **deum:** *deorum*. **hostia:** in apposition to the subject "I" (Sinon). Sinon refers here to the preparatory rites for his sacrifice.

157. **fas mihi:** supply *est*. **fas...iura:** note the contrast between *fas* and *iura* that frames this line. Usually *fas* is "divine law," and *ius* "human law." Sinon thus asserts that divine law empowers him "to break the oaths (*iura*)" he had sworn to the Greeks.

158. **fas odisse...ferre:** supply *est mihi*. **viros:** = *eos*, i.e. the Greeks. **ferre sub auras:** lit. "bear up into the air," i.e. "divulge," "openly proclaim."

159. **si qua tegunt:** *qua* is the neuter accusative plural of the indefinite pronoun. The subject of *tegunt* is *omnia* (158). **nec:** a delayed connective, though it could also be an archaic usage that is equivalent to *non* (Austin).

160. **tu...servataque...Troia (161):** feminine vocative singular, subject of *maneas...serves*. Sinon directly and powerfully addresses Troy (not its people), as Aeneas had at 56. **promissis maneas:** *maneas* (like *serves*) is an optative subjunctive (AG §441). The preposition *in* is omitted, as it commonly is in such phrases as *stare iureiurando, opinione,* and *iudiciis*.

161. **vera:** neuter accusative plural. **feram...rependam:** future active indicatives in future more vivid protases. With *feram* understand *sub auras* to fill out the usage of this verb from 158. Sinon ends this portion of his speech by cleverly suggesting that he will help Troy, a claim that can only tantalize the Trojans to trust him and want to hear more. Similarly he will bring his entire speech to a close at 192-4 with a piece of information that will greatly rouse the Trojans: Calchas had prophesied that the Trojans would conquer Greece, if they should bring the horse into their city.

162. **coepti...belli:** objective genitive with *fiducia*. Latin idiom tends to avoid verbal nouns and, where we use such nouns followed by a genitive, it often employs a noun and past participle in agreement, cf. 413 *ereptae virginis* "the carrying off of the maiden"; 1.515 *res... incognita* "ignorance of the facts"; 5.665 *incensas...navis* "the burning of the ships."

Palladis auxiliis semper stetit. impius ex quo
Tydides sed enim scelerumque inventor Vlixes
fatale adgressi sacrato avellere templo   165
Palladium caesis summae custodibus arcis
corripuere sacram effigiem manibusque cruentis
virgineas ausi divae contingere vittas:
ex illo fluere ac retro sublapsa referri

---

163. **Palladis:** emphatic and in position parallel to *Palladium* in 166. **stetit:** "stood firm in," a strong word; though singular, it has *spes* and *fiducia* as subjects. **ex quo:** understand *tempore*. This phrase correlates with *ex illo* (again supply *tempore*) in 169.

164. **Tydides:** "son of Tydeus," i.e. Diomedes, an important Greek warrior, who later settles in Italy and will decline an alliance with the Latins to fight the Trojans in the Italian war of *Aeneid* 7-12 (cf. 11.225-95). On the patronymic form, see 82 n. **sed enim:** "but indeed," "however"; should be translated at the beginning of the sentence. Vergil is fond of this perhaps archaic phrase (cf. Quintillian 9.3.14) and places it indifferently at the beginning of a clause or after two or three words as here (cf. *Aen.* 1.19; 5.395; 6.28; cf. also *nec enim* at 100). **scelerumque inventor:** suggests the basic nature of Aeneas' characterization of Ulysses. Note that the names of two of the greatest Greek warriors balance this line.

165. **fatale:** see 166 n. for its meaning. **adgressi:** "undertook" + infinitive. *Adgressi* is balanced by another participle (*ausi*) at 168, falling at the same caesura. **sacrato...templo:** ablative of separation.

166. **Palladium:** a statue of Pallas, whose preservation was linked by fate (165 *fatale*) to Troy's safety, provided it stayed in the city. The figure did not represent the goddess armed with helmet, spear, and shield as she is usually represented (e.g. 175), but wearing "maiden fillets" (168) as a sign of her virginity. On the various versions of the Palladium's theft, see Gantz (1993): 638, 642-6. Note that the theft of the Palladium is not actually related to the wooden horse, though a connection is implied (cf. 108 n.). Gransden (1990) 125 writes: "The Trojans put together pieces of narrative, true and false, and make their own credible synthesis"; cf. also Hexter (1990). **summae...arcis:** i.e. the acropolis on which the temple stood. Note the interlocking word order (or synchysis*) with the ablative absolute phrase *caesis custodibus*.

167. **corripuere:** for *corripuerunt*. **sacram effigiem manibusque cruentis:** chiasmus*.

168. **virgineas...vittas:** *virgineas* is a transferred epithet (enallage*): the goddess Pallas was *virginea*, not her *vittas* ("fillets" or "garlands"). The *vittae* worn by maidens differed from that of matrons. The adjective also suggests "purity" and so a contrast with the pollution of "blood-stained hands." **ausi:** supply *sunt*. **contingere:** "touch," "handle," with the implied sense of "defile" (cf. contagion).

169. **ex illo:** again, supply *tempore*, and see 163 n. **fluere...referri:** historical infinitives; *spes* is nominative subject. "The hope of the Greeks (began) to ebb and, sinking backward, receded." The metaphor in *fluere* is from the ebbing of the tide.

spes Danaum, fractae vires, aversa deae mens.   170
nec dubiis ea signa dedit Tritonia monstris.
vix positum castris simulacrum: arsere coruscae
luminibus flammae arrectis, salsusque per artus
sudor iit, terque ipsa solo (mirabile dictu) emicuit parmamque
ferens hastamque trementem.   175
extemplo temptanda fuga canit aequora Calchas,
nec posse Argolicis exscindi Pergama telis

---

170. **fractae:** supply *sunt.* **aversa:** supply *est.* Note the switch from historical infinitive (169) to finite verb within the same sentence. **mens:** lines ending in a monosyllable occur infrequently in Vergil and thus add emphasis to the word. The clipped nature of this line is made even more striking by the elaborateness of the previous six lines.

171. **nec dubiis:** litotes*. **ea signa:** "signs thereof" (i.e. of her anger). **Tritonia:** "Tritonian," i.e. Minerva. One myth had it that the goddess was born at Lake Triton in Africa. **monstris:** i.e. the means by which a divinity can make her feelings known.

172. **positum...:** *positum (erat) (in) castris,* continues the clipped nature of 170. **arsere...:** an example of parataxis*, wherein two independent clauses are placed side by side without a subordinating conjunction (cf. AG §268). Translate: "scarcely had the image been placed..., when glittering flames blazed..." Cf. the similar construction at 692-3: *Vix ea fatus erat... subitoque fragore intonuit.*

173. **luminibus...arrectis:** supply *e* or *ex*; *arrectis* means "raised" or "lifted." Note that this phrase is interlocked (synchysis*) with *coruscae...flammae.* **salsus:** the adjective adds a sense of reality. The sweating of images was a frequent prodigy, but Barchiesi (1998) 136 suggests that here it "breaks the dignified rules of epic supernatural." **artus:** accusative plural, the "limbs" of the image.

174-5. **ipsa...emicuit:** in addition to the sweating of her statue in 173, Pallas herself (*ipsa*) suddenly appears like lightning (i.e. the metaphor in *emicuit*) and disappears three times. **mirabile dictu:** "wondrous to tell"; *dictu* is an ablative of specification (AG §510) formed from the supine of *dico.* **parmamque...hastamque:** as a goddess of war (among other things), Pallas is depicted holding a shield and spear. **–que...-que:** "both...and..."

176. **extemplo:** a formal and archaic adverb, it gives further gravity to the event, whose interpretation is immediate and unquestioned by the Greeks (and Trojans). **temptanda:** supply *esse*; a passive periphrastic infinitive in indirect statement after *canit.* The compulsion implied by this form is another small detail suggesting the credibility of the tale through a proper understading of religious necessity. **fuga:** ablative. **canit:** "proclaims" or "prophesies"; *canere* is often so used (cf. also 124 n.). Oracles were usually delivered in hexameter verse and probably intoned or chanted. Note the switch to primary sequence. **Calchas:** the Greek seer continues to play a central role. Cf. 100.

177. **posse...:** the accusative (*Pergama*) and infinitive (*posse excindi*) construction after *canit* (176) continues here.

omina ni repetant Argis numenque reducant *Subj in ind. st.*
quod pelago et curvis secum avexere carinis.
et nunc quod patrias vento petiere Mycenas,   180
arma deosque parant comites pelagoque remenso
improvisi aderunt. ita digerit omina Calchas.
hanc pro Palladio moniti, pro numine laeso
effigiem statuere, nefas quae triste piaret.   *rel. clause of purpose / of characteristic – use ut*
hanc tamen immensam Calchas attollere molem   185

---

178. **omina ni...:** the protasis of a present general condition in indirect statement. **Argis:** locative of the plural noun *Argi, -orum,* m., the city "Argos." **numen:** here means either the Palladium or the goddess Pallas, whose power is housed in the Palladium. Sinon pretends that the Greeks must seek purification from Pallas back in Greece for their profanation of the Palladium (167) in order to regain her support. This detail may refer to the custom of Roman generals who would return to Rome and "seek fresh auspices" (*auspicia repetere*) if anything "unlucky" occurred on an expedition.

179. **quod:** antecedent is *Palladium* or *numen.* **avexere:** *avexerunt*; indicative, not subjunctive, because the words are an explanatory remark of Sinon's. So too we have Sinon's words at 180-8, but 189-94 are the words of Calchas in indirect statement.

180. **quod:** "as to the fact that...," a use of *quod* very common in letter-writing. Cf. Cicero, *ad Familiares* 1.7 *quod scribis te velle...* "as to the wish you express..." (AG §572). **vento petiere Mycenas:** for this phrase, see 25 n. *Petiere = petiverunt.*

181. **deosque parant comites:** Sinon suggests the gods have deserted the Greeks, who must therefore return home and induce them to join the expedition again. **pelagoque remenso:** ablative absolute; though deponent, *remenso* has a passive sense.

182. **improvisi:** this adjective has an ironic quality. Within the terms of Sinon's story, the Greeks will certainly return *improvisi*, but Sinon also knows that that Greek warriors are at that moment hiding "unforeseen" in the horse. *Improvisi* thus points to another fact that Aeneas the narrator and the reader already know. **digerit:** "arranges," and thus here means "explains." Omens are an expression of the will of the gods, but to the ignorant they seem confused and confusing: the seer arranges the signs so as to explain them.

183. **hanc:** with *effigiem*, is demonstrative and emphatic. **moniti:** sc. the Greeks. **pro numine laeso:** this expands the idea in *pro Palladio*. (Cf. 1.8, where we are told that Juno's offended divinity has caused countless woes for Aeneas and the Trojans.) Note that the explanation given for the horse here differs from that which Sinon suggests at 110-13, where the horse seems to be an offering to the gods for a safe return to Greece, not for appeasing an angry goddess (cf. 17).

184. **piaret:** imperfect subjunctive in a secondary sequence relative clause of purpose.

185. **hanc:** connected to *hanc* (183), and thus still modifying *effigiem*. See 183 n. **immensam... molem:** in apposition to *hanc* at beginning of this line. **Calchas attollere...iussit (186):** supply *nos.*

roboribus textis caeloque educere iussit,
ne recipi portis aut duci in moenia posset,
neu populum antiqua sub religione tueri. *reported speech*
nam si vestra manus violasset dona Minervae,
tum magnum exitium (quod di prius omen in ipsum   190
optative subj. convertant!) Priami imperio Phrygibusque futurum;
sin manibus vestris vestram ascendisset in urbem,
ultro Asiam magno Pelopea ad moenia bello
venturam et nostros ea fata manere nepotes.'

---

186. **roboribus textis:** ablative of description (AG §415), "of interwoven wooden planks." See 112 n. for the meaning of *roboribus*, and 16 n. for the metaphor in *textis*. **caelo:** dative of direction, for *ad caelum*.

187. **ne...posset:** negative purpose clause . **recipi...duci:** present passive infinitives with *posset*.

188. **neu...tueri:** deponent infinitive after *posset* (187), continuing the negative purpose clause. **antiqua sub religione:** "under ancient divine protection." The horse was sent *pro Palladio* and if properly welcomed and worshipped would provide the same protection to Troy as the Palladium had (see 166 n.).

189. **nam...:** supply *Calchas dixit*. A future more vivid conditional (*si vestra manus violaverit dona Minervae, tum exitium erit...*) is reported in secondary sequence indirect speech. *Violaverit* becomes *violasset* (for *violavisset*). Cf. 94 n. **Minervae:** objective genitive, cf. 31 n.

190. **quod...omen:** refers back to *exitium*. **ipsum:** i.e. Calchas, the augur.

191. **convertant:** optative subjunctive (AG §441). **futurum:** supply *esse*; this is the verb of the future more vivid apodosis in indirect discourse (see 189 n.). **imperio Phrygibusque:** dative of reference or disadvantage (AG §376).

192. **sin...:** "but if...", the conditional in indirect speech continues (cf. 189 n. and 191 n.). **vestris vestram:** Sinon emphasizes that the Trojans must bring the horse into the city themselves. **ascendisset:** for the form, cf. 189 n.

193. **ultro:** see 145 n. **Pelopea ad moenia:** i.e. to Greece. Pelops (*Pelopea* is an adjectival form) was the grandfather of Agamemnon and Menelaus. **magno...bello:** ablative of accompaniment. In this line, Sinon says that Asia would bring war on Greece itself.

194. **venturam:** supply *esse*. For the construction, see 189 n. **ea fata:** neuter accusative plural, "this fate," i.e. the possible outcomes for the Trojans' handling of the horse: destruction (*magnum exitium*) or empire (*Pelopea ad moenia*). **manere:** an infinitive in indirect speech with *ea fata* as accusative subject (*manent* in direct speech). Here it means "await" and takes a direct object (*nostros...nepotes*, i.e. the Greeks).

Talibus insidiis periurique arte Sinonis   195
credita res, captique dolis lacrimisque coactis
quos neque Tydides nec Larisaeus Achilles,
non anni domuere decem, non mille carinae.
Hic aliud maius miseris multoque tremendum

---

195. **Talibus insidiis:** the narrator Aeneas shows his own artistry by drawing the Sinon
episode to a close with a reference to his own introduction to it at 65-6 (*accipe nunc Danaum
insidias et crimine ab uno / disce omnis*). The account was in fact a cautionary tale of Greek
treachery and therefore of Greek character. **periuri:** another instance of Aeneas proleptically
revealing the treachery of Sinon.

196. **credita:** supply *est*. **res:** here means "tale." **captique:** supply *sumus* (i.e. we, Trojans). **dolis
lacrimisque coactis:** ablative of means, referring to Sinon's treachery. *Coactis* is a word
specially used of "forced" or "false" tears.

197. **quos:** antecedent is the understood *nos* in *capti sumus* from the preceding line. **Tydides:**
see 164 n. **Larisaeus:** adjectival form of *Larisa* (or *Larissa*), the town in Thessaly from which
Achilles came. The patronymic *Tydides* and the epithet *Larisaeus* add stateliness to the line.
Sinon's omission of Ulysses here is surely pointed. Achilles and Diomedes are defined by
their military excellence, Odysseus by his treachery.

198. **anni...decem:** Troy fell in the tenth year of the war. Note that it is in this year that
Homer's *Iliad* takes place. **domuere:** for *domuerunt*. **mille carinae:** the thousand ships
that set sail against Troy is traditional at least as far back as the Greek tragedian Aeschylus,
Agamemnon 45 (fifth century BCE). **non...non:** more unusual than *neque...neque* and
therefore perhaps more rhetorically evocative. In the end, a deceitful nobody named Sinon
brought Troy down.

199-233: *Twin serpents suddenly emerge from the sea and attack Laocoon and his two sons.*
The scene switches suddenly back to Laocoon. As he performs a sacrifice (presumably regarding
his distrust of the horse), he and his sons are attacked by twin serpents that emerge from the sea.
They ironically become the human sacrifice necessary for the Greeks' return home (cf. 114-29).
See R. M. Smith (1999) 503 on "the systematic perversion of religious sacrifice" in this episode.

Exactly why Laocoon (and his sons) must die is debated, since he is correct that the horse
is a Greek ruse. Servius relates a story that Laocoon was punished for having sex in a sacred
area, one probably associated with Neptune, while Hyginus (probably second century C.E.)
says that Laocoon had married and had children against Apollo's will (see Tracy (1987) and
Austin *ad loc.*). However, there is no clear indication of either of these stories in Vergil, who
seems to suggest that Laocoon is killed for striking the sacred horse with his spear (229-31).
The mode of Laocoon's death also varied, though perhaps the most famous representation
is the marble statue group at the Vatican Museum that probably dates to the Late Republic.
For bibliography, see 1-267 n.

199. **Hic:** temporal adverb. **miseris:** understand *nobis*, dative with the compound verb *obicitur*.
aliud: supply *omen*, which in turn is modified by the two comparative adjectival phrases
maius and *tremendum magis*. **multo:** ablative of degree of difference.

obicitur magis atque improvida pectora turbat.   200
Laocoon, ductus Neptuno sorte sacerdos,
sollemnis taurum ingentem mactabat ad aras.
ecce autem gemini a Tenedo tranquilla per alta
(horresco referens) immensis orbibus angues
incumbunt pelago pariterque ad litora tendunt;   205

---

200. **improvida pectora:** *improvida* conveys the suprise and horror that the Trojans will experience at the deaths of Laocoon and his sons, but it also resonates with Sinon's ironic use of *improvisi* at 182 (see n.). *Pectora* can refer to intellectual and emotional capacity. In Aeneas' story both are put to the test, though the emotional effect of Sinon's speech and of Laocoon's death is perhaps more powerful (e.g. 195-6).

201. **ductus...sorte:** i.e. chosen by lot. Only here do we learn that Laocoon is a priest of Neptune, though he is more traditionally identified as a priest of Apollo. His religious status was not mentioned at 40-56. **Neptuno:** dative of reference.

202. **sollemnis:** "sacred," "sacrificial," modifying *aras*. Though Vergil does not specify what happened to Laocoon after Sinon's sudden entrance at 57, this passage shows that he went to perform a sacrifice (*mactabat*), presumably to consult the gods about the wooden horse. The solemnity of this scene contrasts with the horrific event about to occur. **taurum ingentem:** the depiction of the bull being slaughtered as *ingentem* suggests the importance of the sacrifice, but the size of the bull will be quickly and monstrously surpassed by the serpents about to attack. **ad:** with accusative here means "nearby," "at."

203. **ecce autem:** "But look!" This phrase introduces a dramatic and unexpected incident (cf. 318, 526, 673). **gemini:** modifying *angues* (204); it is also used to describe the serpents (*dracones*) at 225, and is applied to the Atridae (Agamemnon and Menelaus) at 415 (cf. n.) and 500. See Knox (1950) on snake imagery in *Aeneid* 2. **a Tenedo:** the serpents come from Tenedos, and thus foreshadow the eventual attack of the Greeks from that island (255). **tranquilla:** like *sollemnis* (cf. 202 n.), this adjective contrasts with the serpents' violence. **alta:** substantive adjective meaning the "deep" (understand *maria*, i.e. the deep sea). Petronius' description of Laocoon's death in *Satyricon* 89.35-65 (first century CE) looks back to this passage.

204. **horresco referens:** Aeneas' aside underscores the surprise and horror of the event. **immensis orbibus:** ablative of quality. The serpents' monstrousness is again emphasized, just as the horse's had been earlier (cf. 150 *immanis equi*). **angues:** Vergil delays *angues* to the end of 204, though it is modified by *gemini* in 203 (an example of hyperbaton*), thereby adding suspense to the description of the serpents' attack.

205. **pelago:** dative with *incumbunt*, "skim over" (lit. "lean on or over"). The verb here may convey a sense of violence or aggression, as the verb often can (cf. *incubuere mari*, of Aeolus' winds as they build up a storm against Aeneas and his fleet at 1.84). This would add further to the contrast between the sudden and unexpected violence of the serpents and the calm of the sea (cf. *tranquilla per alta* 203). **pariter:** "at the same time," "side by side." **tendunt:** can mean not only to stretch (cf. 29 n.) but also to aim (e.g. a weapon or a glance). Here the latter meaning is used in an intransitive sense: "aim for" or "head toward." Cf. 1.204-5 *per tot discrimina rerum / tendimus in Latium*.

pectora quorum inter fluctus arrecta iubaeque
sanguineae superant undas; pars cetera pontum
pone legit sinuantque immensa volumine terga.
fit sonitus spumante salo; iamque arva tenebant
ardentisque oculos suffecti sanguine et igni   210
sibila lambebant linguis vibrantibus ora.
diffugimus visu exsangues. illi agmine certo

---

206. **quorum:** antecedent is *angues* (204). **fluctus:** here has the sense of "tide," and is thus differentiated from *undas* ("waves"). **arrecta:** while this participle means "upright," it is often used in expressions in Vergil that describe fear-inspiring events or reactions. Cf. 173 *luminibus…arrectis*; 4.280 and 12.868 *arrectaeque horrore comae*. **iubae:** *iubae* ("crests") are traditional features of serpents. *Iuba* is originally the hair on an animal's neck (especially a horse's mane) (e.g. 11.497), but it came to be used of anything that resembled it, such as the plume of a helmet, which of course could be of horse-hair (cf. 412) or, as here, the crest of a serpent.

207. **superant:** the subject is *pectora arrecta iubaeque sanguineae*. **pars cetera:** "the remaining part," i.e. the rest of the serpents' bodies — up until now, Vergil has focused on their chests and heads. Note the alliteration of "s" suggests the serpents' hissing (onomatopoeia*).

208. **pone:** adverb, "behind." **legit:** "skims." From its sense of "plucking," "gathering," *lego* in poetry acquires a secondary sense of "passing over the surface" or "along the edge." Thus *aequor, pontum, vada legere* means "to sail over the sea," and *oram, litus legere* "to coast along." Cf. the analogous use of the word = "to peruse (a book)." **volumine:** "in a coil."

209. **sonitus spumante salo:** note the alliterative imitation (cf. 207 n.). The phrase *fit sonitus* suggests the suddenness of the sound. *Spumante salo* is ablative absolute. **arva:** = *litora*; though the primary meaning of *arvum* is "field" or "ploughed land," in poetry the plural *arva* could be used simply to denote dry land as opposed to water. **tenebant:** not "hold" but here "were reaching." For this meaning of *teneo*, cf. 5.159 *iamque propinquabant scopulo metamque tenebant*.

210. **ardentisque oculos suffecti:** *suffecti* is a passive participle with middle sense and takes a direct object (*ardentisque oculos*), "having suffused their burning eyes with blood and fire" (cf. 1.228 *lacrimis oculos suffusa nitentis*). Note that metaphors of fire and burning will be central to Aeneas' description of Troy's destruction.

211. **sibila…ora:** this artful enclosing adjective-noun phrase concludes the horrifying description of the serpents' initial onslaught.

212. **diffugimus:** short "u" (historical) present tense (AG §469). **visu:** ablative of cause. **illi:** *gemini angues*. **agmine certo:** "with unswerving advance." *Agmen* has two senses: 1.) "an army on the march," 2.) "march," "advance." Here Vergil takes advantage of this double meaning and describes the "advance" of the serpents by a word which also compares them with an "army on the march" as it moves in a long, winding, glittering line.

Laocoonta petunt; et primum parva duorum
corpora natorum serpens amplexus uterque
implicat et miseros morsu depascitur artus;   215
post ipsum auxilio subeuntem ac tela ferentem
corripiunt spirisque ligant ingentibus; et iam
bis medium amplexi, bis collo squamea circum
terga dati superant capite et cervicibus altis.
ille simul manibus tendit divellere nodos   220

213-14. Laocoonta: Greek accusative form, emphatically placed at the beginning of the line. **et:** may have an adversative sense, "yet," "but." Laocoon seems to be the focal point of the action up to this point, so we are perhaps surpised to find that his sons are the serpents' first victims. Laocoon will be killed when he tries to save them (220-2, though see 223 n.) **primum:** adverb. **parva duorum / corpora natorum:** note the interlocking word order (or synchysis*) that mimics the serpents' crushing embrace of Laocoon's children. **amplexus:** perfect participle of the deponent verb *amplector*.

215. artus: masculine accusative plural. **morsu:** ablative of means. **depascitur:** here with *morsu*, the verb probably means not simply "eat" but "devour." Vergil uses it only twice in the *Aeneid*, both times in conjunction with serpents (here and at 5.93). At *Georgics* 3.458, the phrase *artus depascitur* is used of a disease preying on livestock.

216. post: adverb, "then," "afterwards"; coordinates with *primum* at 213. **ipsum:** *Laocoonta*, direct object of *corripiunt* (217). **auxilio:** dative of purpose; "for assistance," i.e. "to help." **subeuntem:** the force of *sub* is the same as in *succurrere, subsidium*: it conveys the idea of support, cf. 467 *subeunt*. Note the effect of the two elisions in this line.

217. corripiunt: emphatically placed; the swiftness and control of the serpents' action contrast with the frantic actions in the preceding line (*auxilio subeuntem ac tela ferentem*). **et iam:** Vergil does not often place two monosyllables at the end of a line, particularly after such a strong pause at the end of the fifth foot, as we find in *ingentibus*. These two words thus stand out expressively.

218-19. bis...bis: adverbs, "twice...twice." Note how the anaphora* helps convey the overpowering strength of the serpents. **medium:** with this accusative masculine singular understand *Laocoonta*, "the middle of Laocoon," i.e. "his waist." **circum...dati (219):** the compound form is separated by tmesis. *Terga circumdati*, which is parallel to *amplexi medium*, is a good illustration of the middle use of the passive participle. For the active use of this verb, cf. Priam as he vainly prepares to resist the Greeks: *arma diu senior desueta trementibus aevo / circumdat nequiquam umeris* (509-10). **collo:** dative with *circumdat*. **superant:** supply *eum* (i.e. Laocoon). This is the second use of *supero* to describe the serpents (cf. 207).

220. ille: Laocoon. The change of subject is at once marked by the prominent position of the pronoun. **tendit:** "strives" or "struggles" (cf. the different senses at 29 and 205). **nodos:** the "knots" with which the snakes have tied themselves around Laocoon.

perfusus sanie vittas atroque veneno,
clamores simul horrendos ad sidera tollit:
qualis mugitus, fugit cum saucius aram
taurus et incertam excussit cervice securim.
at gemini lapsu delubra ad summa dracones   225
effugiunt saevaeque petunt Tritonidis arcem,
sub pedibusque deae clipeique sub orbe teguntur.

---

221. **perfusus:** perfect passive participle; *vittas* is accusative of specification. For the construction, cf. 57 n. The gore (*sanie*) is presumably from the serpents' devouring of Laocoon's sons (215), a detail emphasizing both the horror of the situation and the futility of Laocoon's attempt to resist. The surprise of this attack is perhaps increased by its context: Laocoon is a priest of Neptune and is presumably in the process of sacrificing to him when the serpents emerge from the sea, the god's domain.

222. **simul:** coordinates with *simul* in 220. Laocoon reacts both physically (220) and vocally (here). **clamores...horrendos**: expands on the horror of the preceding lines, while *ad sidera*, an example of hyperbole*, underscores the priest's pain.

223. **qualis mugitus:** accusative plural, object of *tollit*; "such as the bellowings a bull [raises], when..." The bellowing and struggling of a victim at the altar portended disaster. Here Laocoon, who was in the midst of a sacrifice, is now compared to a bull being sacrificed. Laocoon thus metaphorically meets the fate (human sacrifice) that Sinon claims to have avoided (cf. also 221 n.), though it should be noted that Laocoon's death is not actually described through this simile: the bull is struck and flees the altar, but its death is not portrayed. See R. M. Smith (1999) 518-20 on the simile and its implications.

224. **incertam:** the axe (*securim*) is *incertam* ("ill-aimed") because it does not strike the bull dead. **cervice:** ablative of separation with *excussit*.

225. **at:** transfers our attention from Laocoon's presumed death (cf. 223 n.) to the departure of the serpents. **gemini:** cf. 203 n. **lapsu:** ablative of manner; "by slithering," cf. 323 n. Words relating to *labor*, which can mean both slide (i.e. "slither," like a snake) and collapse in ruin (as Troy will), are important for this book: cf. 97, 236, 240, 262, 430, 465, 551, 693, and 695. See Knox (1950). **delubra...summa**: "the highest shrines"; as the next line shows, they stand on the acropolis.

226. **arcem:** for *templum*. The temple stood on the *arx* of the city. **saevaeque:** with *Tritonidis*, genitive singular of *Tritonis*, i.e. Pallas (cf. 171 n.). Pallas is *saeva* not only for her role as a war goddess and perhaps the Trojans' most formidable divine opponent, but also because the Trojans now believe that the serpents had been sent by her to silence Laocoon, who had been suspicious of the horse (cf. 40-53, 229-30). Having completed their job, the *angues* find protection at her statue (227).

227. **sub pedibusque deae:** i.e. under a statue of the goddess. The enclitic –*que* is usually not attached to a monosyllabic preposition but to another element in the prepositional phrase. Statues of Pallas often included a snake at her feet. **teguntur:** probably with middle sense, "conceal themselves."

tum vero tremefacta novus per pectora cunctis
insinuat pavor, et scelus expendisse merentem
Laocoonta ferunt, sacrum qui cuspide robur   230
laeserit et tergo sceleratam intorserit hastam.
ducendum ad sedes simulacrum orandaque divae
numina conclamant.
dividimus muros et moenia pandimus urbis.

---

228. **tum vero:** this combination indicates a strong and immediate response or reaction to an event (cf. 105, 309, 624). **cunctis:** dative of reference or disadvantage; understand *nostrum* (partitive genitive).

229. **insinuat:** "creeps"; just as the snakes *sinuant* (208), so the fear they cause is described as *insinuat*. **scelus expendisse:** a contracted phrase meaning "had paid the (penalty of) crime"; cf. 11.258 *scelerum poenas expendimus omnes*. For the syntax, cf. 230 n. **merentem:** translate adverbially, "deservedly." **scelus:** cf. 231 *sceleratum*.

230. **ferunt:** begins an indirect statement: *ferunt merentem Laocoonta expendisse... sacrum... robur:* its status as a religious offering as opposed to a weapon of war (*machina*) had been debated earlier (cf. 35-9, 45-8, 151). The Trojans now endorse the former interpretation. The death of the man who had tried to uncover the Greek deception is thus misread by the Trojans and ironically convinces them to bring the horse into the city (exactly what Laocoon had earlier argued against). See R. M. Smith (1999) 514-16.

230-1. **qui...laeserit...intorserit:** perfect subjunctives in a primary sequence causal relative clause. Translate: "because he (had) struck...and hurled..." (cf. 248). Laocoon had hit the horse with his spear at 50-3. **tergo:** dative with *intorserit*. In 51, we were told that the horse was struck in its "side" and "belly," not its back. Since *tergum* ofterns seems to be used like *tergus* = "skin," "hide," perhaps here it may stand for any part of the horse's framework, though the potential inconsistency is still present.

232. **ducendum...oranda:** supply *esse*; they are infinitives in indirect statement after *conclamant*. **divae:** *Minervae*.

233. Another half line. See 66 n.

234-49: *The Trojans drag the horse into the city and foolishly celebrate.*

234. **dividimus muros et moenia pandimus:** notice the chiasmus*. The *muri* divided are the city walls, while the *moenia* "laid bare" are the "buildings" within. This line is not inconsistent with 242, which refers to "the gate" at which the horse enters. In ancient towns the gate was merely an opening in the lower part of the wall, and it would be natural to "divide the wall" at a point where there was a gate. **dividimus:** Aeneas uses the first person plural and thus portrays himself as going along with the rest of the Trojans. Only after 268 does he begin to act independently. See 1-267 n.

accingunt omnes operi pedibusque rotarum   235
subiciunt lapsus, et stuppea vincula collo
intendunt: scandit fatalis machina muros
feta armis. pueri circum innuptaeque puellae
sacra canunt funemque manu contingere gaudent:
illa subit mediaeque minans inlabitur urbi.   240
o patria, o divum domus Ilium et incluta bello
moenia Dardanidum! quater ipso in limine portae

---

235. **accingunt:** supply *se*. **operi:** dative of purpose, "for the work" (i.e. of opening the wall). **pedibus**: dative with *subiciunt* ("place underneath"). **rotarum...lapsus (236):** "gliding wheels" (lit. "glidings of wheels"). Note how the word family *lab-* is involved in the violence caused by Ulysses against Sinon (97 *prima mali labes*), by the snakes that attack Laocoon (225 *lapsu*), and by the rolling of the horse into Troy (here and 240). See 225 n.

236. **stuppea vincula:** "hempen ropes." *Stuppea* is an adjectival form of *stuppa* ("hemp" or "tow") that Vergil introduced at *Georgics* 1.309; *vincula* from *vincio* ("bind") were not only physical restraints on animate beings but were things that could bind or restrict inanimate and even abstract ideas. Our phrase here would seem to liken the rope attached to the horse to those used to moor a ship. **collo:** dative, indirect object of the compound verb *intendunt* (cf. 237 n.).

237. **intendunt:** "stretch," "tie tightly." The word is not used loosely for "fasten on," "throw over," but rather describes the "drawing taut" of a rope placed on the horse to haul it into the city — "draw the hempen bands tight upon its neck." **scandit:** "climbs." **machina:** cf. 46 and 151 n.

238. **feta:** with ablative *armis*, standing in for the warriors inside the horse by metonymy*. For the horse as metaphorically* pregnant with soldiers, see also 20 and 52 with notes. **pueri... puellae:** a Roman religious rite may be suggested here, one in which *pueri* and *puellae* play prominent roles. **circum:** adverb.

239. **sacra:** accusative plural, here "hymns." **funem...gaudent:** there may be reference here to the practice of noble youths laying their hands on the tracks of the cars (*tensae*) on which the images of the gods were carried at Rome. **contingere gaudent:** cf. 64 n.; *gaudent* here means "are joyfully eager to." Notice how throughout Vergil dwells on the irony of the Trojans' happiness and celebration.

240. **illa:** i.e. the *fatalis machina* (237), the horse. **mediae...urbi:** dative with *inlabitur*. **minans:** present participle, though here it can be translated adverbially, "threateningly." **inlabitur:** cf. 235 n.

241. **o patria...:** note the pathos of this outburst. **divum:** *divorum*. **bello:** ablative with *incluta*.

242. **Dardanidum:** archaic genitive. On Dardanus, see 59 n. **portae:** this gate is in the lower part of the city wall that was breached in 234.

substitit atque utero sonitum quater arma dedere;
instamus tamen immemores caecique furore
et monstrum infelix sacrata sistimus arce.   245
tunc etiam fatis aperit Cassandra futuris
ora dei iussu non umquam credita Teucris.
nos delubra deum miseri, quibus ultimus esset
ille dies, festa velamus fronde per urbem.
     Vertitur interea caelum et ruit Oceano nox   250
involvens umbra magna terramque polumque
Myrmidonumque dolos; fusi per moenia Teucri

---

243. **substitit:** "stuck," "halted"; understand the horse as subject. Tripping at the threshold was in itself a bad portent; the consequent rattling of the weapons provides another warning. Aeneas emphasizes that each thing happened four times (*quater...quater*), thus underscoring the tragic ignorance of the Trojans as they drag the horse into the city. **utero:** *(in) utero.*

244. **immemores:** "unmindful," i.e. ignoring the significance of the omen in 242-3. **furore:** this is the first attribution of *furor* to the Trojans. It will play an important role in Aeneas' actions throughout the rest of the book.

245. **sacrata...arce:** *(in) arce,* ablative of place; supply *in.* **infelix:** neuter accusative singular, modifying *monstrum.* "Observe how the finality of this line is achieved by slow spondees, alliteration of *s,* use of the powerful word *monstrum,* and juxtaposition of the conflicting religious terms *infelix* and *sacrata*" (Williams).

246-7. **Cassandra:** Apollo gave Cassandra the gift of prophecy to win her over, but she still rejected him. As a result, she was cursed by the god always to prophesy truly but never to be believed. **fatis...futuris:** understand *canendis,* dative of purpose, "to foretell the coming disasters." **non umquam credita:** probably modifying *ora,* not *Cassandra.* **Teucris:** dative of agent common in poetry after perfect passive participles, where in prose we would expect *a* + ablative (AG §375).

248. **deum:** *deorum,* with *delubra.* **miseri, quibus...esset:** the position of *quibus* connects it with *miseri.* For this causal *qui* (= *quippe qui*), cf. 230, 345.

249. **festa...fronde:** ablative of means.

250-67: *At night, while the Trojans are sleeping, the Greek warriors spill out of the horse and open the city gates.*

250. **Vertitur...caelum:** the heavens are regarded as consisting of two hemispheres (one bright and the other dark) that revolve, causing day and night. The line has models in Ennius' *Annales* fragment 205 (Warmington and Skutsch) and Homer's *Odyssey* 5.294. **Oceano:** "from Ocean" (ablative), though Mack (1980) argues that *Oceano* is dative after *ruit* by drawing on the uses of *ruo* elsewhere in Vergil.

252. **Myrmidonum:** see 7 n. **fusi:** *fusus* describes the attitude of one who lies down, without any care or fear of being disturbed; thus "lying at ease." **per moenia:** here, "throughout the (buildings of the) city." See 234 n.

conticuere; sopor fessos complectitur artus.
et iam Argiva phalanx instructis navibus ibat
a Tenedo tacitae per amica silentia lunae   255
litora nota petens, flammas cum regia puppis
extulerat, fatisque deum defensus iniquis
inclusos utero Danaos et pinea furtim
laxat claustra Sinon. illos patefactus ad auras
reddit equus, laetique cavo se robore promunt   260
Thessandrus Sthenelusque duces et dirus Vlixes,
demissum lapsi per funem, Acamasque Thoasque
Pelidesque Neoptolemus primusque Machaon

[handwritten margin notes: "zeugma", "two object", "Homer hers?"]

253. **conticuere:** Vergil here uses the same verb he had to describe the Carthaginians (1) as Aeneas was about to tell his tale. **complectitur artus:** perhaps an echo of the serpents devouring Laocoon's children at 215 (*depascitur artus*). Cf. also the combination of sleep and the snake metaphor at 268-9.

254-9. The relationship between the three verbs (*ibat, extulerat, laxat*) is difficult. It is probably best to take *cum…extulerat* (257)…*laxat* (259) as an inverted *cum*-clause (Williams; AG §546a). The sentence would mean: "And now the fleet…was moving when suddenly the king's ship gave the signal…and Sinon loosens…"

254. **phalanx:** note that the Greeks are described as attacking in their characteristic military formation, though one that long post-dated the Trojan war. **instructis navibus:** "with its ships arrayed for battle." For more on *instruo*, see 152 n.

255. **Tenedo:** see notes on 21 and 203. **tacitae per amica silentia lunae:** Vergil focuses on the calm security that the moonlight provides the Greek fleet as it sails back to Troy in contrast to the terror it is about to wreak on an unsuspecting city.

256-7. **regia puppis:** presumably Agamemnon's ship. **iniquis:** the *fatis* are *iniquis* from the Trojans' perspective.

258-9. **inclusos…Danaos et…laxat claustra:** notice the zeugma*, whereby *laxat* must be construed differently with its two objects: "releases the enclosed Greeks and…loosens the bars." We can also see an example of hysteron proteron*, since the bars would be loosened before the Greeks could be released. **illos:** the Greeks enclosed in the horse. **patefactus:** "opened."

260. **cavo…robore:** ablative of separation.

261. **dirus:** an epithet for Ulysses also at 762. He had been *durus* at 2.7, though by the end of book 3 we see a different understanding of him as *infelix* (3.613, 691).

262. **lapsi:** cf. 225 n.

263. **Pelides:** patronymic modifying *Neoptolemus* (also called Pyrrhus), whose father was Achilles, and grandfather Peleus. He will play a central role later in book 2 (506-58), when he kills Priam. **primusque Machaon:** the force of *primus* is unclear, for Machaon is not the first warrior out of the horse, nor is he *primus* in the sense of "peerless," for he was not a notable warrior.

et Menelaus et ipse doli fabricator Epeos.
invadunt urbem somno vinoque sepultam;   265
caeduntur vigiles, portisque patentibus omnis
accipiunt socios atque agmina conscia iungunt.

---

264. **ipse doli fabricator Epeos:** we had been told at 15 that the horse was built with Pallas' art; here we learn the name of the builder. Epeos' role in building the horse goes back to Homer, *Odyssey* 8.493.

265. **somno vinoque:** probably hendiadys* for "drunken sleep." **sepultam:** "buried," the metaphor looks forward to the destruction awaiting the Trojans (cf. 3.630). Ennius (*Annales* fragment 294 in Warmington, 288 in Skutsch) has the fuller phrase *vino domiti somnoque sepulti* "overcome with wine and buried in slumber."

267. **agmina conscia:** "allied troops."

The Fall of Troy (lines 268-558)

The second major part of book 2 describes the destruction of Troy. As the Greeks rampage through the city, we see Aeneas gradually realizing that Troy's final day has come. The section is framed by violence associated with Achilles: Hector, slain by this greatest of Greek warriors, appears to Aeneas in a dream at the beginning of this section, while Priam's death at the hands of Achilles' son Pyrrhus occurs at the end. If Hector's death and apparition mean the defeat of Troy's military defences (cf. *Iliad* 22; *Aeneid* 2.291-2), Priam's death shows with finality the collapse of Troy's political structure, symbolized gruesomely by the king's decapitation, the image with which this section ends (554-8). In between these two momentous events, we see Aeneas' gut-wrenching reactions to Troy's destruction.

This section is crucial for understanding Aeneas because it displays the origins of the most important themes of his epic. First, we learn from Hector that Aeneas is to assume a new role for his people: he becomes an agent of fate, who must lead his people from Troy to found a new city (289-95). Second, the requirements of fate necessitate a reconfiguration of epic heroism. While heroic action in Homer privileged individual glory (see, e.g., Sarpedon's statement of the "heroic code" at *Iliad* 12.310-28), in Vergil it will take the good of the community as its foremost concern. These changes are difficult for Aeneas, and throughout this section he is continually overcome by his passions to act in a more Homeric mode and die in battle (e.g. 316-17), as he struggles to make sense of Hector's paradoxical (and un-Homeric) injunction to save his city by fleeing it.

Vergil may be the first to represent Priam's grisly death as "the crowning event of the sack of Troy" (Heinze 1915, 1993: 23), and there are numerous other elements in book 2 that differ from previous accounts. For more on Vergil's version of Troy's fall, see Putnam (1965) 28-37, Kenney (1979), Bowie (1990), Gransden (1990), Sklenár (1990), Ross (1998), and Rossi (2002, 2004: 17-53).

Tempus erat quo prima quies mortalibus aegris
incipit et dono divum gratissima serpit.
in somnis, ecce, ante oculos maestissimus Hector   270
visus adesse mihi largosque effundere fletus,
raptatus bigis ut quondam, aterque cruento

268-97. *Hector appears to Aeneas in a vision and urges him to take Troy's tutelary gods and flee the city.*
This scene has an important literary heritage in Homer and Ennius. At *Iliad* 23.65-107 the
shade of Patroclus appears to Achilles to demand burial; at the opening of *Annales*, the poet
Homer appears to Ennius, the father of Roman poetry, as he begins his history of Rome,
starting with the fall of Troy. Hector's appearance is thus grounded in the greatest works of
the Greek and Latin epic traditions. For more on Ennius and his influence in this section,
see the notes on 271 and 274-5. See also Widgodsky (1972): 74, 77-8 for the influence of
Ennian tragedy, and R. A. Smith (2005): 67-9.

268. **quo:** antecedent is *tempus*; ablative of time. Note that the beautiful description of sleep
as a release from mortal cares is ironically juxtaposed against the infiltration of the Greeks
into the city (254-67) and Hector's terrifying wraith and message. **mortalibus aegris:**
dative plural, a Homeric phrase (cf. *Odyssey* 11.19), which contrasts human experience with
the everlasting vitality of the gods. *Aegris* here means "weary."

269. **dono divum:** *dono* is ablative. **serpit:** notice the continuing presence of snake metaphors.
In this case, sleep's slithering helps the Greeks take Troy by surprise.

270. **in somnis:** though *somnus* generally means "sleep," it can be used in such constructions
as *per somnum* and *in somnis* (as here) to mean "in one's dreams." Cf. 1.353-4 *in somnis
inhumati venit imago / coniugis*. Note that Aeneas does not awaken until 302 (*excutior
somno*). **ecce:** suggests the quick change of circumstances from quiet to the horror that
will engulf the remainder of the book. **ante oculos:** understand *meos* (i.e. Aeneas'). Aeneas
stresses Hector's visual presence (cf. also 271 *visus adesse mihi*). **Hector:** son of king Priam
and the greatest of the Trojan warriors; *Iliad* 22 describes his duel with Achilles and his
subsequent death (cf. 268-558 n.). Note the elisions in this line, which help convey Aeneas'
horror and surprise as he sees Hector.

271. **visus…:** governs the infinitives *adesse…effundere*; supply *est*. There is a complex recall of
Ennius here. *Visus adesse mihi* echoes *visus Homerus adesse poeta* from *Annales* 1 (fragment
5 in Warmington, 3 in Skutsch), while *effundere fletus* resonates with Lucretius' description
of Homer, which itself refers back to the same Ennian passage: *speciem lacrimas effundere
salsas* (*De Rerum Natura* 1.125).

272. **raptatus bigis:** *bigae* (from *bi-* + *iuga* = two yokes) was a two-horse chariot; *rapto* conveys
a strong sense of vehemence, "dragged violently away." Achilles fastened Hector's corpse
to his chariot and dragged it back to the Greek camp on the Trojan shore (Homer, *Iliad*
22.395-404, 464-5). This event is the subject of one of the pictures Aeneas sees at Carthage
at 1.483. There may be another Ennian echo, this time from the *Andromache*: *vidi, videre
quod me passa aegerrume, Hectorem curru quadriiugo raptarier* (fr. 91-2 in Warmington, 78-9
in Jocelyn). **ut quondam:** "as once (he had been)." Note the heavily spondaic character of
this line.

pulvere perque pedes traiectus lora tumentis.
ei mihi, qualis erat, quantum mutatus ab illo
Hectore qui redit exuvias indutus Achilli,   275
vel Danaum Phrygios iaculatus puppibus ignis;
squalentem barbam et concretos sanguine crinis
vulneraque illa gerens, quae circum plurima muros
accepit patrios. ultro flens ipse videbar
compellare virum et maestas expromere voces: 280

midteram

---

273. **perque pedes traiectus lora tumentis:** *lora* cannot be an accusative of specification with
a passive participle, since it is Hector's *pedes*, not the *lora*, that are pierced. Instead, *lora* is
a retained accusative. Thus, "having thongs passed through his swelling feet." Note the
effective alliteration* of "p" in *pulvere perque pedes*. **tumentis:** by referring to swelling feet,
Vergil seems to adopt the post-Homeric account that Achilles dragged Hector alive around
Troy (cf. Sophocles, *Ajax* 1029-31).

274-5. **ei mihi, qualis erat:** the interjection *ei* is more common in tragedy than epic, and
often occurs with *mihi* ("woe is me") as here. This is probably a quotation from Ennius'
Annales (fragment 1 (*ex incertis scriptis*) in Warmington, 442 in Skutsch), where it seems
to describe Homer's apparition (cf. 268-97 n.). If so, this connection would give Hector's
appearance still more power and authority. **illo Hectore:** *illo* points us to the greatness of
Hector before his death as told in the *Iliad*. The enjambment* of *Hectore* gives the name
emphasis. **redit:** the present, instead of the perfect, is graphic and vivid; Aeneas pictures
Hector "as he returns" (for the tense, cf. 663 n. on *obtruncat*). **exuvias indutus:** *indutus*
has a middle sense (unlike *traeictus* in 273) and takes *exuvias* as object. The *exuvias* are
presumably Achilles' armor that Hector had stripped from the body of Patroclus (cf. *Iliad*
17.125). **Achilli:** genitive singular. For this form (as opposed to *Achillis*), see 7 n.

276. **puppibus:** dative of direction. In *Iliad* 15, Hector leads the Trojan charge to set fire to
the Greek ships.

277. **squalentem...illa:** note that the details of Hector's appearance are graphically presented
in a set of three phrases (tricolon*), and that the line has an expressive spondaic quality (cf.
272 n.).

278. **gerens:** refers back to *qualis erat* (274), "what a (terrible) sight he was!...displaying a..."
Gerens is used not only of things that you can take off such as *arma*, but of the eyes, face,
forehead or the like, where we might say "displaying." **quae...plurima...accepit (279):**
"which he received in plenty."

279. **ultro:** here "first" (i.e. without waiting for Hector to speak). **flens ipse:** "weeping myself,"
i.e. in addition to Hector's crying (cf. 271). In the Classical world, tears were consistent with
heroic character. Cf. 3.348 where Helenus weeps for joy as he meets and recognizes Aeneas
and his men, and 5.173 where Gyas weeps with passion at being passed in a race. **videbar:**
captures Aeneas' uncertainty in comprehending what he experienced. Cf. also his use of
this verb at 730, as he is fleeing the city.

280. **compellare:** "address," not to be confused with *compellere* (3), "bring together," "compel."

'o lux Dardaniae, spes o fidissima Teucrum,
quae tantae tenuere morae? quibus Hector ab oris
exspectate venis? ut te post multa tuorum
funera, post varios hominumque urbisque labores
defessi aspicimus! quae causa indigna serenos   285
foedavit vultus? aut cur haec vulnera cerno?'
ille nihil, nec me quaerentem vana moratur,
sed graviter gemitus imo de pectore ducens,

---

281. **o lux Dardaniae, spes o…:** *lux* here means "hope," "protector." Aeneas' emotional response to Hector is conveyed by the repetition of "*o*" in something like a chiastic construction. *Dardanus* was the founder of Dardania in the Troad and ancestor of Priam, and Troy was often called *Dardania*. This phrase may recall a line from Ennius' tragedy *Alexander*: "*o lux Troiae, germane Hector*" (fragment 76 in Warmington, 69 in Jocelyn). See 285 n.

282. **tenuere:** supply *te*. In 281-6, Aeneas surprisingly does not seem aware that Hector has been killed. Perhaps Aeneas/Vergil is conveying the confusion that often characterizes dreams? The lapse is intriguing.

283. **exspectate:** vocative of passive participle. **ut:** exclamatory usage; its particular force here is "how gladly," and should be translated closely with *aspicimus* (285).

285. **defessi aspicimus:** again the visual aspect of the scene is emphasized with *aspicimus*, while the dream-quality is further suggested by *defessi*. **quae causa…** cf. 282 n. These questions may recall Ennius' *Alexander*: "*Quid ita cum tuo lacerato corpore/ miser es aut qui te sic respectantibus/ tractavere nobis?*" (fragment 77-9 in Warmington, 70-2 in Jocelyn). These Ennian lines are part of a prophecy by Cassandra (cf. 246-7 n.) about the death of Hector, his mutilation, and the destruction of Troy. Since Aeneas seems to have forgotten about Hector's death and mutilation, the Ennian allusion here and at 281 (see n.) may thus add to the power and accuracy of Hector's (and Cassandra's) words regarding Troy's fall. See Widgosky (1972): 77. **indigna:** when used of a person suffering, it means "undeserving," but when of the thing suffered, "undeserved" and so "cruel," "shameful." **serenos:** is usually an epithet of the sky or the weather, and means "sunny" with the associated idea of "calm." The adjectives *indigna* and *serenos* are pointedly contrasted.

286. **foedavit vultus:** cf. *patrios foedasti funere vultus* at 539, which refers to the violence done by Achilles' son to another Trojan leader.

287. **ille nihil:** *ille* = Hector; supply *dixit*. The omission of a word that is syntactically needed but can be easily inferred is called ellipsis*. **nec…moratur:** *non* (or another negative) + *moror* is an idiom that means "pay no attention to" or "disregard." Cf. 5.400 *nec dona moror*. There might be a play with *tantae morae* (282) in *moratur*: Aeneas asked what had delayed Hector; here Hector will not waste his time (*non moror*) on such useless questions.

288. **gemitus…pectore:** Hector's reaction here is closely approximated by Aeneas' (temporally later) to the picture in Carthage of Hector being dragged to his death: *gemitum dat pectore ab imo* (1.485; cf. 272 n.)

'heu fuge, nate dea, teque his' ait 'eripe flammis.
hostis habet muros; ruit alto a culmine Troia.   290
sat patriae Priamoque datum: si Pergama dextra
defendi possent, etiam hac defensa fuissent.
sacra suosque tibi commendat Troia penatis;
hos cape fatorum comites, his moenia quaere
magna, pererrato statues quae denique ponto.'   295
sic ait et manibus vittas Vestamque potentem
aeternumque adytis effert penetralibus ignem.
    Diverso interea miscentur moenia luctu,
et magis atque magis, quamquam secreta parentis
Anchisae domus arboribusque obtecta recessit,   300
clarescunt sonitus armorumque ingruit horror.

---

289. **nate dea:** *nate* is vocative of the past participle of *nascor* (3); *dea* is an ablative of source (AG §403.2a).

290. **ruit…:** the phrase expresses an utter fall, "from top to bottom" (cf. 603). Note the starkness of Hector's revelation about Troy's capture.

291-2. **sat…datum:** supply *est a te*. *Patriae* and *Priamoque* are datives of indirect object. **dextra:** here "right hand" = "valor"; ablative of means. **possent…fuissent:** mixed contrafactual conditional, present in protasis (imperfect subjunctive) but past in apodosis (pluperfect subjunctive). **hac:** is deictic; sc. *dextra*, referring to Hector's own "valor."

293. **sacra…penatis:** *sacra* (neuter plural) are "sacred objects." The *penates* are the gods of the Roman household, though as *patriosque…penates* they represent the *penates* of the city of Troy. These objects are not actually handed over by Hector to Aeneas, since this is just a dream. Cf. 320-1 n.

294-5. **hos…fatorum comites:** *comites* is predicate accusative, modifying *hos* (i.e. *sacra* and *penates*). **his:** dative; understand *sacris et penatibus*. Notice the polyptoton* (*hos…his*). Hector here gives Aeneas the mission that will occupy him throughout the epic.

296-7. **vittas Vestamque…ignem:** presumably the *sacra* of line 293. *Vittas Vestamque* is perhaps an instance of hendiadys*: "(an image of) Vesta wearing a fillet." **aeternumque…:** the fire that was kept continually burning on the altar of Vesta at Rome was supposed to have been brought by Aeneas from Troy to secure the continual existence of the state. This scene ends with great artistry: *manibus…ignem* comprise a tricolon crescendo*, and 297 is a variation on a golden line*.

298-317. *Aeneas views the conflagration of Troy and immediately prepares for battle.*

298. **Diverso:** adjective with *luctu*, but with the sense of "everywhere." **miscentur moenia luctu:** Vergil is fond of using *misceo* to convey the idea of confusion, cf. 329, 487. **moenia:** "city walls," but here "city" by synecdoche*.

299-300. **secreta…arboribusque obtecta:** the *–que* connects the two participial phrases describing the *domus* (*secreta* here = "secluded"). **recessit:** "was set back."

301. **armorum:** i.e. of battle (by metonymy*). **ingruit:** supply *nobis*, "advances upon us."

excutior somno et summi fastigia tecti
ascensu supero atque arrectis auribus asto:
in segetem veluti cum flamma furentibus Austris
incidit, aut rapidus montano flumine torrens   305
sternit agros, sternit sata laeta boumque labores
praecipitisque trahit silvas: stupet inscius alto
accipiens sonitum saxi de vertice pastor.

---

302. **excutior somnis:** it is only at this point that Aeneas wakes up. **summi fastigia tecti:** *fastigia* alone can mean rooftop. By including *summi tecti*, Aeneas emphasizes that he climbed to the highest point of the roof, presumably so that he can have the best view of the city (cf. 458 *evado ad summi fastigia culminis*). Note the frantic nature of Aeneas' actions: he is awakened and rushes to the rooftop all in the same sentence (302-3).

303. **ascensu:** this word is more frequent in prose and is used by Vergil only here. Like *summi tecti* in 302, *ascensu* is technically unnecessary for the meaning of the line (as *supero* will already imply something like "climbing") but it may add emphasis to Aeneas' effort to reach the highest (and thus best) lookout position on the roof (cf. 302 n.). **supero:** verb, "reach." **arrectis auribus:** "with ears pricked up." (cf. *arrecta* used of the serpents' *pectora* at 206). Note the alliteration* of "a" and the harsh elisions that perhaps convey Aeneas' hurried climb, while the coincidence of ictus and word accent by the end of the line contributes to the sense that Aeneas finally has come to a standstill (*asto*).

304-8. **veluti cum:** "even as when..." This magnificent epic simile, comparing Aeneas to a shepherd watching in disbelief as a fire burns a field or a flood rushes down a mountain, is based on Homer, *Iliad* 4.452-6: "Wildly as two winter torrents raging down from the mountains,/ swirling into a valley, hurl their great waters together,/ flash floods from the wellsprings plunging down in a gorge/ and miles away in the hills a shepherd hears the thunder/ so from the grinding armies broke the cries and crash of war" (Fagles). In Vergil's recreation of this simile, the shepherd's (and thus Aeneas') horror at unexpected destruction is emphasized, while the Homeric simile describes armies already in battle. Aeneas is *inscius* (307), as he stands agape (*stupet*), details capturing his emotional state as he witnesses Troy's destruction from his rooftop view.

304. **furentibus Austris:** ablative absolute with temporal sense. On *Austris*, see 111 n.

305. **rapidus...torrens:** *rapidus* is formed from *rapio* and here means not so much "rapid" or "quick" as "flowing so vehemently that it drags things along with it." *Montano flumine* is an ablative of separation or source, and the phrase should be construed closely with *rapidus... torrens*: "a torrent violently whirling from a mountain stream."

306. **sternit...sternit:** the repetition of a word from the end of clause at the beginning of the next is a rhetorical figure called anadiplosis. See also 108 n. **laeta:** a common epithet of crops, "joyous," "bounteous." **labores:** "things produced by labor," i.e. the crops. Cf. 1.455 *manus* "objects of handiwork" and 6.683 *manus* "exploits."

307. **praecipitis:** adjective with adverbial sense; drags the trees down "headlong." **inscius:** because the shepherd (like Aeneas) has just been roused by the sound, and is still dazed and ignorant of its cause. See 304-8 n.

tum vero manifesta fides, Danaumque patescunt
insidiae. iam Deiphobi dedit ampla ruinam   310
Volcano superante domus, iam proximus ardet
Vcalegon; Sigea igni freta lata relucent.
exoritur clamorque virum clangorque tubarum.
arma amens capio; nec sat rationis in armis,
sed glomerare manum bello et concurrere in arcem   315

---

309. **fides:** "truth," "proof"; supply *est*. As Aeneas stands on the top of the roof, he sees the city under attack, which proves the truth of Hector's words (289-95).

310. **insidiae:** this must refer to Sinon's ruse and the Trojan horse and thus be a retrospective characterization, since Aeneas does not here specifically identify the horse/Sinon as the cause of Troy's fall, nor could he from his rooftop view. He only learns this at 328-30. **Deïphobi:** Deiphobus was Hector's brother, who had married Helen after Paris' death. He will appear, gruesomely disfigured, in the underworld at 6.494-547. **dedit…ruinam:** "has made" or "caused ruin," i.e. has fallen in ruin; cf. 482 *dedit fenestram*.

311. **Vulcano superante:** "fire," the god of fire (who supports the Greeks) here stands for fire itself (metonymy*; cf. 306 n.); *superante* has a double force of "vanquishing" and "towering over." Fire will be one of the most important destructive forces in Vergil's description of Troy's fall. Rossi (2004) 24-30 argues that Vergil's use of this image differs from previous treatments of Troy's fall but is part of the more general topos of the *urbs capta*. **proximus:** "neighboring."

312. **Vcalegon:** "Ucalegon's house"; the name of the owner identifies the house by metonymy*. Cf. 3.275 *Apollo* "the temple of Apollo." Ucalegon is mentioned as a Trojan elder at *Iliad* 3.148, where we also find several other Trojans who appear in *Aeneid* 2: Thymoetes (32) and Panthus (318). **Sigea:** "Sigean," "relating to Sigeum," a promontory near Troy, across from Tenedos (see 21, 255).

313. **clamorque virum clangorque tubarum:** note the alliteration* and assonance* in this impressive phrase.

314. **arma amens capio:** note the similarity to the opening of the epic (*arma virumque cano*). *Amens* represents the first of a number of references in this book to Aeneas' frenzy, which will continually conflict with the fulfillment of his fate. Aeneas' struggle with his passions will last until the final act of the *Aeneid*, the slaying of Turnus, where Aeneas is *furiis accensus et iral terribilis* (12.946-7). Cf. also 268-558 n. and 316 n. **nec sat rationis:** supply est; *rationis* is partitive genitive with *sat* and expands on the idea in *amens*. This is an important moment: Aeneas' initial reaction is to fight, though Hector had just counseled against this (289-95).

315. **glomerare:** dependent on the sense of "desire" in *ardent animi* (plural form with singular sense). *Glomerare* (from *glomus*, "ball-shaped mass") originally meant "shape into a ball," but came to be used of gathering things, people, animals, etc. into dense masses or crowds, as here (*manum* = "armed force," "band of men"). Vergil may be the first writer to use it with regard to people. **bello:** dative of purpose.

cum sociis ardent animi; furor iraque mentem
praecipitat, pulchrumque mori succurrit in armis.
    Ecce autem telis Panthus elapsus Achivum,
Panthus Othryades, arcis Phoebique sacerdos,
sacra manu victosque deos parvumque nepotem   320
ipse trahit cursuque amens ad limina tendit.   *vul·*
'quo res summa loco, Panthu? quam prendimus arcem?'
vix ea fatus eram gemitu cum talia reddit:
'venit summa dies et ineluctabile tempus

---

316. **animi:** though *animus* can mean either mind or heart (i.e. passion), the latter is suggested here, particularly since it is in contrast to *ratio* in 314. This line thus juxtaposes the passions (*animi* and *furor iraque*) and rationality (*mentem*). **furor…:** cf. 314 n.

317. **pulchrum…:** i.e. *succurrit pulchrum (esse) mori in armis. Succurrit* begins an impersonal accusative and infinitive statement. For a similar idea, cf. *dulce et decorum est pro patria mori* (Horace, *Odes* 3.2.13, published 23 BCE).

318-69. *Panthus, flying from the citadel, tells Aeneas that Troy has fallen. These words incite Aeneas to rush to battle with the comrades he can find.*

318. **Ecce autem:** cf. 203 n. **Achivum:** = *Achivorum* (cf. 14 n.).

319. **Panthus:** see 312 n. According to Servius, Panthus was taken from Delphi and brought to Troy, where he became a Trojan priest of Apollo. **Othryades:** patronymic; not much is known about this Othryas. **arcis Phoebique sacerdos:** a kind of hendiadys*, "priest of (the temple of) Phoebus Apollo on the citadel (*arcis*)" of Troy. Note that this grand identification of Panthus occupies a full line.

320-1. **trahit:** takes three objects (*sacra, victos deos, parvum nepotem*) in tricolon crescendo*, but with the first two it means "carries," while with the third it = "drags." This is an instance of zeugma*, whereby one verb takes two or more objects, though its sense is strictly appropriate for just one (here *nepotem*). The resulting image looks forward to the more elaborate picture of Aeneas fleeing the city at the end of book 2 (lines 707-25). At 293 Hector told Aeneas to take control of the *sacra* and *penatis*, but it is only here that Aeneas must be given them (though Vergil does not explicitly tell us), since Panthus has come carrying them, and Aeneas has them at 717 (see n.). **amens:** so Aeneas had described himself at 314; the parallel between these two men is strengthened further. **limina:** i.e. of Anchises' house. **tendit:** for this usage, cf. 205 n.

322. **quo res summa loco:** "Where is the main battle?" **quam prendimus arcem?** *arcem* here means "position of defense," not the citadel of the city (mentioned at 33, 245, 319); *prendimus* is perfect ("have we seized") or present ("are we seizing"). Note the clipped nature of these questions.

323. **gemitu:** the ablative used almost adverbially, "with a groan." Cf. 225 *lapsu*, 498 *cumulo* "in a heap." For groaning associated with the deceit of the horse and the fall of Troy up to this point, cf. also 53, 73, 288.

324. **venit summa dies:** *venit* is emphatic; *summa* here = "last," "final." Cf. the phrase *Troiae supremum…laborem* (11). **ineluctabile:** "inescapable," a word first attested in Vergil.

Dardaniae. fuimus Troes, fuit Ilium et ingens 325
gloria Teucrorum; ferus omnia Iuppiter Argos
transtulit; incensa Danai dominantur in urbe.
arduus armatos mediis in moenibus astans
fundit equus victorque Sinon incendia miscet
insultans. portis alii bipatentibus adsunt, 330
milia quot magnis umquam venere Mycenis;
obsedere alii telis angusta viarum
oppositis; stat ferri acies mucrone corusco
stricta, parata neci; vix primi proelia temptant
portarum vigiles et caeco Marte resistunt.' 335
talibus Othryadae dictis et numine divum

---

325. **fuimus…fuit:** the perfect of *sum* is often used euphemistically. Someone who "has been" "is not" and so "is dead," "is non-existent." Cf. 3.11 *ubi Troia fuit*. Again, the verb at the beginning of these two clauses is emphatic, made doubly so by its repetition in different personal forms (polyptoton*; cf. 294-5 n.).

326-7. **ferus…:** the placement of *ferus* at the beginning of this sentence is probably emphatic, given the usage of *fuimus* and *fuit* in 325. This line refers to the belief that the gods abandoned a conquered city (cf. 351 n.). Jupiter is here described as not merely having departed but having gone over to the enemy. **Argos:** accusative of place to which (AG §427.2). **incensa:** "set ablaze," i.e. "burning."

329. **miscet:** "spreads," thus causing the grief that is described with *miscentur* at 298.

330. **insultans:** modifies Sinon and is emphatically placed. **portis…bipatentibus:** dative with *adsunt*. *Bipatentibus* = "having both halves open," i.e. "wide-open." **alii:** "some" (i.e. of the Greeks); it is coordinate with *alii* ("others") at 332.

331. **magnis…Mycenis:** ablative of source.

332. **obsedere:** for *obsederunt*. **angusta viarum:** for *angustas vias*, "narrow streets." For this construction, cf. 725 *per opaca locorum* and 1.422 *strata viarum*.

333-4. **oppositis:** "hostile," modifying *telis* (332). **stat ferri acies mucrone corusco/ stricta:** a difficult phrase meaning "a (battle) line of steel of gleaming blade stands drawn." *Mucrone corusco* is ablative of quality; *stricta* modifies *acies* grammatically and can do this semantically, when *acies* means "sword blade." But here *acies* means "battle line," and thus *stricta* in sense really attaches to *ferri*, which is what is drawn (out of the scabbard). **neci:** dative of purpose, "for slaughter," i.e. "to kill us."

335. **caeco Marte:** like *Vulcano* at 311, *Marte* refers to the primary sphere of this god, and thus here means "war" by metonymy*. *Caeco* = "aimless," thus referring to the confusion of the situation, not the darkness of the night. *Caecus* is often used metaphorically, e.g., as an epithet of "fear," "passion," "frenzy," or the like.

336. **Othryadae:** see 319 n.

in flammas et in arma feror, quo tristis Erinys
quo fremitus vocat et sublatus ad aethera clamor.
addunt se socios Rhipeus et maximus armis
Epytus, oblati per lunam, Hypanisque Dymasque   340
et lateri adglomerant nostro, iuvenisque Coroebus
Mygdonides — illis ad Troiam forte diebus
venerat insano Cassandrae incensus amore
et gener auxilium Priamo Phrygibusque ferebat,
infelix qui non sponsae praecepta furentis   345
audierit!
quos ubi confertos audere in proelia vidi,

---

337. **quo tristis Erinys:** supply *vocat* (338). *Quo* is an adverb, "to what place," "whither."
Erinys is a synonym for Fury. Furies are destructive goddesses of the underworld; here one is
inciting the madness of war. **feror:** throughout book 2, the passive of *fero* is used to convey
frenzied action, over which Aeneas has seemingly little control.

338. **sublatus:** past participle of *tollo* (3).

339. **socios:** predicate accusative, "as comrades."

340. **oblati per lunam:** *offero* in the passive can mean "appear"; *per lunam* is formed on the
analogy of *per noctem*.

341. **adglomerant:** understand *se* from 339.

342. **Mygdonides:** nominative; a patronymic describing Coroebus. Homer mentions a
Mygdon, king of the Phrygians, at *Iliad* 3.186. **illis...diebus:** not simply equivalent to *eo
tempore*; *ille* must be emphatic — "in those (last fatal) days." **forte:** Vergil emphasizes that
Coroebus was in Troy "by chance."

343. **insano:** not merely a general epithet of love; it has special force because Coroebus' love
brought him to his death. **incensus:** note this participle is used both of passion (as here) and
of the burning of Troy (cf. 327 *incensa*).

344. **gener:** "son-in-law." As we learn from the noun *sponsae* (345), Cassandra had been
betrothed to Coroebus, but, as far as we can tell, they did not marry. *Gener* must be taken
as "future" or "would-be son-in-law." Cf. 4.35, where *mariti* are "suitors," not "husbands."

345-6. **infelix:** Vergil is fond of thus placing an adjective at the commencement of a line
with a pause after it, thus giving it great emphasis, cf. 372 *inscius* and 529 *saucius*. **qui
non...audierit:** causal relative clause, explaining why Coroebus is *infelix*. Cassandra had
doubtless warned him of the danger involved in his courtship of her, but her prophecies
were doomed to be ignored (see 246-7 and n.). **furentis:** "mad" in the sense of "inspired,"
for inspiration involves the loss of self-control, the god taking possession of the inspired
person and this possession being accompanied by the outward signs of madness (see, e.g.,
6.77-80).

347. **quos...:** "and when I saw them in close ranks (*confertos*) bold (*audere*) for battle..." *Quos*
refers to the warriors of 339-42 who have joined Aeneas.

incipio super his: 'iuvenes, fortissima frustra
pectora, si vobis audentem extrema cupido
certa sequi, quae sit rebus fortuna videtis;   350
excessere omnes adytis arisque relictis *abl. abs.*

ind. quest.

di quibus imperium hoc steterat; succurritis urbi
incensae: moriamur et in media arma ruamus.
una salus victis nullam sperare salutem.'
sic animis iuvenum furor additus. inde, lupi ceu   355

---

348. **super:** adverb, "in addition." The men were already daring (*audere*), but Aeneas strives to embolden them still further, cf. 355. **his:** supply *verbis*. (To take *super his* together as "after these things" would make less sense, since there is nothing to which "these things" can refer.)

349-50. **si vobis...sequi:** supply *est*. **audentem:** object of *sequi*, it takes *extrema* (neuter plural, "desperate acts") as its direct object. The reading *audentem*, suggested by Servius, is preferable to *audendi*, which has much greater manuscript authority but is more difficult to construe. See Gardiner (1987). **sit:** subjunctive in a primary sequence indirect question dependent upon *videtis*.

351. **excessere...:** for *excesserunt*. There was a regular formula (*carmen quo di evocantur*) for summoning the gods of a besieged city to leave it, a practice called *evocatio*. Aeneas here echoes Panthus' claim about Jupiter at 326 (see n.). **omnes:** modifies *di* (352). **adytis... relictis:** ablative absolute.

352. **quibus:** ablative of means.

353. **incensae:** emphatically placed. **moriamur et in media arma ruamus:** *moriamur* and *ruamus* are hortatory subjunctives. Either this is an instance of hysteron proteron*, whereby the logical order of action is reversed ("Let us dash into the fray and die"), or *et...ruamus* is an explanatory clause ("let us die, and let us do so by rushing into the fray"). In either case, note the assonance* of the long vowel *a*, perhaps underscoring the urgency of Aeneas' words to his comrades.

354. **una salus victis:** dative of possessor construction (AG §373); supply *est*. **sperare:** infinitive in apposition to and thus explaining the *una salus*.

355. **animis:** "courage," to which is now added "frenzy" (*furor*). **lupi ceu...:** these words introduce a simile and are based on the Gr. *lukoi hos* (cf. Homer, *Iliad* 11.72, 16.156). Normally there is a coincidence of word accent and verse accent in the fifth and sixth feet of hexameter lines. Here, however, the monosyllabic *ceu* disrupts it in the sixth foot, giving this line a special tension that is not resolved by line end. Cf. the powerful effect of *aversa deae mens* (170). On the simile, see Lyne (1987) 212-14, who discerns dramatic irony, and Horsfall (1995) 113-14. Other wolf similes occur at 9.59-64, 565-6 (both of Turnus), and 11.809-13 (of Arruns).

raptores atra in nebula, quos improba ventris
exegit caecos rabies catulique relicti
faucibus exspectant siccis, per tela, per hostis
vadimus haud dubiam in mortem mediaeque tenemus
urbis iter; nox atra cava circumvolat umbra.   360
quis cladem illius noctis, quis funera fando
explicet aut possit lacrimis aequare labores?
urbs antiqua ruit multos dominata per annos;
plurima perque vias sternuntur inertia passim
corpora perque domos et religiosa deorum   365
limina. nec soli poenas dant sanguine Teucri;
quondam etiam victis redit in praecordia virtus
victoresque cadunt Danai. crudelis ubique
luctus, ubique pavor et plurima mortis imago.

356. **quos:** object of both *exegit* (357) and *exspectant* (358). **improba:** here means "reckless," "uncontrollable." *Improbus* is a favorite word with Vergil: it expresses an absence of all moderation, of all regard for consequences or for the rights of others (cf. 80). So, e.g., a famished wolf about to attack a sheepfold is *asper et improbus ira* (9.62, cf. 355n.); and Amor is "insatiate" in his tyranny (*improbe Amor, quid non mortalia pectora cogis!* 4.412).

357. **caecos:** cf. 335 n.

358. **siccis:** "thirsty," i.e. for blood. **per tela, per hostis:** observe the other repetitions in this passage: 361 *quis...quis*; 364-5 *perque...perque*; 368-9 *ubique...ubique*. Cf. 306 n. as well.

359-60. **mediaeque...:** "and hold our course for the heart of the city"; *mediae...urbis* is genitive. **nox...:** *atra nox* can be a metaphor* for "death," but here the darkness of the actual night should also be understood. *Cava* has the sense of "enfolding" and modifies *umbra*. For this line, cf. the description of Marcellus at 6.866: *sed nox atra caput tristi circumvolat umbra*.

361-2. **quis...fando/ explicet:** *explicet* is a potential subjunctive; *fando* recalls Aeneas' initial recollection of his sufferings as *infandum...dolorem* in line 3. Cf. also *quis talia fando* (6). Aeneas introduces another stage of his actions as Troy fell. Note the anaphora* involving *quis* (cf. 306 n. and 358 n.).

363. **urbs antiqua ruit...:** this passage resonates with the coda to Priam's death at 554-8. The phrase also recalls the description of Carthage at 1.13 (*Vrbs antiqua fuit*), a city still under construction in book 1. See Reed (2007): 128-47 on Vergil's treatment of the theme of ancient cities and its significance for his representation of Rome.

365-6. **religiosa deorum/ limina:** the temples of the gods are not even free from slaughter. The first syllable of *religiosa* is long (cf. 151 n.). **dant sanguine:** "pay the penalty with their blood."

367. **quondam:** "at times." **victis...in praecordia:** *victis* is dative of reference (instead of possessive or subjective genitive), "into the hearts of the conquered."

368. **cadunt:** as often, "fall dead," "be slain."

369. **luctus:** supply *est* (as with *pavor* and *imago*). **pavor:** the final syllable is lengthened in arsis. The arsis is the part of the metrical foot that receives the verse accent (ictus). When

Primus se Danaum magna comitante caterva   370
Androgeos offert nobis, socia agmina credens
inscius, atque ultro verbis compellat amicis:
'festinate, viri! nam quae tam sera moratur
segnities? alii rapiunt incensa feruntque
Pergama: vos celsis nunc primum a navibus itis?'   375
dixit, et extemplo (neque enim responsa dabantur
fida satis) sensit medios delapsus in hostis.

---

a short vowel falls at the arsis, that vowel, particularly if it precedes the main caesura, is sometimes lengthened. Cf. *obruimur* in 411. **plurima mortis imago:** "many a form of death," i.e. death in many a form. Note the use of the adjective *plurima* at the beginning and near the end of this short passage (364-9) describing Troy's destruction (cf. 363). These lines culminate in a powerful tricolon.*

370-401. *Aeneas and his comrades kill the Greek Androgeos and put on Greek armor.*

370-1. **Primus:** cf. 32 n. **se...offert:** not merely "meets" but "comes to meet." Cf. 372 n. **socia:** predicate adjective: *credens (nostra) agmina (esse) socia.* **Androgeos:** a Greek nominative form. This warrior is otherwise unknown.

372. **inscius:** cf. 345-6 n. **ultro:** "of his own will," see 145 n. Aeneas emphasizes the unwitting nature of Androgeos' mistake. Androgeos lacks the guile of Sinon who had contrived his own capture, which was described in similar language: *se ignotum venientibus ultro... obtulerat* (59-61). **compellat:** cf. 280 n. **amicis:** adjective. Like Priam's *dictis amicis* (147), Androgeos' *verbis amicis* will prove devastating to him.

373. **moratur:** supply *vos* as object. Cf. Aeneas' words to Hector at 282: *quae tantae tenuere morae?* **tam sera:** modifies *segnities* (374), but can be translated adverbially (cf. 1 n.), "so long," "so late."

374. **segnities:** "sloth," "idleness"; primarily a prose word, it helps color Androgeos' (ignorant) rebuke of the soldiers. **alii...vos (375):** the prominent position of these words at the beginning of their clauses marks their contrast. **rapiunt...feruntque:** the ordinary phrase is *ferre et agere* (e.g. Liv. 22.3 *res sociorum ferri agique vidit*). *Ferre* is strictly used of "carrying off" portable property and *agere* of "driving away" captives or cattle, but here any distinction between *rapiunt* and *ferunt* is unnecessary. Translate as "plunder and pillage." **incensa:** for the meaning, see 326-7 n.

375. **vos:** contrasted with *alii* (374). **celsis:** a standard epithet for ships. **primum:** adverb, "for the first time" (i.e. "just now").

376-7. **neque enim:** "for...not." **fida:** here "assuring." **sensit...delapsus:** an imitation of the Greek construction after verbs of "feeling," "knowing," etc., wherein a nominative participle is used to refer back to the subject: "he felt that he had fallen" (cf. *Georgics* 2.510 *gaudent perfusi sanguine fratrum*). The more expected Latin construction would involve an accusative and infinitive (i.e. *sensit se delapsum esse*). Note that *delapsus* is another verb related to *labor* (cf. 225 n.). **medios:** cf. 123 n.

obstipuit retroque pedem cum voce repressit.
improvisum aspris veluti qui sentibus anguem
pressit humi nitens trepidusque repente refugit   380
attollentem iras et caerula colla tumentem,
haud secus Androgeos visu tremefactus abibat.
inruimus densis et circumfundimur armis,
ignarosque loci passim et formidine captos
sternimus. aspirat primo Fortuna labori.   385
atque hic successu exsultans animisque Coroebus
'o socii, qua prima' inquit 'fortuna salutis

---

378. **retroque...:** "and (shrinking) backwards checked his foot and voice (*cum voce*)." **pedem cum voce repressit:** a mannerism not unlike zeugma*, because we are to construe *repressit* differently when taken with *pedem* and *cum voce*.

379. **aspris:** = *asperis*, a harsh instance of syncope (contraction of a vowel or syllable in the middle of a word). Construe *aspris* with *sentibus*, ablative of cause, explaining why the snake was *improvisum*. Elsewhere the lack of foresight is the plague of the Trojans (cf. 182). For the simile, cf. Homer, *Iliad* 3.33-5: "And he faded back into the Trojan troops/ With cheeks as pale as if he had seen —/ Had almost stepped on—a poisonous snake/ In a mountain pass" (Lombardo). Given the destruction connected to snakes in book 2, there may be dramatic irony in associating a snake with a Trojan, cf. Lyne (1987) 210-12.

380. **humi nitens:** "pressing down" or "stepping on the ground"; *humi* is locative. Note the rhythmic contrast between the firm stomp on the snake with the spondaic *nitens* and the quick dactylic retreat in *trepidusque repente refugit*.

381. **attollentem...tumentem:** both participles modify *anguem* (379). *Attollo* originally means "raise something up" physically; Vergil seems to be the first writer to use it in the sense of arousing passion (cf. 12.4 *attollitque animos*). **caerula colla tumentem:** *tumentem* is intransitive, thus making *caerula colla* an accusative of respect. *Caerula* = "greenish blue," a traditional adjective describing the color of serpents that goes back to Ennius.

382. **haud secus:** "not otherwise," a standard phrase returning the focus back to the main narrative after a simile. **abibat:** with conative force, "as he tried to get away" (he, of course, did not succeed in doing so).

383. **circumfundimur:** "we surround (him, i.e. Androgeos)," a middle use (lit. "we pour ourselves around"); see 64 n., 227 *teguntur* "hide themselves," 302 *excutior* "I rouse myself," 393 n., 401 *conduntur*, 510-11 *ferrum/ cingitur* (cf. 520 *cingi telis*), 633 *expedior*, 707 *imponere* "place yourself on."

384-5 **ignarosque loci:** *loci* is objective genitive. **passim...sternimus:** Aeneas and his Trojan band commit widespread slaughter, whereas in 364 they had witnessed it. **aspirat:** with dative, "blows favor on" or "favors."

386. **hic:** adverb, "then." **successu exsultans animisque:** note the different uses of the two ablatives: "elated by their success and in high spirits." The "success" causes exultation and exultation is exhibited "in high spirits."

387. **qua:** "where(ever)."

monstrat iter, quaque ostendit se dextra, sequamur:
mutemus clipeos Danaumque insignia nobis
aptemus. dolus an virtus, quis in hoste requirat?   390
arma dabunt ipsi.' sic fatus deinde comantem
Androgei galeam clipeique insigne decorum
induitur laterique Argivum accommodat ensem.
hoc Rhipeus, hoc ipse Dymas omnisque iuventus
laeta facit: spoliis se quisque recentibus armat.   395
vadimus immixti Danais haud numine nostro
multaque per caecam congressi proelia noctem

---

388. ostendit se dextra: the construction is a natural variation of the ordinary *ostendit se dextram*. Cf. 1.314 *sese tulit obvia*; 3.310 *verane te facies…adfers*. *Dextra* (a nominative adjective modifying *fortuna*) indicates favor ("on the right side," i.e. "propitious"), which is already implied in *aspirat* (385).

389. mutemus…: the idea in *mutemus clipeos* is restated in *Danaumque insignia nobis/ aptemus* (390), an example of theme and variation*, of which Vergil is fond. **insignia:** this word is used of those parts of dress or armor which serve to "distinguish" the wearer (as in such phrases as *imperatoris insignia, pontificalia insignia, regia insignia*). Such "marks of distinction" usually denote superior rank or dignity: here, however, *Danaum insignia* describes those portions of their armor (such as helmets, shields, swords, cf. 392-3) that distinguish the Greeks from the Trojans.

390. dolus…: a rhetorically terse indirect question, suggesting the excitement and quick pace of decision in the midst of battle. The full construction would be something like (*utrum*) *dolus* (*sit adhibendus*) *an virtus, quis…* On *dolus*, cf. 44 n. **in hoste:** this use of *in* + ablative means "in the case of," "when dealing with"; before Vergil, it seems to have been more common in prose. Cf. 541. **requirat:** potential subjunctive.

391. ipsi: "they themselves" (i.e. the Greeks, although they are our foes). **comantem…galeam (392):** the adjective *comans* means "having hair"; when applied to a helmet, it means "plumed."

392. Androgei: genitive singular, as if from *Androgeus*. **clipeique insigne decorum:** *insigne* here is the "emblem" or "ornament" on the shield (cf. 7.657-8 *clipeoque insigne paternum / centum anguis…gerit*) and not the shield itself, as it perhaps is in 389 (see n.).

393. induitur: "puts on," a middle usage (cf. 383 n.).

394. hoc: accusative neuter, "the same thing" (i.e. put on Greek armor). **ipse:** we do not know anything of Dymas and therefore cannot say why he is thus specially distinguished.

396. haud numine nostro: "(guided) not by our own gods." This phrase has at least two meanings that cannot be easily separated: 1.) "by the Greek (i.e. not our own) gods" and, by extension, 2.) "by hostile gods" (i.e. the gods of our enemies). By putting on the Greek armor they are supposed to pass under the guidance of the Greek gods, but because these gods are hostile, the Trojans are led to fresh disaster. See 410-12.

397. multa…proelia: *conserimus* (398) + *proelia* (*bellum, pugnam*, etc.) = "join in battle." **congressi:** "having approached to fight."

conserimus, multos Danaum demittimus Orco.
diffugiunt alii ad navis et litora cursu
fida petunt; pars ingentem formidine turpi   400
scandunt rursus equum et nota conduntur in alvo.
    Heu nihil invitis fas quemquam fidere divis!
ecce trahebatur passis Priameia virgo
crinibus a templo Cassandra adytisque Minervae

---

398. **Orco:** dative of direction, for *ad Orcum*. The infernal god Orcus here stands in for the "underworld."

399-401. Note Aeneas' seemingly exaggerated picture of the Greek warriors cutting and running as he and his comrades move to attack — even through Troy is in the grip of defeat. In Homer, the Greeks are generally tenacious and relentless fighters.

399. **diffigiunt...petunt (400):** another instance of theme and variation* (cf. 389 n.)

400. **fida:** the *litora* are "trustworthy," "safe," because their ships were nearby. **formidine turpi:** "shameful fear." **pars:** coordinates with *alii* in 399 ("some...others..."); it is used as a collective noun with the plural verbs *scandunt...conduntur* (401).

401. **alvo:** i.e. the belly of the wooden horse, but it can also mean "womb," which might once again draw on the metaphor* of pregnancy employed earlier (cf. 238 n.). Note that *alvo* is feminine and modified by *nota*. That some Greeks would flee back into the horse is suprising, both because it would seem unheroic and because it would do nothing to secure their safety. See Harries (1989).

402-52. *They see Cassandra dragged from Minerva's temple, and their deceptive use of Greek armor is discovered. Aeneas rushes to Priam's palace with two comrades.*

402. **fas:** supply *est*, forming an impersonal accusative and infinitive (here *quemquam fidere*) construction. **nihil:** adverbial accusative, "in no way." Their own gods were unpropitious to the Trojans: Aeneas and his comrades for a while seemed to have secured the protection of the Greek gods by putting on Greek armor (396 n.). They now find that the gods are not so easily misled.

403. **passis...crinibus (404):** "with hair dishevelled," ablative absolute. *Passis* is from *pando* (3), "spread out" (not *patior*). Since suppliants would unbind their hair, there is a suggestion that Cassandra was in the midst of supplication when the Greeks tore her from the temple (see 404 n.). Oilean Ajax was later punished for this deed, as Juno tells us at 1.39-45. **Priameia virgo:** a lofty and learned way to name Cassandra, who was one of Priam's fifty daughters.

404. **a templo...adytisque:** the use of both of these words emphasizes the sacrilegious character of the act. *Templum* refers to the temple as a whole, while *adytum* (Gr. *aduton*, "the unenterable place") is the innermost shrine in which the image of the deity was kept. Cassandra was said to have been clinging to the image of the goddess, and Ajax (son of Oileus) used such violence that he dragged the image away with her. The subject was frequently represented in Greek art. The violation of suppliants at altars will reach its highest sacrilege with the slaughter of Priam and another of his children, his son Polites (506-58).

ad caelum tendens ardentia lumina frustra,   405
lumina, nam teneras arcebant vincula palmas.
non tulit hanc speciem furiata mente Coroebus   *abl. abs.*
et sese medium iniecit periturus in agmen.
consequimur cuncti et densis incurrimus armis.
hic primum ex alto delubri culmine telis   410
nostrorum obruimur oriturque miserrima caedes
armorum facie et Graiarum errore iubarum.
tum Danai gemitu atque ereptae virginis ira

obj. gen.

405-6. lumina frustra,/ lumina: note the repetition of *lumina*, which is grammatically unnecessary but creates a powerful emotional effect (epanalepsis*). Here it underscores the pathos of Cassandra's attempts to appeal to the gods with her eyes, since she could not stretch her hands toward heaven because they were bound (*arcebant vincula palmas*). The placement of *frustra* in between *lumina…lumina* adds to the passage's pathos. **tendens:** for the meaning, see 205 n.

407. non tulit: the understatement of this litotes* contrasts with Coroebus' rage, *furiata mente*. Note that *furor* here will hasten his death (cf. 244 n.). On Coroebus' relationship to Cassandra, see 344 n.

408. medium…in agmen: cf. 377 *medios…in hostis* and 123 n.

409. consequimur…incurrimus: again note the theme and variation* (cf. 389 n.), a device used rather frequently in this section of the book. This line also seems to be a variation of 383, perhaps a sign that this passage was in need of further revision.

410-11. telis/ nostrorum obruimur: Aeneas and his band are still disguised as Greeks and thus are attacked by the Trojan army. Note that the final syllable of *obruimur* is lengthened because of its position in arsis (cf. 369 n.). **oriturque:** *orior* more often denotes some kind of physical rising (e.g. sun, person from bed, etc.), less often of an event that occurs, as here. **miserrima:** because the slaughter (*caedes*) is inflicted by friends.

412. facie: ablative of cause, as is *errore* ("deception"; cf. 48). **Graiorum errore iubarum:** serves to explain the phrase *armorum facie*; the horse-hair plumes of the Greek helmets betray the Trojans wearing them.

413. gemitu atque ereptae virginis ira: *ereptae virginis* is an objective genitive with *ira*; *gemitu* and *ira* are both ablative and probably form a hendiadys*, "with a raging shout at the rescue of the maiden" (lit. "rescued maiden," cf. 643 n.). The Greeks' reaction here suggests that Coroebus had at least temporarily rescued Cassandra, though he falls at Minerva's altar at 424-6.

undique collecti invadunt, acerrimus Aiax
et gemini Atridae Dolopumque exercitus omnis;   415
adversi rupto ceu quondam turbine venti
confligunt, Zephyrusque Notusque et laetus Eois
Eurus equis; stridunt silvae saevitque tridenti
spumeus atque imo Nereus ciet aequora fundo.
illi etiam, si quos obscura nocte per umbram   420
fudimus insidiis totaque agitavimus urbe,
apparent; primi clipeos mentitaque tela
agnoscunt atque ora sono discordia signant.

omit

414-15. acerrimus Aiax: cf. 403 n. **gemini:** cf. 203 n. The *Atridae* ("the sons of Atreus," i.e. Agamemenon and Menelaus) are called *gemini* not because they were twins, but because they were famous for their joint effort in the siege of Troy. Cassandra will be given to Agamemnon as a prize of war, and they will both be killed upon his return to Mycenae by his wife Clytemnestra and her lover Aegisthus. Note the tricolon* describing the Greek troops.

416. adversi: adjective, here "face-to-face." **ceu quondam:** "even as at times"; the phrase introduces a simile. **rupto...turbine:** ablative absolute. *Rumpo* in the passive, as here, can mean "bursts forth"; *turbine* here means "hurricane."

417-18. Zephyrus...Notus...Eurus: the West, South and East winds, thus explaining *adversi...venti* (416). **Eois...equis:** ablative with *laetus* ("exulting in..."); the East wind comes riding his chariot. The adjective *Eous* is derived from the Greek word for "dawn," but could also mean "East" (as here), since it is from this direction that the Sun rises. **stridunt silvae saevit:** note the expressive alliteration*. **tridenti:** the trident is normally a symbol of Neptune, but here Nereus wields one.

419. Nereus: the sea-god. **fundo:** *fundus* means "bottom," but was often used for the "bottom" or "depths of the sea."

420-1. illi...si quos: "those whom..." (lit. "those men, if any..."), referring to those whom the Trojans, dressed as Greeks, had routed (see 391-401). **insidiis:** i.e. wearing enemy armor (cf. 391-5); ablative of means. **totaque...urbe:** "throughout the whole city," ablative of place where (AG §429.2). **agitavimus:** "hunted," so commonly *agitare feras*.

422. apparent: the long separation of this verb from its subject *illi* in 420 (i.e. hyperbaton*) conveys a sense of surprise, since the Trojans had earlier routed the Greeks here described. **primi:** take adverbially. Up to this point all had been confusion (cf. 416-19), with Greeks and Trojans armed alike. Now when these newcomers appear, "they first recognize the shields and deceitful weapons" which the Trojans wore. The effect is instantaneous: the confusion, which had up until this point saved the Trojans, ceases and "straightway we are overwhelmed by their number" (424).

423. ora...: "mark our lips (i.e. speech) as differing in sound (from their own)." *Signant* here seems to mean *agnoscunt*, but this is an unusual usage of this verb, which more normally means "indicate."

ilicet obruimur numero; primusque Coroebus
Penelei dextra divae armipotentis ad aram   425
procumbit; cadit et Rhipeus, iustissimus unus
qui fuit in Teucris et servantissimus aequi
(dis aliter visum); pereunt Hypanisque Dymasque
confixi a sociis; nec te tua plurima, Panthu,
labentem pietas nec Apollinis infula texit.   430
Iliaci cineres et flamma extrema meorum,
testor, in occasu vestro nec tela nec ullas

---

424. **numero:** understand *Danaorum*. **primus:** cf. 32 n.

425. **dextra:** ablative, understand *manu*. **Penelei…:** a Greek genitive singular. **divae armipotentis:** i.e. Pallas/Minerva. **ad aram:** for this phrase, see 202 n.

426. **cadit et:** for the delay of *et*, see 73 n. **iustissimus unus:** "most just of all men." *Unus* which has by itself a superlative force is sometimes added to superlatives or expressions equivalent to a superlative to give emphasis; cf. 1.15 *magis omnibus unam;* 3.321 *felix una ante alias.*

427. **servantissimus:** "most protecting of"; it is the superlative of *servans*, an adjective seemingly created by Vergil. **aequi:** "justice." Neuter adjectives could be used substantively, especially when an abstract idea is involved, as here (cf. also 141 *veri* "truth").

428. **dis aliter visum:** supply *est*. "It seemed otherwise to the gods," a comment by Aeneas, expressing Rhipeus' death as part of the gods' plan, though it might also convey a sense of incomprehension that the gods did not save such a good man. This latter interpretation resonates with the poet's questioning of divine wrath at 1.8-11. For the significance of this phrase for understanding Vergil's gods, see Johnson (1999).

429. **a sociis:** because the Trojans Hypanis and Dymas had been dressed in Greek armor. **plurima…pietas (430):** *plurima* (here "abundant") emphasizes the inability of *pietas* to help the Trojans during the collapse of their city. The direct address or apostrophe* to Panthus here builds up the emotional power that will reach a climax in Aeneas' words in 431-4.

430. **labentem:** construe circumstantially or temporally. **infula:** a headband, wrapped in wool, that was worn by priests. Its sacred character might have been expected to provide protection. **texit:** *tego* here = "protect," not simply "cover."

431. **flamma extrema meorum:** the burning town became the funeral pyre of those who fell. *Iliaci cineres* and *flamma extrema* are vocative.

432. **testor…:** "I call you to witness that in your ruin I did not avoid…" What follows is an accusative (supply *me*) and infinitive (*vitavisse…meruisse*) construction. The personal pronoun can be omitted, as here, when there is no ambiguity, cf. 4.492-3 *testor…invitam accingier.*

vitavisse vices Danaum et, si fata fuissent
ut caderem, meruisse manu. divellimur inde,
Iphitus et Pelias mecum (quorum Iphitus aevo   435
iam gravior, Pelias et vulnere tardus Vlixi),
protinus ad sedes Priami clamore vocati.
hic vero ingentem pugnam, ceu cetera nusquam
bella forent, nulli tota morerentur in urbe,
sic Martem indomitum Danaosque ad tecta ruentis   440
cernimus obsessumque acta testudine limen.

---

433. **vices Danaum:** "hazards of (encountering) the Greeks." *Vices* is frequently used in connection with the changes of fortune. Hirtzel and Mynors punctuate differently by placing a comma after *vices*, and thus construing *Danaum* with *manu* (434). *Danaum*, however, makes good sense with *vices*, while *manu* can be taken to indicate Aeneas' own hand (i.e. valor).

434. **ut caderem:** a substantive clause of purpose (AG §563d) after the idea in *si fata fuissent* but conceptually carried on to *meruisse manu*. "If my fate had been that I should fall, by my own valor I earned it" (i.e. the right to fall). **meruisse:** cf. 432 n. **divellimur**: a strong word whose emphatic position stresses that what happened to Aeneas was caused by the violence of the fray; with *inde*, it also vigorously marks the change of scene.

435-6. **Iphitus et Pelias mecum:** the subject of *divellimur*. Nothing else is known of these two comrades with whom Aeneas had become separated from the other Trojans. **aevo/ iam gravior:** supply *erat*; "was already somewhat disabled from old age." **vulnere...Vlixi:** "from a wound inflicted by Ulysses." *Aevo* and *vulnere* are ablatives of cause.

437. **sedes:** accusative plural, here means "palace." **vocati:** supply *sumus*.

438. **hic:** adverb. **ingentem pugnam:** governed by *cernimus* (441 and see 440 n.). **ceu cetera nusquam/ bella forent:** clause of comparison (AG §524). *Forent = essent* (AG §170a).

439. **nulli...urbe:** continues the *ceu* clause of comparison.

440. **sic Martem...:** Vergil repeats and expands the idea of *ingentem pugnam* (438); "so do we behold Mars uncontrolled..." **tecta:** i.e. Priam's roof.

441-5. Vergil describes an assault at and around the gate of the palace that has two goals: first, to burst open the gates (441); second, to scale the walls (440-1, 442-4). The besieged Trojans are mainly on the roof, though a contingent is positioned behind the gate (450) in case it is forced open. The gate seems to stand slightly back from the line of the front of the house, leaving an open space, which is flanked by the walls and forms the *vestibulum* mentioned in 469.

441. **acta testudine:** "by the advancing roof of shields," lit. "by the tortoise brought up against it." The *testudo* consists of a body of men who locked their oblong shields together over their heads so as to form a sloping roof over themselves in order to assault a fortified position.

haerent parietibus scalae postisque sub ipsos
nituntur gradibus clipeosque ad tela sinistris
protecti obiciunt, prensant fastigia dextris.
Dardanidae contra turris ac tota domorum   445
culmina convellunt; his se, quando ultima cernunt,
extrema iam in morte parant defendere telis;
aurátasque trabes, veterum decora alta parentum,
devolvunt, alii strictis mucronibus imas
obsedere fores, has servant agmine denso.   450
instaurati animi regis succurrere tectis
auxilioque levare viros vimque addere victis.

---

442. **parietibus:** note the scansion. The first "i" is consonantal, making the "a" long; the "e" is short. **postisque…:** "right up under the very doors they force their way by climbing" (*gradibus*, lit. "by the steps" or "rungs" of the ladders). The phrase emphasizes the boldness of the assault as being made exactly where the defense was strongest.

443-4. **clipeosque…protecti obiciunt:** *protecti* may be either "thus protected," or it may be used in a middle sense, "protecting themselves." Note the emphatic picture of the all-out effort of the Greeks. They not only climb (*nituntur gradibus*) with both their legs, but they also use each hand for a different function. The juxtaposition of *sinistris* and *dextris* at the end of each line underscores the exertion.

445. **contra:** adverb, "on the other hand," "in turn"; Aeneas now focuses our attention on the Trojan reaction to the Greek assaults on Priam's palace. The Trojan defense of the walls and roof (445-9) and the gate (449-50) stand in chiastic opposition to the Greek assaults on these areas at 442-4 and 441 respectively (Williams). **turris:** accusative plural.

446-7. **his…telis:** i.e. the turrets and pieces of roof covering (445-6). **ultima:** neuter plural, here "the end," an idea expanded by *extrema…morte* (447). Aeneas emphasizes the desperation of the Trojans, who tear apart for weapons the very palace they are trying to defend.

449-50. **alii:** while lines 445-9 show some Trojans defending the roof, 449-50 describe other Trojans (*alii*) standing behind the palace "doors below" (*imas fores*). **obsedere:** for *obsederunt*. **has:** sc. *fores*.

451. **instaurati animi…:** the verbal idea in *instaurati animi (nostri)* governs the three infinitives that follow (cf. 64 n.).

452. **viros:** i.e. the Trojans defending the palace.

Limen erat caecaeque fores et pervius usus
tectorum inter se Priami, postesque relicti
a tergo, infelix qua se, dum regna manebant,   455
saepius Andromache ferre incomitata solebat
ad soceros et avo puerum Astyanacta trahebat.
evado ad summi fastigia culminis, unde
tela manu miseri iactabant inrita Teucri.
turrim in praecipiti stantem summisque sub astra   460
eductam tectis, unde omnis Troia videri
et Danaum solitae naves et Achaica castra,

453-68. *Aeneas and his comrades rush to the roof of the palace and overturn a tower onto the Greeks below.*

453-4. **pervius usus / tectorum inter se Priami:** a very difficult phrase. It means "a passage connecting the halls of Priam with one another" (lit. "a traversable use of Priam's halls among themselves"). The "halls of Priam" are probably his own palace and that of Hector and Andromache. They were connected by this private "gate in the rear" (*postes relicti a tergo*), which "had been left" undefended by the Trojans inside and unobserved by the Greeks, who were unfamiliar with the palace.

455. **infelix:** describing Andromache. **qua:** "by which," referring back to the gate in 454.

457. **soceros:** "her parents (-in-law)," i.e. Priam and Hecuba, though *socer* usually means "father-in-law." **avo:** "grandfather," i.e. Priam. **Astyanacta:** Greek accusative form. Astyanax was the son of Andromache and Hector. When Troy falls, he will be thrown to his death from the city walls. The three are famously portrayed as Hector leaves for battle at *Iliad* 6.399-502. **trahebat:** the use of *traho* instead of *duco* suggests that the boy can barely keep up with his mother; cf. 320-1 *parvumque nepotem / ipse trahit.*

458. **evado:** "I climb up"; for *e/ex* in compounds meaning "upwards," "on high," cf. 461 *eductam* "rising high"; 553 *extulit.* The use of *evado* at the beginning of this line without any kind of phrase connecting to the action that precedes is startling. With *evado*, we must understand something like "by this passage," referring to the *postes...a tergo*, described at 454-7. Servius suggests understanding *hac* (i.e. *hac evado*). **summi fastigia culminis:** "the top of the highest roof." For *fastigium*, cf. 302 n.

460. **turrim:** object of the participle *adgressi* (463) and the main verbs *convellimus* (464) and *impulimus* (465). **in praecipiti:** "on a sheer edge," the phrase describes the position of anything when, if it falls, there is nothing whatever to stop its fall. **summis...tectis (461):** ablative after *eductam.*

461-2. **unde...castra:** *videri* is a complimentary infinitive with *solitae (sunt)*, which has three subjects (*Troia, naves, castra*). The appropriate forms of *solitae* are to be understood.

adgressi ferro circum, qua summa labantis
iuncturas tabulata dabant, convellimus altis
sedibus impulimusque; ea lapsa repente ruinam   465
cum sonitu trahit et Danaum super agmina late
incidit. ast alii subeunt, nec saxa nec ullum
telorum interea cessat genus.
     Vestibulum ante ipsum primoque in limine Pyrrhus
exsultat telis et luce coruscus aëna;   470

463-4. **circum:** adverb, "all around" (the turret). **qua summa…:** Trojans use their crowbars (*ferro*) where these "topmost stories" (*summa tabulata*) spring from the roof. **labantis iuncturas:** "yielding joinings." **altis sedibus:** "from its lofty place." Notice that the use of dactyls from 464 to 466 helps convey the fall of the turret.

465-6. **ruinam…trahit:** cf. 631. This phrase is extremely graphic: when anything high falls after swaying back and forth, it does not fall in separate pieces or collapse, but the highest part seems to lean forward and then suddenly to "drag after it" the rest in its fall.

467. **ast:** an archaic form of *at*. **alii:** i.e. other Greeks. **subeunt:** Cf. 216 n.

468. **cessat:** singular because of its subject *ullum telorum…genus*, but it is also to be understood with *saxa* (467). Another half-line, cf. 66 n.

469-505. *Pyrrhus bursts through the palace doors*. In this section, Achilles' son Pyrrhus enters the action. He is a carefully drawn figure, embodying many of the destructive metaphors in book 2: he is compared to a snake (471-5), a violent flood of water (496-9, cf. the storm in *Aeneid* 1); he flashes almost like fire (cf. *coruscus*, 470); he embodies the violence of his father (*vi patria*, 491). But this is not all that makes Pyrrhus terrifying. Set against his violence are glimpses at the complete vulnerability of Priam, his palace, and his family when confronted by this terrifying Greek warrior. For more on Pyrrhus and the imagery in this book, see Knox (1950), Putnam (1965) 34-7, and 471-5 n. On the structure of these lines, Kenney (1979) 114-17 discerns "a very striking example of ring-composition," whereby the passage from 469-500 is enclosed by images of Pyrrhus raging (469-70, 499-500), and the events in between are arranged symmetrically with the interior of Priam's palace described at the center (483-90).

469. **Vestibulum:** for the geography of the palace and the assault, see 441-5 n. **primoque in limine:** rough restatement of the idea in *Vestibulum ante ipsum* (i.e. theme and variation*). **Pyrrhus:** also called Neoptolemus (549), he was the son of Achilles and Deidamia. He was born and raised on the island of Scyros (cf. 477) and led its contingent to Troy after his father's death. Pyrrhus' deeds after the war and his eventual murder are told by Andromache at 3.321-36.

470. **telis et luce…aëna:** "with weapons and bronze reflection," hendiadys* for "with shining bronze weapons." **coruscus:** may be a word play (paronomasia*) on the meaning of Pyrrhus' name in Greek, "Flame-colored," which also resonates with the importance of fire imagery in this book (cf. 469-505 n.). **exsultat:** here probably means "exults." However, since this verb can also mean "dances," it may evoke "an association with the form of dance known as the Pyrrhic" (Williams), a type of war-dance.

qualis ubi in lucem coluber mala gramina pastus,
frigida sub terra tumidum quem bruma tegebat,
nunc, positis novus exuviis nitidusque iuventa,
lubrica convolvit sublato pectore terga
arduus ad solem, et linguis micat ore trisulcis.   475
una ingens Periphas et equorum agitator Achillis,
armiger Automedon, una omnis Scyria pubes
succedunt tecto et flammas ad culmina iactant.

471-5. qualis ubi…: this simile has an important model in *Iliad* 22.93-5, describing Hector as Achilles approaches to fight: "As a snake in the hills, guarding his hole, awaits a man —/ bloated with poison, deadly hatred seething inside him,/ glances flashing fire he coils round his lair…" (Fagles). Vergil, however, has made an important reversal: "the snake is now a symbol of aggression and it is the son of Achilles who is the aggressor, the father of Hector who is presently being attacked" (Kenney (1979) 106). Vergil's simile also resonates with lines from the *Georgics*: 473 and 475 directly quote *Georgics* 3.437 and 439, from a passage which describes the danger of snakes to a shepherd resting in the fields, while 474 adapts *Georgics* 3.426, which depicts an amphibious serpent. For the influence of the Hellenistic poet Nicander here, see Kenney (1979) 107-8.

471. in lucem: "towards the light"; the words strictly go with the verb of motion *convolvit* (474) but are placed at the beginning of the simile to connect it with *luce* (470). *Ad solem* (475) repeats the motif. **coluber:** a largely poetic word for "snake," used by Vergil less frequently than *anguis* and *serpens*. **mala:** "poisonous." **pastus:** from *pascor* ("feed on").

472. tumidum: "swollen," perhaps with poison from the *mala gramina* (471) it has eaten. **quem:** relative pronoun with *coluber* (471) as antecedent.

473. nunc…: cf. 471-5 n. **positis…exuviis:** ablative absolute, but like the ablative *iuventa*, it expresses the cause behind the adjective it is associated with (*novus* and *nitidus* respectively). **iuventa:** the noun *iuventa* may be an ellipsis for *iuventa aetas* and is used much less frequently than *iuventus* by Vergil. **novus:** may allude to Pyrrhus' other name N̲eoptolemus (in Greek = "New Warrior"), which is used at 500.

474. lubrica…: this line adapts *Geo.* 3.426: *squamea convolvens sublato pectore terga* (cf. 471-5 n.)

475. micat: "flickers," "darts." *Micare* is strictly used of a quick jerky movement backwards and forwards; the meaning "to sparkle" is only secondary.

476-7. una…una: *una* is the adverb and here means "together (with Pyrrhus)." **Periphas:** an unimportant warrior at *Iliad* 5.842. **Achillis:** genitive singular. **armiger Automedon:** in apposition to *equorum agitator Achillis*; Automedon appears as such at *Iliad* 16.145 and 17.536. Compound adjectives like *armiger* (*arma* + *gero*) often suggest lofty diction. **Scyria:** see 469 n.

478. tecto: dative with *succedunt*. Since Pyrrhus has come to the entrance (453), *tecto* here means "dwelling" by metonymy*. *Culmina* = "roof."

ipse inter primos correpta dura bipenni
limina perrumpit postisque a cardine vellit   480
aeratos; iamque excisa trabe firma cavavit
robora et ingentem lato dedit ore fenestram,
apparet domus intus et atria longa patescunt;
apparent Priami et veterum penetralia regum,
armatosque vident stantis in limine primo.   485

---

479. **ipse:** i.e. Pyrrhus (469), to whom our attention is now returned. **inter primos:** a detail emphasizing Pyrrhus' fearlessness in battle. **dura:** describes both the material of which the doors (*limina*) are made and also the character of the resistance it offered. **bipenni:** ablative. *Bipennis* is an adjective formed from *bi* and *penna*, and literally means "having two wings." However, when applied to an axe, it means a "double-edged axe," and could be used substantively as such, as here. Note that the phrases *correpta...bipenni* and *dura... limina* are interlocked (synchysis*).

480. **limina:** here "doors"; cf. 479 n. **perrumpit...vellit:** the presents mark action still going on and incomplete, "is striving to burst through...and rend." In contrast are the perfects *cavavit* (481) and *dedit* (482).

481. **aeratos:** the enjambment* of this word and the use of *dura* (479) and *firma robora* (481-2) underscore the doors' sturdiness — and thus also Pyrrhus' strength, because he penetrates them. **trabe:** "wood panel" (of the door).

482. **dedit:** cf. 310 n. and 480 n. **lato...ore:** ablative of quality. *Os, oris*, n. ("mouth") could also be used metaphorically to mean an "opening," as here.

483-4. **apparet...apparent:** note the pictorial power of the repetition of the verb in different forms (polyptoton*) that helps emphasize the horrific violence about to occur in this stately palace. **penetralia:** "chambers"; like *veterum*, this word suggests awe, as it was often used of a god's shrine, e.g. 5.744 *penetralia Vestae*.

485. **armatos:** see 449-50. **vident:** the subject seems to be "the Greeks," even though the interior of the palace had been the subject of the preceding two verbs (483 *apparet*; 484 *apparent*). It is possible, however, that the Trojans could be the subject: they peer through the hole in the doors and see Greek warriors. **in limine primo:** "on the very threshold" (i.e. on the other side of the hole just made through the doors).

at domus interior gemitu miseroque tumultu
miscetur, penitusque cavae plangoribus aedes
femineis ululant; ferit aurea sidera clamor.
tum pavidae tectis matres ingentibus errant
amplexaeque tenent postis atque oscula figunt.　　　　490
instat vi patria Pyrrhus; nec claustra nec ipsi
custodes sufferre valent; labat ariete crebro

486-505. According to Servius, this passage and thus Vergil's representation of the fall of
Troy at some level are modeled on Ennius' depiction of the destruction of Alba Longa in
the *Annales*. Scholars also discern similarities to Livy's description of Alba's sack (1.29). See
Rossi (2004) 23-4, who also suggests (40-4) that Vergil's emphasis on the palace's interior
and on the Trojan women's lament is part of the topos of the *urbs capta* (cf. 507). For the
influence of Ennius' tragedy *Andromacha*, see Reed (2007): 101-6.

486. **at domus interior:** the phrase contrasts what is going on in the house with what is going
on outside and probably does not describe any particular part of the house. It thus expands
upon *apparet domus intus* (483), the description of which includes what is just inside the
front doors of the palace (485 *in limine primo*) as well as the inner court (484 *penetralia*).

487. **miscetur:** cf. 298 n. **cavae...aedes:** "hollow" or "vaulted halls"; the adjective suggests
the idea of "echoing."

488. **ululant:** an onomatapoietic* word meaning "howl"; it is used here of the halls themselves.
ferit aurea sidera: hyperbole* that helps set the grandeur of the heavens against the
destruction of Priam's palace.

489. **tectis...ingentibus:** "throughout the vast halls." For this ablative, cf. 421 *tota urbe*.

490. **postis:** accusative plural. Since the *postis* of the palace doors have just been breached (480)
and are about to be torn out (493), the *postis* which the women kiss here are probably other
doors or even "columns" (on this usage of *postis*, cf. Horace, *Odes* 3.1.45-6: *cur invidendis
postibus...|moliar atrium?*).

491. **instat:** emphatically placed; the hostile sense of this verb is further emphasized by *vi
patria*. **patria:** adjective referring to Achilles, Pyrrhus' father (see 268-558 n. and 469 n.).
ipsi: emphasizes that the *custodes*, the people who are supposed to be able to protect those
inside the palace, cannot (*nec...sufferre valent*) because of the overwhelming onslaught they
experience.

492. **valent:** besides "to be powerful" or "well," *valeo* + infinitive can mean "to have the
strength to...," as here. **ariete crebro:** "incessant battering" (lit. "frequent battering-ram").
While Pyrrhus plies his axe (479 *bipenni*), his followers aid him by battering the door. Note
that *ariete* here is trisyllabic: the "i" is consonantal, as in 16 *abiete* and 442 *parietibus*.

ianua, et emoti procumbunt cardine postes.
fit via vi; rumpunt aditus primosque trucidant
immissi Danai et late loca milite complent.   495
non sic, aggeribus ruptis cum spumeus amnis
exiit oppositasque evicit gurgite moles,
fertur in arva furens cumulo camposque per omnis
cum stabulis armenta trahit. vidi ipse furentem
caede Neoptolemum geminosque in limine Atridas,   500

---

493. **emoti procumbunt cardine postes:** at 480 the Greeks began pulling out the doorposts, which are finally dislodged (*emoti*) here. The *cardo* does not resemble a modern "hinge," nor is the *postis* the same as a modern "door-post." Ancient doors were not hung on hinges but turned on two pivots with one socket in the *limen* or sill, the other in the *limen superum* or lintel. The term *cardo* can be used either of the pivot or of the socket in which it moves. Since the bar (491 *claustra*) fastening the two halves does not give, the Greeks must "wrench the posts from their supporting sockets" to knock down the doors.

494. **fit via vi:** note the emphatic repetition of *vi* in the same metrical position as in 491. **rumpunt aditus:** "they burst an entrance." *Aditus* is a cognate accusative (AG §390). This is another example of theme and variation* (cf. 409 n.), since it repeats the idea in *fit via vi*. **primos:** presumably the *custodes* of 492. **trucidant:** means not simply "slaughter" but to do so especially violently — "butcher." It is primarily a prose word (occurring only at 12.577 elsewhere in Vergil) and thus helps underscore the bestial nature of Pyrrhus.

495. **milite:** "soldiers" (cf. 20 n.).

496-9. This simile recalls one describing Diomedes in battle at *Iliad* 5.87-92: "For he stormed across the plain like a winter torrent at the full, which with its swift flood sweeps away the embankments; this the close-fenced embankments do not hold back, nor do the walls of the fruitful vineyards stay its sudden coming when the storm of Zeus drives it on; and before it in multitudes the fair works of men fall in ruin" (Wyatt). See Kenney (1979) 109-12 for detailed discussion of the simile.

496. **non sic:** "not thus" (i.e. "not with such violence"). The words introduce a simile (see 496-9 n.) that can only imperfectly suggest the actual scene. **aggeribus ruptis:** ablative absolute; *aggeribus* probably means "dam," though it could also mean "river banks" and thus be similar to *oppositas...moles* in the next line. **cum:** temporal.

497. **oppositas...moles:** "opposing river banks." **gurgite:** here must mean "violent torrent," and not simply "water" or "stream," as *gurges* often does.

498. **fertur...:** *fertur* carries the sense of overwhelming and uncontrollable fury in this book. Observe the alliteration* and the dactylic movement of the line, perhaps suggesting the water's gushing. **cumulo:** for the meaning of this ablative, see 323 n.

499-500. **vidi ipse...:** emphatic (cf. 5). Note that Aeneas is still on the palace roof looking down at the inside of the palace. **furentem / caede:** both Pyrrhus and the river in the simile (*furens*, 498) are infected by *furor*. **Neoptolemum:** cf. 473 n. **Atridas:** cf. 414-15 n.

vidi Hecubam centumque nurus Priamumque per aras
sanguine foedantem quos ipse sacraverat ignis.
quinquaginta illi thalami, spes tanta nepotum,
barbarico postes auro spoliisque superbi
procubuere; tenent Danai qua deficit ignis.   505
     Forsitan et Priami fuerint quae fata requiras.

perf. in ind. quest.

501. **vidi:** anaphora*, cf. 499. **centumque nurus:** *nurus* is accusative plural. Priam is said to have had fifty sons and fifty daughters. The sons were married, and each had a marriage-chamber (503 *quinquaginta thalami*) in the palace. *Centum nurus* must therefore refer to Priam's fifty daughters plus these fifty daughters-in-law. In describing the whole group with one word, Vergil uses *nurus* instead of simply *natae*. **per aras:** "among the altars," cf. 550.

502. **sanguine foedantem…:** a reference to the slaughter of Priam at the altar described in 506-58. **ignis:** object of *foedantem*. **quos ipse sacraverat:** relative clause describing *ignis*; Priam (*ipse*) is the subject of *sacraverat*.

503. **illi:** "those famous"; they are described at *Iliad* 6.242-50. **spes tanta nepotum:** in apposition to *thalami*.

504. **barbarico:** here denotes "Phrygian," "Trojan." This Greek adjective was used without pejorative associations to indicate those who did not speak Greek, and thus meant "non-Greek." For example, when Plautus (*Trinummus* 19) wishes to say that he has translated a Greek play into Latin, he writes "*Plautus vertit barbare.*" Reed (2007): 104 writes that "the use of the adjective allies Trojan ancestors to Roman descendants on one side of an ethnic boundary whose other side is occupied by the Greeks." **postes:** note again the emphasis on the door(posts). Cf. 493.

505. **procubuere:** emphatic enjambment*; the verb conveys the completed nature of the actions described at 493 (*procumbunt*). **Danai…ignis:** note the equation of destructive fire with the Greeks. **qua:** "where."

506-58. *Pyrrhus pursues and kills Polites near the altar where his parents have sought refuge, and then slays Priam.* Priam's death clearly serves as a symbol for Troy's defeat, but it does something more. Priam is brutally and profanely slain at an altar by Pyrrhus. The scene thus also encapsulates for Aeneas the terrible criminality of the Greeks, which before now had been primarily represented by the actions of Ulysses and Sinon.

     The slaying of Priam by Pyrrhus was an important part of the poetic tradition of the sack of Troy. Vergil's treatment largely follows the version that had Priam killed at the altar of Zeus Herkeios (as in the early Greek epic poet Arctinus) rather than being taken from the altar and then slain (as in the early Greek epic poet Lesches). But at the very end of the passage, with its tragic image of Priam's decapitated body lying on the shore, Vergil seemingly alludes to yet another tradition — that Priam had actually been brought to the Trojan shore and murdered at Achilles' tomb. Servius says this is the version in a play by the tragedian Pacuvius (second century BCE), which is now lost. Knauer (1964a) and Bowie (1990) have also identified important references to Hector's death in the *Iliad*, while Rossi (2004) 44-9 has explored tragic and historiographical subtexts. See also Heinze (1915,

urbis uti captae casum convulsaque vidit
limina tectorum et medium in penetralibus hostem,
arma diu senior desueta trementibus aevo
circumdat nequiquam umeris et inutile ferrum   510
cingitur, ac densos fertur moriturus in hostis.
aedibus in mediis nudoque sub aetheris axe
ingens ara fuit iuxtaque veterrima laurus

1993: 25-6), Austin (*ad loc.*), and Sklenár (1990). For the tradition of Priam's death in art, which often joined his death with that of his grandson, Astyanax, see Gantz (1993) 649-57.

506. **requiras:** potential subjunctive with *forsitan*. **fuerint:** perfect subjunctive in a primary sequence indirect question. **et:** here means "also." Aeneas, who has been narrating since line 3, addresses Dido (his primary audience) with a question (cf. *requiras*) for the only time in this book, and thus sets off the death of Priam as a set-piece (506-58).

507. **uti:** "as," "when"; with this meaning, *ut* takes the indicative (AG §543). It can be distinguished from the present infinitive of the deponent *utor*, because this verb has a long "u." The *uti* here is an archaic form of *ut* that provided a convenient metrical alternative and was also used in the late Republic and Empire for its archaic flavor. **urbis...captae:** cf. 486-505 n.

508. **medium:** agrees with *hostem*, but translate with *penetralibus*. Cf. 67 n. and 512. Note the tricolon* of things Priam sees, beginning with *urbis...captae casum* (507) and ending with the enemy in his very home. **tectorum:** here means "palace."

509. **diu:** take with *desueta*, "long unused." **senior:** "rather old." Aeneas emphasizes Priam's age with the comparative adjective of *senex*, used substantively. **aevo:** ablative of cause explaining *trementibus*.

510. **umeris:** modified by *trementibus* (509), it is dative with the compound verb *circumdat*.

511. **cingitur:** middle voice (cf. 383) and thus can take an object (*inutile ferrum*). Cf. the passive use of this verb at 520. **densos:** modifies *hostis* and adds more pathos to the futility of Priam's attempt and to the certainty of his death (*moriturus*; cf. *periturus* 408). **fertur:** "is rushing," i.e. until Hecuba draws him back. Again *fertur* implies loss of control. Note that just as Vergil had described what Priam had seen in 507-8 with a tricolon* structure, so does he also group his three actions in response: *circumdat* (510)...*cingitur...fertur* (511). The tempo will change in 512-14, where each line is structured by a pair of phrases (e.g. *aedibus in....sub aetheris axe* (512); *ingens ara...veterrima laurus* (513); *incumbens...complexa* (514).

512. **aedibus...axe:** Aeneas/Vergil describes an enclosed court, unroofed but surrounded by a pillared portico (528) and rooms opening into the portico, and with an altar of *Zeus Erkeios* "the god of the homestead" in the center. **nudo:** here "open."

513. **iuxtaque:** adverb, "and next to it" (i.e. the altar). **veterrima laurus:** should also be construed with *fuit* and is modified by *incumbens* and *complexa* (*laurus* is f.) in 514. See also 511 n.

incumbens arae atque umbra complexa penatis.
hic Hecuba et natae nequiquam altaria circum,   515
praecipites atra ceu tempestate columbae,
condensae et divum amplexae simulacra sedebant.
ipsum autem sumptis Priamum iuvenalibus armis
ut vidit, 'quae mens tam dira, miserrime coniunx,
impulit his cingi telis? aut quo ruis?' inquit.   520
'non tali auxilio nec defensoribus istis
tempus eget; non, si ipse meus nunc adforet Hector.
huc tandem concede; haec ara tuebitur omnis,

---

514. **arae:** dative with *incumbens*. **umbra:** ablative of means.

515. **hic:** adverb referring to the area described in 512-14. **nequiquam:** an archaic word that helps convey the gravity and futility of their situation and actions. **altaria circum:** anastrophe*. The altar was a sacrosanct place of refuge.

516. **praecipites:** "driven headlong." **atra...tempestate:** ablative of means or time when.

517. **condensae et...amplexae:** refer back to *Hecuba* and her *natae* (515). **divum:** = *divorum* (cf. 648).

518. **ipsum:** intensifies *Priamum*. **Priamum iuvenalibus:** given the description of Priam above as somewhat decrepit in 509-10, this juxtaposition of words seems almost oxymoronic, pointing once again to the futility of Priam's attempt to stop Pyrrhus' youthful violence.

519. **ut:** "when." **vidit:** Hecuba is the subject. **mens...dira:** "monstrous idea" or "intent"; again we see the idea that madness is driving the action.

520. **impulit...:** supply *te* (i.e. Priam). **cingi:** passive, not middle as in 511 (see n.). **quo:** adverb, "(to) where," "whither."

521-2. **tali auxilio...defensoribus istis...:** ablative with *eget*. *Istis* is demonstrative but probably not derisive, since Hecuba had just called Priam *miserrime coniunx* (519). She points to his armor and weapons and says "the situation does not need such defenders." **non, si ipse meus nunc adforet Hector:** "no, even if my own Hector were here to help." *Adforet* is imperfect subjunctive (= *adesset*) in a present contrafactual protasis. Hecuba means that the only resort they have is to seek refuge at the altar (as they will do) – and this would be the case, even if Hector were there. Cf. Hector's own words on the futility of resistance (291-2).

523. **tandem:** here = "please." "It...adds a note of pleading to the imperative" (Austin). **omnis:** accusative plural; with it understand *nostrum* (partitive genitive of *nos*), which would refer to Hecuba, Priam, and their daughters. *Omnis* is emphatic, as is *simul* in the next line: they will all live or die together.

*2nd pers.
sing.*

aut moriere simul.' sic ore effata recepit
ad sese et sacra longaevum in sede locavit.   525
     Ecce autem elapsus Pyrrhi de caede Polites,
unus natorum Priami, per tela, per hostis
porticibus longis fugit et vacua atria lustrat
saucius. illum ardens infesto vulnere Pyrrhus
insequitur, iam iamque manu tenet et premit hasta.   530
ut tandem ante oculos evasit et ora parentum,
concidit ac multo vitam cum sanguine fudit.

---

524. **moriere:** second person singular future indicative deponent. **simul:** "at the same time" (i.e. as we do). Note the change in Priam's actions. At first, he is ready to fight the Greeks; in the end, without further words, he is drawn to the altar by Hecuba. **ore effata:** *ore* is tautologous since it is already implied by *effata*, though Vergil often uses *ore* with verbs of speaking, perhaps to elevate the tone. The verb *effata* goes back to Ennius, and may thus add gravity.

525. **sese:** accusative reflexive pronoun, referring back to Hecuba, the subject of *recepit*. **longaevum:** describing Priam. His old age and thus his frailty are again emphasized (cf. 509 *senior*).

526. **Ecce autem:** cf. 203 n. **elapsus Pyrrhi de caede:** *caede* (instead of, e.g., *manibus*) is a surprising turn of phrase. *Pyrrhi* is subjective genitive. This scene perhaps recalls Achilles' pursuit of Hector (like Polites, another son of Priam) around the walls of Troy in *Iliad* 22.

527. **unus natorum Priami:** Priam was said to have had fifty sons and fifty daughters (cf. 501 n.). *Unus* is set against the unspecified number of *tela* and *hostes* that Polites avoids.

528. **porticibus longis:** for this ablative, cf. 420-1 n. and 771. With *longis* Aeneas/Vergil once again emphasizes the desperation and perhaps futility of Polites' flight for safety. **fugit:** "u" is short (i.e. present tense). **vacua:** indicates that his search for help is vain because the Trojans have fled the halls.

529. **saucius:** cf. 345-6 n. **ardens:** note the fire metaphor* once again; cf. 470 n. **infesto vulnere:** *vulnere = telo*, the entire phrase thus boldly means "with hostile weapon" (i.e. his weapon is ready to strike a wound at any moment).

530. **insequitur:** the chase is now described from Pyrrhus' perspective (529-30); 526-9 had described Polites'. The placement of *insequitur* pointedly contrasts with *saucius* describing Polites at the beginning of the preceding line. **iam iamque...:** implying not that Pyrrhus actually catches Polites, but that Pyrrhus is always on the verge of catching and stabbing him. Cf. 12.754-5 *iam iamque tenet similisque tenenti/ increpuit malis* of a hound hunting a deer. **hasta:** ablative of means.

531. **ut:** "when," "as." **tandem:** finally Polites breaks away from Pyrrhus, only to fall, dying, in front of his parents Priam and Hecuba. **evasit:** "escaped," "emerged," presumably from the *porticibus longis* and *vacua atria* of 528.

532. **concidit:** = "fell," "was killed" (perfect tense).

hic Priamus, quamquam in media iam morte tenetur,
non tamen abstinuit nec voci iraeque pepercit: *Active*
'at tibi pro scelere,' exclamat, 'pro talibus ausis   535
di, si qua est caelo pietas quae talia curet,
persolvant grates dignas et praemia reddant
debita, qui nati coram me cernere letum
fecisti et patrios foedasti funere vultus.   *M-term*
at non ille, satum quo te mentiris, Achilles   540
talis in hoste fuit Priamo; sed iura fidemque
supplicis erubuit corpusque exsangue sepulcro

---

533. **hic:** temporal adverb. **in media iam morte:** the expression is proverbial for being in imminent danger of death; cf. Cicero, *In Catilinam* 4.18 *ex media morte reservatum*.

534. **abstinuit:** "refrained" (from an action), an intransitive use of this verb. **voci iraeque:** hendiadys* for "wrathful words"; dative with *pepercit*, from *parco* (3).

535. **at tibi:** this use of *at* is very frequent in curses; it marks a sudden outburst of words that will not be controlled. The pronoun is also regularly placed immediately after *at* to emphasize the person at whom the curse is directed.

536. **si qua est:** *qua* is the nominative feminine singular of the indefinite adjective and modifies *pietas*, the "righteousness" of the gods which redresses wrong. **quae...curet:** relative clause of characteristic.

537. **persolvant...reddant:** the main verbs of the sentences are optative subjunctives (AG §441) and can be taken sarcastically.

538. **qui...:** *tibi* (Pyrrhus) in line 535 is the antecedent of this relative clause. Word order for translation: *qui fecisti me cernere letum nati coram*. **fecisti me cernere:** a rare construction used instead of a substantive clause of result (i.e. *fecisti ut cernerem*; see AG §568).

539. **patrios:** emphatic. **foedasti:** a contracted form (i.e. syncope) of *foedavisti*.

540. **satum quo...:** = *(e) quo mentiris te satum (esse)*. Pyrrhus' conduct showed him to be no true son of Achilles. **non ille...talis...fuit:** Priam contrasts Pyrrhus' criminal behavior with the honorable treatment that he (Priam) received when he went to Achilles to beg for Hector's body back, an event depicted in the paintings at Carthage (1.484) and retold in *Iliad* 24. For a more flattering depiction of Neoptolemus, see Odysseus' praise of him to his father Achilles in the underworld (*Odyssey* 11.506-37).

541. **in hoste fuit Priamo:** cf. 390 n. By using *Priamo* instead of *me*, Priam emphasizes his preeminence among the Trojans. **fidem:** this word often means "protection," as in the phrases *in fidem et clientelam se committere, in alicuius fidem ac potestatem venire, di vestram fidem!*, and here *iura fidemque* seems to mean "claim to protection."

542. **erubuit:** "blushed at," i.e. "respected" (cf. 540 n.). Many intransitive verbs thus acquire a secondary meaning and become transitive, cf. 31 *stupet* "is amazed at"; 3.394 *horresce* "shudder at"; and so *exire, evadere* = "escape from"; 6.177 *festinant* "perform hurriedly." **sepulcro:** dative of purpose, "for burial."

reddidit Hectoreum meque in mea regna remisit.'
sic fatus senior telumque imbelle sine ictu
coniecit, rauco quod protinus aere repulsum,   545
et summo clipei nequiquam umbone pependit.
cui Pyrrhus: 'referes ergo haec et nuntius ibis
Pelidae genitori. illi mea tristia facta
degeneremque Neoptolemum narrare memento.   *imperative*
nunc morere.' hoc dicens altaria ad ipsa trementem   550
traxit et in multo lapsantem sanguine nati,
implicuitque comam laeva, dextraque coruscum
extulit ac lateri capulo tenus abdidit ensem.

---

544. **sic fatus:** supply *est*. **sine ictu:** practically synonymous with *imbelle*. Priam's physical weakness (*senior, imbelle sine ictu*) is again emphasized, making his righteous outrage even more poignant. Cf. 525 n.

545. **rauco:** "echoing." **protinus:** emphasizes the weakness of Priam's spear cast. **aere:** for "shield."

546. **umbone pependit:** the *umbo* is a projecting boss in the centre of the shield, intended to cause a weapon to glance aside. Here we must suppose that it is strengthened or covered with leather, which the spear just pierces and in which it is caught so as to "hang in vain from the boss." *Pependit* seems to contradict the idea in *repulsum* in 545 and is perhaps an indication of the roughness of this passage.

547. **cui Pyrrhus:** supply *fatur*; *cui* refers back to Priam. **ergo:** i.e. since you condemn my actions. **referes...ibis:** hysteron proteron*. These futures are used almost as imperatives: "(you shall) go and bear your tale." Sklenár (1990) 72-3 has insightful comments on the effectiveness of Pyrrhus' retort to Priam.

548. **Peliadae genitori:** datives. Achilles, Pyrrhus' father (*genitori*), was in turn the son of Peleus (*Peliadae*, Greek patronymic). **illi:** emphatic, "to him (i.e. Achilles) remember to tell my savage deeds and that Neoptolemus is no true son of his." **mea tristia facta:** *tristia* is sarcastic.

549. **degeneremque Neoptolemum:** supply *esse*. **memento:** imperative.

550-1. **morere:** present imperative of the deponent verb *mori*. **hoc:** refers back to Pyrrhus' words at 547-50. **altaria ad ipsa trememtem/ traxit:** Pyrrhus drags Priam to the altar itself (*ipsa*) for slaughter – thereby heightening the criminality of the act, as *in multo lapsantem sanguine nati* also does.

552-3. **laeva, dextraque:** i.e. *manu*. With his left hand, Pyrrhus grabs Priam by the hair, while his right hand stabs the king with a flashing sword (*coruscum...ensem*). For the potential wordplay between Pyrrhus and *coruscus*, see 470 n. **tenus:** preposition that normally follows its ablative object (here = *capulo*), "up to the hilt." **lateri:** dative with *abdidit*; it is equivalent to *in latus* (cf. 19 n.). **extulit:** cf. 458 n.

haec finis Priami fatorum, hic exitus illum
sorte tulit Troiam incensam et prolapsa videntem   ✓555
Pergama, tot quondam populis terrisque superbum
regnatorem Asiae. iacet ingens litore truncus,
avulsumque umeris caput et sine nomine corpus.

---

554. **haec finis:** supply *est*. **Priami fatorum:** the "fate of Priam" became proverbial as an instance of a great reversal of fortune. The pathos and simplicity of these closing words deserve attention. **hic exitus...tulit:** "this end took him away"; it is a variation on *haec finis Priami fatorum.*

555. **sorte tulit:** *sorte* = "fate." For the meaning of *tulit*, cf. 554 n. and 600 *tulerint.* **videntem:** modifies *illum* (Priam).

556. **tot...populis terrisque:** ablatives with *superbum*. The numerous subject peoples and lands raise him to the proud position in which he can be described as "lord of Asia."

557-8. **Asiae:** here the lands of Asia Minor, around the city of Troy. **iacet...:** these lines enact Priam's reversal of fortune, from great ruler to headless corpse. Vergil may here allude to the murder of Pompey upon his arrival at Egypt in 48 BCE. See Bowie (1990) and Sklenár (1990). **litore:** (*in*) *litore*. Earlier Priam had been slain inside the palace at an altar (550-3). *Litore* may be a reference to the tradition that Priam was killed at Achilles' altar on the Trojan shore. For more on Pompey as well as the various traditions of Priam's death, cf. 506-58 n. **umeris:** ablative of separation with the participle *avulsum.*

The Flight from Troy (lines 559-804)

In the final section of book 2, Aeneas decides to leave his fallen city, but he is continually distracted from doing so: when he sees Helen hiding at the temple of Vesta, he is overcome by a desire to kill her; when his father refuses to leave the city, he feels he must stay and fight; and when he loses track of his wife Creusa on the way out of Troy, he decides to rush back into the city to find her. In each case, Aeneas is momentarily tempted to risk death again in battle, but these temptations are overcome by important revelations (Venus: 594-620; omens: 679-704; the shade of Creusa: 776-89) that emphasize the necessity of his flight and Jupiter's role in promoting his fate.

In creating these stumbling blocks to Aeneas' departure from Troy, Vergil has creatively engaged the literary tradition. Venus' revelation and Creusa's appearance both seem to look back to important Homeric passages (cf. 589-633 n. and 725-95 n.), while the omen involving Ascanius' burning hair bears some similarity to a story about the Roman king Servius Tullius (cf. 679-724 n.). By ultimately heeding these signs and revelations, Aeneas emerges as a figure of *pietas*, for it is in this section of book 2 that he is explicitly presented with the plan of the gods and of the fate he will pursue in the remainder of the epic. For more information on the artistic and literary evidence for Aeneas' flight from Troy, see Austin (*ad loc.*) and Gantz (1993) 713-17. For the influence of *Iliad* 6, see Hughes (1997).

> At me tum primum saevus circumstetit horror.
> obstipui; subiit cari genitoris imago,   560
> ut regem aequaevum crudeli vulnere vidi
> vitam exhalantem; subiit deserta Creusa

559-66. *The sight of Priam's slaying makes Aeneas think of his own father and family.* This passage serves as a transition from the fall of Troy to Aeneas' flight from the city. Up until this point, Aeneas has been little concerned with the safety of his family. Rather he has been trying to protect the city more generally from the onslaught of the Greeks.

559. **At:** marks the transition from Aeneas' witnessing of Priam's slaying to his reaction. **primum:** "for the first time." Only now does Aeneas, who had been engaging in battle, experience *horror*. **circumstetit:** note that the *saevus horror* is treated as a physical entity.

560. **subiit:** supply *me* (or *mihi*), as in 562 and 575. **genitoris:** Aeneas' father Anchises.

561. **ut:** "as," "when." **aequaevum:** modifying *regem* (i.e. Priam), "of like age" (with repsect to Anchises).

562. **vitam exhalantem:** *vitam*, an abstract noun, is given a physical presence. Cf. *horror* in 559. **subiit:** again supply *me* (or *mihi*). Note the anaphora* with *subiit* (560). *Subiit* has three subjects: *deserta Creusa, direpta domus, parvi casus Iuli*. **Creusa:** Aeneas' wife, though the tradition about her name and role in the mythological tradition varied. For more on Creusa see 725-95 and n.

et direpta domus et parvi casus Iuli.
respicio et quae sit me circum copia lustro.
deseruere omnes defessi, et corpora saltu   565
ad terram misere aut ignibus aegra dedere.
Iamque adeo super unus eram, cum limina Vestae

---

563. **direpta domus:** *diripio* (*dis* + *rapio*), "tear apart," or, as here, "plunder." The house has not in fact been plundered, as we learn in what follows. **domus:** though the "u" is short (i.e. nominative singular), it is lengthened in arsis (cf. 369 n.). Thus scan the "u" as long. **Iuli:** an alternate name for Aeneas' son Ascanius, which Vergil also uses (e.g. 598). *Iulus* probably developed in the late Republic to associate Ascanius with the Julian *gens*. The connection of the Julians to Iulus, Aeneas, and thus to Venus was of fundamental importance to the political ideology of Julius Caesar and his adopted son, Augustus.

564. **respicio:** Aeneas has been gazing down from the roof to the altar where Priam has just been killed. He now looks back behind him on the roof to take stock of his situation. **quae...copia:** primary sequence indirect question dependent on *lustro* "survey." **me circum:** anastrophe*.

565-6. **deseruere:** for *deseruerunt*; understand *me*. **saltu:** ablative of means. Cf. 323 n. **misere...dedere:** perfect tense. **aegra:** here "weary," "exhausted," not "sick"; it modifies *corpora*.

567-88. *Aeneas glimpses Helen hiding at Vesta's temple and wants to kill her.* This passage has been the subject of much controversy. Though it does not appear in the major manuscripts, Servius *auctus* (i.e. the Servian commentary as expanded probably in the seventh/eighth century CE, cf. 34 n.) quotes the passage in a note on line 566, and claims that it was part of Vergil's epic but was deleted by his literary executors (cf. 66 n.). To some, these lines seem inconsistent with what comes before and after. For example, a different account is given of Helen's actions during Troy's fall at 6.511-27, where she is described as guiding the Greeks. To others, Venus' words at 594 and 601 seem references to this disputed passage (e.g. 574-5), references that would be difficult to explain if these lines are deleted. The arguments for and against authenticity are numerous and varied, but the issue cannot be decided with certainty. For the ancient evidence, see Austin (*ad loc.*) and Rowell (1966). For the argument against authenticity, see Heinze (1915, 1993: 26-30), Goold (1970) and Murgia (1971, 2003). In support of Vergilian authorship, see Austin (1964) 217-19, Reckford (1981), Conte (1986) 196-9, E. L. Harrison (1990) 48-50, Egan (1996), and Syed (2005) 74-9.
    The question of Vergilian authenticity aside, Aeneas' near slaying of Helen is not part of earlier treatments of Troy's fall, and seems to be an adaptation of a tradition found in the *Little Iliad* (cf. 1-267 n.) that Menelaus almost killed his former wife Helen, when he finds her during the sack of Troy. See, e.g., Heinze (1915, 1993: 28) and Gransden (1990) 131.

567. **Iamque adeo:** Vergil frequently places *adeo* second in a clause to strengthen the preceding word. Here it emphasizes the transition in the narrative, which is marked by *iamque,* as being an important one. **super...eram:** tmesis for *supereram*. **limina:** object of *servantem* (568). **Vestae:** the Roman goddess of the hearth was also associated with virginity, as were her priestesses the Vestal Virgins. Helen's refuge at her temple thus increases her brazenness and Aeneas' outrage.

servantem et tacitam secreta in sede latentem
Tyndarida aspicio; dant clara incendia lucem
erranti passimque oculos per cuncta ferenti.   570
illa sibi infestos eversa ob Pergama Teucros
et poenas Danaum et deserti coniugis iras
praemetuens, Troiae et patriae communis Erinys,
abdiderat sese atque aris invisa sedebat.
exarsere ignes animo; subit ira cadentem   575

---

568. **servantem...latentem:** modifying *Tyndarida* (569). Aeneas places great emphasis on
Helen's hiding (*tacitam, secreta, latentem*). *Servo* here must mean "stay near," not "guard"
or "watch."

569. **Tyndarida:** singular accusative of the Greek patronymic *Tyndaris, -idos,* f., "daughter
of Tyndareus." Helen was the child of Leda and Jupiter (who was disguised as a swan at
the time of her conception), but Tyndareus was Leda's human husband, and thus Helen's
"father" as well. **dant clara incendia lucem:** Vergil contrasts Helen's attempt at hiding
(567-9) with the brightness of the destruction of Troy, which her affair with Paris ultimately
entailed (though cf. 601-3).

570. **erranti...ferenti:** datives; supply *mihi* (i.e. Aeneas). Notice Vergil's use of two parallel
participles to enclose the line (cf. 568). Since Aeneas only descends at 632, we must imagine
him still on the roof here.

571-3. **sibi infestos...praemetuens:** these lines form an elaborate participial phrase to express
in tricolon* the things Helen (*illa*) fears. Take *sibi* as dative with *infestos*. **Erinys:** cf. 337 n.;
a strong word for the denunciation of Helen, one also found at Aeschylus, *Agamemnon* 749.
patriae: i.e. Greece. The adjective *communis* thus emphasizes Helen's criminality: she is so
bad that the Greeks and Trojans both hate her. The harsh feelings that she inspires among
both Trojans and Greeks can also be seen at *Iliad* 3.159-60, 241-2.

574. **abdiderat...sedebat:** note the differing tenses. **invisa:** this word may either be (1) the
participle of *invideo*—"she was crouching a hateful being," or (2) from *in* and *visus*—"she
was crouching (so as to be) unseen." The use of the word at 601 and 647 as "hateful" suggests
this meaning here. Moreover, it would be strange to describe her as "unseen" at the very
moment she is discovered, whereas the description of her as "hateful" naturally precedes the
outburst of hate described in the next line. **aris:** probably an ablative of place where (AG
§426; in poetry, the preposition *in* is often omitted for this usage) to be construed with
both *abdiderat* and *sedebat*; it could also, however, be taken as a dative with *invisa*. Perhaps
both interpretations are at play.

575. **exarsere:** = *exarserunt.* **animo:** ablative of place where, again without the preposition *in.*
subit ira: construe *ira* ("angry longing") with the infinitive *ulcisci* in 576 (cf. 64 n.), and take
the resulting phrase as subject of *subit,* which governs an implied *me* (or *mihi*), as in 560.

ulcisci patriam et sceleratas sumere poenas.
'scilicet haec Spartam incolumis patriasque Mycenas
aspiciet, partoque ibit regina triumpho,
coniugiumque domumque patris natosque videbit
Iliadum turba et Phrygiis comitata ministris?   580
occiderit ferro Priamus? Troia arserit igni?
Dardanium totiens sudarit sanguine litus?
non ita. namque etsi nullum memorabile nomen

---

576. **sceleratas...poenas:** a very difficult construction. *Sceleratas* probably refers to Helen's crimes, not the punishments themselves (*poenas*), and thus is a kind of transferred epithet (or enallage*) that means "punishment for her crime"; cf. also *feminea...poena* (584) and *merentis...poenas* (585-6). Williams (*ad loc.*) and others maintain that the phrase means something like "punishment wicked to inflict" or "sacrilegious vengeance," i.e. because it involves a suppliant at an altar.

577. **scilicet:** "doubtless," "of course"; it conveys Aeneas' disgust at the thought of Helen surviving the war and returning to Greece. The sentence is really affirmative in form, and its interrogative character comes from its sarcastic tone. **patriasque Mycenas:** Helen is from Sparta, where her husband Menelaus is king, but he was originally from *Mycenae* (feminine plural), where his brother Agamemnon rules.

578. **partoque ibit regina triumpho:** *parto* from *pario* (3). *Triumpho* is anachronistic, imagining the Greek Helen in a decidedly Roman ceremony. The triumph was an official military parade for a general who had won a significant victory. Cf. the representation of Augustus' triple triumph (29 BCE) at the center of Aeneas' shield (8.714-28).

579. **coniugiumque...natosque:** *coniugium* stands in for *coniugem*, i.e. Helen's Greek husband Menelaus. **patris:** Helen's father Tyndareus (cf. 569). **natos:** in Homer, Helen only had one child, a daughter named Hermione (*Od.* 4.12-14), though some sources suggest that she also had a son called Nicostratus. It should perhaps be taken as "offspring."

580. **Iliadum:** genitive plural of *Ilias, -adis, f* ("Trojan woman"). **turba...Phrygiis... ministris:** ablatives to be construed with the nominative *comitata* (from *comito*), modifying Helen, the implied subject of the sentence. The captive Trojan women would become her "servants" (*ministris*).

581-2. These three questions are to be construed as a set. The future perfect indicative describes events that precede those conveyed by a simple future (here *videbit*, 579). Translate "Will it be for this (i.e. that this result might follow) that Priam has fallen by the sword...?" **sudarit:** is a contracted (or syncopated) form of *sudaverit*. *Sudare* (1) means "to sweat" but is used here metaphorically for the blood from battle that soaks the shore.

583. **non ita:** understand *erit*. The future is used here with the sense of an imperative. **namque etsi...laudem:** present general condition. **nomen:** "reputation," "fame." The sentence, because it betrays the heroic concern for a good reputation, gives voice to the intense hatred, anger, and outrage that Aeneas experiences.

feminea in poena est nec habet victoria laudem,
exstinxisse nefas tamen et sumpsisse merentis   585
laudabor poenas, animumque explesse iuvabit
ultricis flammae et cineres satiasse meorum.'/
talia iactabam et furiata mente ferebar,

---

584. **feminea:** ablative, cf. 576 n. Here an adjectival form conveys what would be translated as an objective genitive ("the punishment of a woman"). **victoria:** the potential slaying here is viewed as a kind of symbolic mini-victory, even though the war will be lost.

585-6. **nefas:** "unspeakable crime," here used of a person, "a sinful creature." By describing Helen as such, Aeneas dehumanizes her and thus suggests that he will not suffer infamy for killing her, even though she is a woman (cf. 584). **exstinxisse...sumpsisse:** perfect infinitives, both dependent on *laudabor*, which here has the force of *cum laude dicar* and so is followed by an infinitive. The future indicatives (*laudabor, iuvabit*) with perfect infinitives (*exstinxisse, sumpsisse, exple(vi)sse, satia(vi)sse*) help underscore (better than potential subjunctives would have) the contemplated pleasure that Aeneas would experience at slaughtering Helen. **merentis...poenas:** "just punishment," cf. 576 n. *Sumo poenas* is a standard idiom for "exact punishment" for a crime. It would, however, be a crime to kill Helen, a suppliant, at the altar – e.g. Pyrrhus' slaughter of Priam at an altar only underscores his *impietas*.

586-7. **animumque explesse iuvabit/ ultricis flammae:** a difficult sentence for which there is no completely satisfactory explanation. The reading *flammae*, a correction in later manuscripts for *famam* or *famae*, offers the best solution. In this case, *explesse* would govern the genitive *ultricis flammae*, the entire clause meaning "and I will rejoice to have filled my soul with avenging fire"; *flammae* would imply something like "fury" (cf. 575 *ignes*). The use of the genitive with *explesse*, however, is not attested elsewhere, though verbs and adjectives expressing fullness are commonly followed by a genitive (cf. 1.215 *implentur... Bacchi*). Renehan (1973) argues for the authenticity of *flammae* but doubts that Vergil is its author (cf. 567-88 n.).

588. **iactabam:** *iacto* (1), originally meant "toss," but also took on the metaphorical meaning of "speak" or "utter," and here must mean "utter wildly." **talia:** understand *dicta*. **ferebar:** difficult. It cannot mean motion, because Aeneas is still on the roof and does not descend until line 632 (*descendo*). Perhaps it is to be taken metaphorically, "I was carried away (i.e. crazed)." **furiata mente:** Aeneas' impulse to kill is driven by his state of fury (*furor*).

cum mihi se, non ante oculis tam clara, videndam
obtulit et pura per noctem in luce refulsit   590
alma parens, confessa deam qualisque videri
caelicolis et quanta solet, dextraque prehensum
continuit roseoque haec insuper addidit ore:
'nate, quis indomitas tantus dolor excitat iras?

589-633. *Aeneas' mother Venus restrains him and reveals that the gods are behind Troy's destruction.*
Perhaps the most important moment in book 2. Venus stops Aeneas from killing Helen,
and in the process she provides her son with an important revelation: the gods and fate are
destroying Troy; Aeneas must yield to their will. He is given an understanding of events
on an entirely new level. His role is to carry out the divine plan of which the destruction of
Troy is just the beginning (and most painful part) for Aeneas.

Various intertextual influences have been seen here. Venus' restraint of Aeneas resonates
with *Iliad* 1.188-222, where Athena holds Achilles back from slaying Agamenon. Venus'
removal of the cloud from Aeneas' vision so he can see the overall divine dimension
behind Troy's destruction echoes (and contrasts) with *Iliad* 5.121-32, where Athena allows
Diomedes temporarily to distinguish between god and human on the battlefield. The near
killing of Helen also has a parallel in Euripides' *Orestes*. For more on this passage, see
Knauer (1964a), E. L. Harrison (1970, 1990), Reckford (1981), Conte (1986), Hershkowitz
(1998) 80-5, and Johnson (1999).

589-92. **cum...solet:** a long and convoluted *cum*-clause; the main structure is *alma parens
mihi se videndam obtulit*. Venus (*alma parens*) is the subject as well as the reflexive direct
object (i.e. *se*) of *obtulit*. Thus *non...clara, confessa deam, qualis...solet* all refer to Venus. Her
willingness to appear as herself here contrasts with her encounter with Aeneas at 1.314-410:
there she is disguised as a huntress and is ultimately reproached by him, when he realizes
her identity upon her departure.

589. **mihi:** dative of agent with the gerundive *videndam*, which modifies *se* and expresses
purpose.

590. **pura per noctem in luce:** again the contrast between light and dark, central to the
narrative of the fall of Troy. See 569 n. **refulsit:** "gleamed," "sparkled."

591. **alma parens:** emphatic enjambment*. **confessa deam:** not for *confessa se deam esse*, but
deam (here "godhead," "divinity") is boldly put as the direct object. **qualisque...solet:**
"in form (*qualis*) and in stature (*quanta*) as she usually appears to the gods." Not merely
superior beauty but superior size characterizes ancient gods and heroes.

592-3. **dextraque prehensum / continuit:** Venus is still the subject; with *prehensum*
understand *me* (i.e. Aeneas); with *dextra* (ablative) understand *manu* (cf. 291), i.e. Aeneas'
hand. **roseo...ore:** Venus' lips are often rose-colored. **haec:** sc. *dicta*. **insuper:** "in addition."

594. **nate:** vocative. **quis:** the interrogative pronoun, but it is often used as the interrogative
adjective and here should here be understood with *tantus dolor*.

quid furis aut quonam nostri tibi cura recessit? 595
non prius aspicies ubi fessum aetate parentem
liqueris Anchisen, superet coniunxne Creusa
Ascaniusque puer? quos omnis undique Graiae
circum errant acies et, ni mea cura resistat,
iam flammae tulerint inimicus et hauserit ensis. 600
non tibi Tyndaridis facies invisa Lacaenae
culpatusve Paris, divum inclementia, divum,

---

595. **furis:** again, Aeneas' maddened state of mind is characterized in terms of intense passion. Cf. also *iras* in 594. **quonam:** interrogative adverb, "(to) where"; **nostri:** objective genitive of *nos*, it goes with *cura,* while *tibi* is dative of reference.

596-7. **non:** = *nonne,* an interrogative adverb that expects the answer "yes" (*num* expects "no"). **prius:** "first" (adverb). **parentem:** Anchises. **liqueris...superet:** subjunctives (perfect and present respectively) in primary sequence indirect questions dependent on *aspicies. Liqueris* is from *linquo* (3). **coniunxne:** the delayed position of *-ne,* which continues the indirect question, is unusual but may add emphasis to *coniunx* (i.e. Creusa).

598. **quos...circum:** the delayed preposition *circum* takes *quos* and *omnis* as objects. *Quos* is a connecting relative pronoun (AG §308f.) that refers back to Anchises, Creusa, and Ascanius.

599-600. **ni...resistat,...tulerint...et hauserit:** present contrary-to-fact condition, usually with the imperfect subjunctive, but here, as sometimes in poetry, with primary sequence subjunctives (*resistat* = present; *tulerint, hauserit* = perfect). Note the emphatic contrast of tenses: the present of continuous effort versus the perfect which marks the quick ruin which would at once follow any relaxation of effort on Venus' part. **hauserit:** "draw blood," "wound." **mea cura:** in contrast to *nostri...cura* (595), Venus here says that she is helping the very people Aeneas has been ignoring (i.e. his family; cf. 596-8).

601-603. An important revelation to Aeneas that encourages him to look at the fall of Troy in a different way. In seeing Helen, he has focused his anger on the human aspect of Troy's fall, but Venus here tells him that fate and the gods are behind Troy's destruction. The theme of Aeneas' gradual understanding of fate is central to his characterization and culminates in the shield Venus gives him at the end of book 8.

601. **tibi:** dative with *invisa.* **Tyndaridis:** see 569 n. **Laecenae:** adjectival form of *Laconia,* equivalent to Sparta.

602. **culpatusve:** "deserving of blame," "reprehensible." The enclitic *–ve* should be construed with *non* (601): "neither...nor." **divum inclementia, divum...:** the asyndeton* before the initial *divum* and the force of the repeated *divum* (cf. epanalepsis*) strongly contrasts this entire clause with what precedes and should be translated as "but..." Vergil seems to have invented the word *inclementia* for this passage. As we will see at lines 610-16, Neptune, Juno, and Pallas Athena are exacting revenge on Troy for past wrongs. On the effective repetition of *divum,* cf. *lumina frustra,/lumina* at 405-6.

has evertit opes sternitque a culmine Troiam.
aspice (namque omnem, quae nunc obducta tuenti
mortalis hebetat visus tibi et umida circum   605
caligat, nubem eripiam; tu ne qua parentis
iussa time neu praeceptis parere recusa):
hic, ubi disiectas moles avulsaque saxis
saxa vides, mixtoque undantem pulvere fumum,
Neptunus muros magnoque emota tridenti   610
fundamenta quatit totamque a sedibus urbem
eruit. hic Iuno Scaeas saevissima portas

---

603. **evertit:** a singular verb, but it should be construed with the subjects *facies*, *Paris*, and *inclementia*. **opes:** *ops, opis, f.*, here means "riches" (of Troy). **sternitque a culmine:** for the image of Troy falling from its height, cf. 465-6 n.

604-7. To help Aeneas see the true causes of Troy's destruction, Venus provides her son with a view of the involvement of the gods that is unclouded by human frailties.

604-5. **aspice:** is connected in sense with the description initiated by *hic* (608). **quae...caligat:** relative clause modifying *omnem...nubem* (606). **obducta:** *obducta* ("drawn over") governs the phrase *tuenti...tibi* (dative of reference or disadvantage). **mortalis...visus:** accusative plural.

606-7. **tu ne...time neu...recusa:** *time* and *recusa* are imperatives in a "neither...nor..." (*ne... neu*) construction. The pronoun *tu* is unnecessary; its presence adds emphasis. Normally, a negative prohibition is expressed with *noli* + infinitive. **ne qua:** *qua* modifies *iussa* and is the neuter accusative plural of the indefinite adjective. **parere:** object infinitive of *recusa*. **parentis...parere:** there is perhaps a wordplay (paronomasia*) here by associating *părens* with the verb *părere* ("to obey"), though they are not etymologically related.

608. **hic:** adverb. **saxis:** ablative of separation. **moles:** here perhaps "buildings."

609. **mixtoque undantem pulvere fumum:** *undantem* means "billowing"; the dust (*pulvere*) is from the falling buildings. Note the interlocking word order (synchysis*) that mimics the idea in *mixto*.

610. **Neptunus:** Neptune and Apollo helped Laomedon (Priam's father) build the walls of Troy but were cheated out of their pay. As a result, the sea-god sought the destruction of Troy in the Trojan War (though Apollo, despite his anger, still supported the Trojans). Here Neptune uproots the walls he had built. **magnoque...tridenti:** ablative.

611. **quatit:** perhaps refers to the epithet "Earth-shaker" that Homer often uses of Poseidon. **sedibus:** here "base," "foundation."

612. **Iuno...saevissima:** she is the bitterest enemy of Troy. For the reasons of her hatred for the Trojans, see 1.12-28. **Scaeas...portas:** the most famous of the gates of Troy. They were called *Scaean* "because they were on the west, i.e. the left hand side (Gr. *skaios*) looking north. Thus they faced the Greek camp" (Williams). Laomedon was said to be buried on top of these gates, and Troy's safety depended on the protection of this tomb (cf. Servius *ad* 2.13 and 2.241).

prima tenet sociumque furens a navibus agmen
ferro accincta vocat.
iam summas arces Tritonia, respice, Pallas   *abl. respect*   615
insedit nimbo effulgens et Gorgone saeva.
ipse pater Danais animos virisque secundas
sufficit, ipse deos in Dardana suscitat arma.
eripe, nate, fugam finemque impone labori.
nusquam abero et tutum patrio te limine sistam.'   620
dixerat et spissis noctis se condidit umbris.

---

613. **prima:** points to Juno's primary role in the destruction of Troy, though the word also
draws attention to the suffering of Aeneas and the Trojans throughout the epic. See also 612
n. **sociumque...agmen:** refers to the Greeks who are her helpers in the destruction of Troy;
thus *socium* = "allied." **furens:** describes her role in destroying Troy but also applies to her
nature as a force of *furor* throughout the epic.

615. **Tritonia...Pallas:** cf. 171 n. Pallas was a central supporter of the Greeks in the Trojan
War. In addition to aiding the most important Greek warriors (most notably Ulysses), she
is associated with the ruse of the Trojan Horse (cf. 15 n.). Though this is the only place in
the epic where she is seen taking action, she plays an important role throughout. See Spence
(1999).

616. **insedit:** perfect of *insideo*, which here takes the accusative *summas arces* (615). **nimbo
effulgens et Gorgone saeva:** a difficult phrase. *Saeva* here is probably a nominative
describing Pallas, the entire phrase meaning "shining forth from a cloud and fierce with the
Gorgon." The *nimbus* might then be a storm cloud or a dark cloud that usually veils deities
from sight (cf. 12.416 *Venus obscuro faciem circumdata nimbo*). Either of these meanings
is preferable to "halo" (Servius *auctus*, cf. 567-88 n.) or to the variant *limbo* ("hem"), also
offered in Servius. **Gorgone:** ablative singular of *Gorgo*. Pallas had the head of a Gorgon
on her shield. Gorgons were monstrous women with snakes instead of hair and could turn
people to stone. Medusa was the only mortal one and was slain by Perseus.

617-18. **viris:** accusative plural, "strength" (from *vis*, not *vir*). **ipse...ipse:** *ipse* itself is emphatic;
its repetition here is doubly so. Aeneas emphasizes Jupiter's role in rousing both the Greeks
and the gods in their destruction of Troy. We are not given a specific reason here as to why
Jupiter takes such an active role, but the implication may be that he is upholding fate, not
playing favorites. **in Dardana...arma:** *in* + accusative = "against." **arma:** here stands in for
"troops," "army" by metonymy*.

619. **eripe, nate, fugam:** the phrase reinforces Hector's similar injunction at 289: *heu fuge,
nate dea, teque his...eripe flammis.* Cf. 268-558 n. **nate:** once again Venus emphasizes his
divine lineage, despite the animosity (just described) of Jupiter, Neptune, and Pallas toward
the Trojans. **labori:** dative after *impone*.

620. **patrio limine:** supply *in*. *Patrio* refers to Anchises.

621. **spissis...umbris:** supply *in*. The adjective *spissis* means "thick" or "dense," attributing to
the shadows an almost physical presence.

apparent dirae facies inimicaque Troiae
numina magna deum.
  /Tum vero omne mihi visum considere in ignis
Ilium et ex imo verti Neptunia Troia;   625
ac veluti summis antiquam in montibus ornum
cum ferro accisam crebrisque bipennibus instant
eruere agricolae certatim; illa usque minatur
et tremefacta comam concusso vertice nutat,
vulneribus donec paulatim evicta supremum   630
congemuit traxitque iugis avulsa ruinam.

622-3. **dirae facies:** "terrifying forms" or "shapes." **inimicaque...deum:** *inimica* is a predicate adjective, while *magna* is attributive — "the mighty powers of the gods appear fighting against Troy." Since Aeneas has just described the physical presences of Neptune, Juno, Pallas, and Jupiter, *numina* probably refers more generally to their awesome strength. This is a half line that brings the scene of Venus' revelation to an awe-inspiring close.

624. **Tum vero omne...:** Vergil vividly represents Troy's destruction as culminating in one universal crash, and proceeds to emphasize the idea by this simile of a tree which is long attacked, then quivers and rocks, and at last sinks, crashing to the ground. **visum:** supply *est*. **considere:** here, "sink," "collapse."

625. **ex imo:** "from its depths" or "base." **verti:** passive infinitive of *verto* (here "overturn," "knock down"). **Neptunia:** Cf. 610 n. With *Neptunia Troia* understand *visa est*.

626-31. This simile is perhaps modelled on one at *Iliad* 4.482-8, describing the death of Simoeisius at the hands of Ajax: "...and down in the dust he fell like a lithe black poplar/ shot up tall and strong in the spreading marshy flats,/ the trunk trimmed but its head a shock of branches./ A chariot-maker fells it with shining iron ax/ as timber to bend for handsome chariot wheels/ and there it lies, seasoning by the river..." (Fagles). Vergil employs other tree similes at 4.441-6 and 5.448-9.

626. **ac veluti...cum:** "even as...when."

627. **bipennibus:** see 479 n. **instant:** "strive" + infinitive.

628. **illa:** i.e. the ash tree (*ornum* 626). **usque:** "continually." **minatur:** here, "threatens" to fall.

629. **comam:** accusative of respect after *tremefacta*. **nutat:** "totter" (intransitive).

630. **vulneribus:** the blows of the axes are violently depicted as "wounds." **evicta:** from *evinco*, "defeat utterly" — here the prefix *e/ex* means not "out" but "thoroughly." **supremum:** "one last time" (adverbial accusative) .

631. **traxit...ruinam:** for this phrase see 465 n. **iugis avulsa:** in the end the tree is not simply cut down but is uprooted.

descendo ac ducente deo flammam inter et hostis
expedior: dant tela locum flammaeque recedunt.
    Atque ubi iam patriae perventum ad limina sedis
antiquasque domos, genitor, quem tollere in altos   635
optabam primum montis primumque petebam,
abnegat excisa vitam producere Troia
exsiliumque pati. 'vos o, quibus integer aevi *gen of Specification*
sanguis,' ait, 'solidaeque suo stant robore vires,

---

632. **descendo:** it is only now that Aeneas descends from the roof of Priam's palace. **ducente deo:** ablative absolute explaining how Aeneas managed to escape through the enemy to his father's house. *Deo* must be construed generically for "divinity" and not "male god," since it indicates Venus; we would have expected *dea*. This is a long-standing textual problem. **flammam inter...hostis:** *inter* governs both *flammam* and *hostis*.

633. **expedior:** passive with middle sense, "I extricate myself," and thus "I escape." **dant tela locum:** under Venus' guidance, Greek weapons (and the flames of burning Troy) "give place" to Aeneas, thus allowing him to go unharmed to his father's house.

634-70. This is our introduction to Anchises, Aeneas' father by the goddess Venus. He is initially portrayed as hopeless, old, and weak. This characterization, however, contrasts with the important role he will play in helping Aeneas lead the Trojans from their fallen city and in interpreting the many signs and portents they will encounter during their travels in book 3.

634-49. *When Aeneas reaches home, Anchises refuses to leave.*

634. **ubi...perventum:** supply *est a me*; an impersonal passive construction (cf. AG §208d). **patriae:** "father's" (i.e. Anchises). **sedis:** as often, means "house," cf. 760.

635-6. **antiquasque domos:** whereas the phrase *patriae...ad limina sedis* is used to convey the goal of the action involved in *perventum*, *antiquasque domos* stresses the ancient splendor of the house itself. Vergil uses the plural *domos* "sometimes to suggest grandeur," instead of the singular *domum*, even when the meter does not require it (Austin). **tollere in altos/ optabam primum montis...:** *montis* is accusative plural. Aeneas is responding to Venus' concern about Anchises (596-7). He will eventually carry Anchises out of Troy (see, e.g., 707-8). **optabam primum...primumque petebam:** notice the chiastic structuring of the line. **primum:** adverb.

637. **abnegat:** "refuse" + infinitive. **producere:** "lead forth" or "prolong." **excisa...Troia:** ablative absolute, explaining *abnegat*.

638. **pati:** with *abnegat* (637); Anchises would view life after Troy's fall as something to endure, not enjoy. **quibus:** dative of possessor, referring to the antecedent *vos*; supply *est*. **integer aevi:** modifies *sanguis* (639) and means "unimpaired by age" or "youthful." *Aevi* is probably a genitive of specification (AG §349 d; cf. 5.73 *aevi maturus* "ripe in regard to time"; Hor. *Odes* 1.22.1 *integer vitae* "upright in regard to life.")

639. **sanguis:** "vigor" or "vitality." **solidae...vires:** elaborates the idea in *integer aevi sanguis*. Instead of *sunt* in the dative of possessor construction with *quibus*, Vergil employs *stant*, which is perhaps more emphatic.

vos agitate fugam.   640
me si caelicolae voluissent ducere vitam,
has mihi servassent sedes. satis una superque
vidimus excidia et captae superavimus urbi.
sic o sic positum adfati discedite corpus.
ipse manu mortem inveniam; miserebitur hostis   645
exuviasque petet. facilis iactura sepulcri.
iam pridem invisus divis et inutilis annos
demoror, ex quo me divum pater atque hominum rex

---

640. **fugam:** Anchises is the third person to enjoin Aeneas to flee (cf. Hector at 289 and Venus at 619).

641. **me:** contrasts emphatically with *vos* (640). **voluissent...servassent (642):** past contrafactual condition; *servassent* = *servavissent*. **ducere vitam:** a metaphor from spinning; every person "draws out" the thread of existence until the appointed hour.

642. **sedes:** Vergil uses both the singular and plural to mean "house" (cf. 634). **satis... superque:** the construction understood is *satis superque est quod...* ("it is enough and more than enough that..."). **una...excidia (643):** plural for singular. This is a reference to the sack of the city by Hercules, to whom Laomedon had promised his daughter Hesione in marriage. When Laomedon renged on the promise, Hercules stormed the city. For Laomedon's treachery toward the gods, cf. 610 n.

643. **captae superavimus urbi:** *superare* is used here exactly as *superesse* with the dative and means "survive." **captae...urbi:** "the capture of the city" (cf. 162 n.).

644. **sic o sic:** repetition of *sic* for dramatic effect. **positum adfati discedite corpus:** Anchises urges them to regard him not as a frail old man lying stretched upon a bed but as a corpse already laid out (*positum*) upon a bier: *adfati* refers to the last "greeting and farewell" addressed to the dead at the close of a funeral. (Cf. Cat. 101.10 *ave atque vale*.)

645. **manu:** this is an ablative of means and probably = "conflict." Anchises is not describing suicide, but voicing his intention to fight. The next words explain what he means further: a Greek enemy will ruthlessly slay him for the sake of his armor. **miserebitur hostis:** sc. the objective genitive *mei*. The verb *miserebitur* is ironic, since the enemy will not show Anchises any special pity. Rather from Achises' perspective death by the Greeks will seem an act of pity because it will relieve him of the burden of seeing Troy defeated.

646. **facilis iactura sepulcri:** this is a truly un-Roman idea. Throughout antiquity, the "loss of burial" is regarded as almost the greatest loss that can befall a person: when Anchises speaks of it as a "light" thing, his words startle by their utter hopelessness.

647. **iam pridem:** construe with *demoror*. **divis:** dative with *invisus* (*sum*). **annos demoror (648):** because Anchises has lived so long past his crippling by Jupiter (see 649 n.), which made him hateful to the gods and useless, he has delayed the course of the years.

648. **ex quo:** supply *tempore*: "from the time when," "since." **divum pater atque hominum rex:** an Ennian phrase for Jupiter.

fulminis adflavit ventis et contigit igni.'
    Talia perstabat memorans fixusque manebat.   650
nos contra effusi lacrimis coniunxque Creusa
Ascaniusque omnisque domus, ne vertere secum
cuncta pater fatoque urgenti incumbere vellet.
abnegat inceptoque et sedibus haeret in isdem.
rursus in arma feror mortemque miserrimus opto.   655
nam quod consilium aut quae iam fortuna dabatur?
'mene efferre pedem, genitor, te posse relicto
sperasti tantumque nefas patrio excidit ore?
si nihil ex tanta superis placet urbe relinqui,

---

649. **fulminis...ventis:** because Anchises had proclaimed his love for the goddess Venus, he was struck by Jupiter's lightning. **adflavit:** "blasted."

650-70. *Unwilling to flee without his father, Aeneas prepares to rush again to battle.*

650. **memorans:** "recalling"; functions like an infinitive dependent on *perstabat*—he persisted in recalling such things (*talia*). **fixusque:** i.e. with respect to his resolve.

651. **nos:** plural for singular. **contra:** adverb. **effusi lacrimis:** supply *sumus*; lit. "were poured forth in tears," a very strong expression, as though they wholly melted into tears. We would have expected *effudimus lacrimas* (cf. 271 n.).

652-3. **ne...vellet:** either an indirect command or a fear clause following the verbal idea in *effusi lacrimis*, which implies beseeching or fear. **vertere:** here "overturn" or "ruin" with *cuncta* as direct object. **incumbere:** lit. "to lean" or "press on" (with dative), though here with the sense "to add weight to" a doom already pressing in on them (*fato...urgenti*).

654. **abnegat:** emphatically placed, reinforcing Anchises' initial stubbornness (cf. 637 *abnegat*). **incepto:** ablative with *in*. The phrase *inceptoque et sedibus...in isdem* forms a zeugma* with *haeret* that joins physical (*sedibus*) and abstract (*incepto*) ideas. **sedibus... isdem:** i.e. Anchises' house.

655. **rursus in arma feror:** refers back to 337, where the phrase *in arma feror* occurs as Aeneas rushes off to fight the Greeks instead of fleeing Troy, which had been Hector's injunction (289). Here he ignores the same advice he has just received from his mother Venus (619). Again, the verb *fero* in the passive implies rash or violent action; cf. 337, 498, and 511.

656. **quod...quae:** interrogative adjectives with *consilium* and *fortuna* respectively.

657-8. **mene:** *me* is emphatically placed at the beginning of the line and is the object of *sperasti*; *-ne* is the enclitic interrogative. *Spero* with present infinitive = "expect." Note that Aeneas' reply begins abruptly, without even a verb to indicate the change to direct speech. **te...relicto:** ablative absolute. **nefas:** Anchises' suggestion is so called because it would violate the ideal of *pietas* for Aeneas to leave his father to die in Troy.

659. **placet:** "it is resolved," an impersonal usage. Note the pointed contrast between *nihil* and *ex tanta...urbe*.

> et sedet hoc animo perituraeque addere Troiae   660
> teque tuosque iuvat: patet isti ianua leto,
> iamque aderit multo Priami de sanguine Pyrrhus,
> natum ante ora patris, patrem qui obtruncat ad aras.
> hoc erat, alma parens, quod me per tela, per ignis
> eripis, ut mediis hostem in penetralibus utque   665
> Ascanium patremque meum iuxtaque Creusam
> alterum in alterius mactatos sanguine cernam?

660-1. **sedet:** here used to express fixity of purpose. It is equivalent to *stat* (cf. 750 and n.). **hoc:** neuter nominative, "this," referring to Anchises' decision to stay in Troy. **animo:** *(in tuo) animo.* **iuvat:** supply *te*; *addere* follows and takes *teque tuosque* (661) as objects. **isti... leto:** datives, "to that death of yours" (i.e. that you have decided upon). Here *isti* conveys a sense of frustration.

662. **iam:** here with the future tense (*aderit*), it means "soon," not "now" or "already." **multo Priami de sanguine Pyrrhus:** *sanguine* is a vivid substitution for "slaying"; *multo* emphasizes the goriness of Priam's demise. Just as Priam's death had earlier reminded Aeneas of his father Anchises, so now Anchises' decision to remain in Troy brings to Aeneas' mind the terrible slaying by Pyrrhus, who is here envisaged as actually coming to Anchises fresh from (*de*) the blood of Priam.

663. **natum...aras:** Aeneas emphasizes the two crimes he witnessed Pyrrhus commit: 1.) slaying Polites in front of his father, whom he then 2.) slaughtered at an altar. **patris, patrem:** note the differing vowel lengths in these two inflected forms of *pater*. The "a" is by nature short, but a short vowel followed by a mute and a liquid (here "t" and "r") can be either long or short. Here we see both possibilities (the former short, the latter long). The asyndeton between *patris, patrem* separating the line into two halves and the juxtaposition of *natum* and *patrem* at the beginning of each half underscore the impiety of Pyrrhus through the accumulation of his crimes. **obtruncat:** denotes especially callous "slaying"; translate as "butcher" (cf. 494 *trucidant* with n.). The present tense is not only more vivid than the past here (cf. 274-5 n.) but also suggests that Pyrrhus' killing spree is still unfinished. Pyrrhus' violence may also be suggested by the three elisions in this line, the last with *qui* being particularly rare.

664-7. **hoc...cernam:** a difficult syntactic construction in which Aeneas suddenly addresses his mother Venus. The phrase *quod me...eripis* is literally "as to the fact that you are saving me"; it is here used as equivalent to a simple noun serving as the subject of *erat. Hoc* is then a predicate and is explained by the clause *ut...cernam.* Translate: "Was this (the purpose), dear mother, (for) which you are saving me from sword and fire, that I may see...." **iuxta:** "next to one another" (adverb). **mactatos:** accusative plural, modifying the joint object *Ascanium patremque meum...Creusam.* **alterum in alterius...sanguine:** "one in the blood of the other," further modifying the joint object, even though this idiomatic phrase occurs in the singular. **cernam:** we might have expected a secondary sequence subjunctive since *erat* is imperfect; however, because the overall sense of the sentence is present, the primary sequence subjunctive is used.

arma, viri, ferte arma; vocat lux ultima victos.
reddite me Danais; sinite instaurata revisam
proelia. numquam omnes hodie moriemur inulti.'   670
    Hinc ferro accingor rursus clipeoque sinistram
insertabam aptans meque extra tecta ferebam,
ecce autem complexa pedes in limine coniunx
haerebat, parvumque patri tendebat Iulum:
'si periturus abis, et nos rape in omnia tecum;   675
sin aliquam expertus sumptis spem ponis in armis,

---

668. **arma, viri:** recalls the opening of the poem, *arma virumque*. The dramatic repetition of *arma* emphasizes the renewed frenzy of Aeneas' decision to fight instead of fleeing. Here we have the man of *Aen.* 1.1 (*virumque*) actually calling for *arma*. **ferte:** Aeneas suddenly turns from his address to his mother (664) to a generalizing imperative. **lux ultima:** "last light" or "death." *Ultima* and *victos* emphasize what Aeneas views as the ultimate futility of fighting for Troy now.

669. **Danais:** dative plural. **sinite...revisam:** *sino* (3) usually takes an accusative and infinitive construction, but here it governs a present subjunctive in indirect command (*ut* omitted) — *sinite (ut) revisam.* For the omission of *ut*, cf. the common phrases *fac abeas, velim facias, licet venias,* and also Terence, *Andria* 5.3.30 *sine te hoc exorem.* **instaurata:** used proleptically — Aeneas will "renew" the battle by reseeking it.

670. **numquam...hodie:** cf. *Eclogues* 3.49 *Numquam hodie effugies. Numquam* loses its sense of time and becomes an emphatic negative.

671-78. *Creusa begs Aeneas not to desert their family.*

671. **accingor:** here passive, as in 520 and 614 (cf. the middle use of *cingitur* at 511). **clipeo:** here "the handle of my shield" — the arm was passed through a strap or handle in the centre of the shield inside. **sinistram:** supply *manum*.

672. **insertabam...ferebam:** note the switch from present (671 *accingor*) to imperfect (*insertabam...ferebam*), the latter verbs explaining Aeneas' actions at the time of Creusa's unexpected appeal in the lines that follow. **aptans:** "as I bind it." **me...ferebam:** periphrasis for "I raced out of the house."

673. **ecce autem:** cf. 203 n. **complexa pedes:** usually the suppliant clasps the knees; the substitution of the feet here marks her as at once beseeching him and hindering his departure. **coniunx:** Creusa.

674. **haerebat:** note the emphatic enjambment*, perhaps suggesting Creusa's insistence. **patri:** for *ad patrem*, refers to Aeneas. *Patri* is emphatic: not "to me" but "to his father," because it is to the paternal affection of Aeneas that she appeals by her act.

675. **si...:** present general condition. **et:** "also," "as well." **in omnia:** i.e. "to death or whatever may befall us."

676. **sin:** = *si non*, "but if (you do) not..." **aliquam:** with *spem*. **expertus:** "having tried them (sc. *arma*) before."

hanc primum tutare domum. cui parvus Iulus,
cui pater et coniunx quondam tua dicta relinquor?'
    Talia vociferans gemitu tectum omne replebat,
cum subitum dictuque oritur mirabile monstrum.   680
namque manus inter maestorumque ora parentum
ecce levis summo de vertice visus Iuli
fundere lumen apex, tactuque innoxia mollis
lambere flamma comas et circum tempora pasci.

---

677. **primum:** adverb. **tutare:** present singular imperative of the deponent verb *tutor* (1).

678. **coniunx quondam tua dicta:** "once called your wife." Creusa uses this phrase because Aeneas was about to leave her and meet his death. **relinquor:** present with future sense, literally to be taken with the speaker, Creusa (Aeneas' *coniunx*), but third person forms of the verb (*relinquitur*) must be understood for the subjects *parvus Iulus* (677) and *pater*.

679-725. *Omens involving Ascanius encourage Aeneas, Ascanius, and Creusa to leave.* The omen of Ascanius' burning hair seems to have been invented by Vergil and is perhaps based on the famous story about the sixth king of Rome, Servius Tullus (Livy 1.39; cf. Ovid, *Fasti* 6.636); for possible Lucretian influence, see 116 n. (At 7.71-80, a similar portent will involve Lavinia, the Latin princess over whom the Italian war will be fought in the second half of the epic.) Anchises' interpretation of the omen represents a turning point in his characterization. Initially reconciled to Troy's destruction, he now takes on an important role in the Trojans' flight from Troy.

    The passage closes with Aeneas, his father on his shoulders carrying the *penates* and Ascanius at his side (721-4). This image powerfully captures Aeneas' *pietas* and was a popular subject in art; for references, see Gantz (1993) 714-16.

679. **Talia:** refers back to Creusa's speech.

680. **subitum dictuque...mirabile:** both adjectives are to be construed with *monstrum*; *dictu* is the ablative of the supine of *dico* (3) and goes with *mirabile*, "wondrous to tell" (see AG §510).

681. **manus...ora:** both direct objects of the preposition *inter*. Creusa is on her knees holding up Iulus to Aeneas, and thus the boy is "between the hands and faces of his sad parents." Vergil offers a vivid picture of father, mother, and son.

682. **levis...apex (683):** the subject of the verb *visus* (*est*). *Apex* is strictly used of the point in which the cap of a flamen (a type of priest) ended, but it is here used for a sort of "tongue (cf. *lambere*) of fire." Perhaps the shape of the flame resembles that of a priest's hat (*apex*), thereby suggesting the prophetic sign.

683. **tactuque innoxia:** might mean "harmless to be touched" (cf. 680 *dictu mirabile*), but seems more fittingly to be "harmless with its touch" (i.e. the flame touches the hair but does not burn it). **mollis:** with *comas*.

684. **tempora:** "temples" (of head). **pasci:** passive infinitive of *pasco* (3) with middle sense; it usually means "feed" or "graze," but here it is closer to "dance" or "play." The infinitives *lambere* and *pasci* are complementary infinitives with an understood *visa est* (adapted from 682 *visus*) for which *innoxia flamma* is subject.

nos pavidi trepidare metu crinemque flagrantem   685
excutere et sanctos restinguere fontibus ignis.
at pater Anchises oculos ad sidera laetus
extulit et caelo palmas cum voce tetendit:
'Iuppiter omnipotens, precibus si flecteris ullis,
aspice nos, hoc tantum, et si pietate meremur,   690
da deinde augurium, pater, atque haec omina firma.'
   Vix ea fatus erat senior, subitoque fragore
intonuit laevum, et de caelo lapsa per umbras
stella facem ducens multa cum luce cucurrit.

685-6. **trepidare:** "shake" or "tremble," combining the ideas of fear and eagerness. Their fear is emphasized by both *pavidi* and *metu*. **trepidare...excutere...restinguere:** historical infinitives (cf. 98 n.) with nominative subject (*nos pavidi*). *Excutere* and *restinguere* carry the additional sense of trying (conative): "they try to shake off...to put out..." **sanctos...ignis:** the fire is *sanctos* because it is a divine portent (cf. 682 n.), though it is not fully accepted as such until 699-700.

687. **at pater Anchises...laetus:** note Anchises' sudden change of heart from despair to happiness, as he is seemingly the first to understand the meaning of the portent. His role as interpreter of portents will continue in book 3.

688. **caelo:** dative of direction, equivalent to *ad caelum*. **cum voce:** = *dixit*.

689. **si flecteris:** a present general protasis; *flecteris* is present passive, not future because the "*e*" in "*-eris*" is short. **precibus...ullis:** ablative of means.

690. **hoc tantum:** "only this (do I pray)"; a verb like *precor* must be supplied. **pietate:** ablative of cause with *meremur* (2), which applies not simply to Anchises but to his family more generally. Anchises thus suggests the worthiness of his prayer due to his family's *pietas*, the defining value of Aeneas.

691. **deinde:** this word emphasizes the idea that there is a natural sequence: first due reverence to the gods and then due reward from them. **augurium:** Anchises asks for an omen (i.e. an *augurium impetrativum*) to confirm the one that had been sent by the gods unasked (i.e. an *augurium oblativum*). *Augurium* is the reading of Probus and the one Servius seems to have had. It makes good sense here, though Mynors prefers the manuscript reading *auxilium*. **firma:** imperative, "confirm"; i.e. confirm the first omen by a second, and thus show that the first sign was not an accidental event but the sure indication of divine will.

692. **ea:** understand *verba*. **subitoque fragore...:** note the parataxis*. Instead of "and suddenly," translate as "when suddenly...'

693. **intonuit laevum:** *laevum* is cognate accusative after *intonuit* (AG §390b); thunder on the left was a good omen in Roman augury. **et de caelo...:** Jupiter then sends a second omen of a shooting star (*de caelo lapsa per umbras stella*) to confirm the first (i.e. the flame in Iulus' hair).

694. **facem ducens multa cum luce:** *facem* for *lucem*. Lit. a star "trailing a torch accompanied with much light."

illam summa super labentem culmina tecti   695
cernimus Idaea claram se condere silva
signantemque vias; tum longo limite sulcus
dat lucem et late circum loca sulphure fumant. /
hic vero victus genitor se tollit ad auras
adfaturque deos et sanctum sidus adorat.   700
'iam iam nulla mora est; sequor et qua ducitis adsum,
di patrii; servate domum, servate nepotem.
vestrum hoc augurium, vestroque in numine Troia est.
cedo equidem nec, nate, tibi comes ire recuso.'

---

695. **labentem...signantem** (697): both modify *illam* (i.e. *stellam*). **summa...culmina:** neuter accusative plural, object of the preposition *super*.

696. **Idaea...silva:** supply *in*. Ida is a mountain at Troy.

697. **signantemque vias:** the shooting star illuminates its path as it falls on Mt. Ida. These words should be understood closely with *claram*: it is by its "brightness" that the star "marks its path." **tum:** i.e. after the star's departure. **longo limite sulcus:** the path (*limes*) the star had taken seemed like a glistening furrow (*sulcus*) which had been ploughed in the sky. *Sulcus* thus refers to the tail of light that trails the star.

698. **circum:** adverb.

699. **hic vero:** this adverbial phrase points to Anchises' sudden change of heart. **victus:** here not "conquered" but "persuaded" (i.e. finally to leave Troy, as Aeneas had advised). **se tollit ad auras:** i.e. Anchises stands up. Until this point, Anchises had been seated (654) and almost laid out on a couch (644); at the first omen he "lifted his eyes and hands to heaven" (687-8), but now "he raises himself toward heaven."

700. **sanctum:** like the *ignis* in 686, the *sidus* is also taken as a divine omen.

701. **iam iam:** with this emphatic repetition, Anchises reverses his earlier decision to remain at Troy. **nulla mora:** stresses the promptness of his obedience, as does the present *sequor* ("I follow," not *sequar* "I will follow") and the still more emphatic *adsum*. *Adsum* is the word used by anyone who is asked for (e.g. a slave) and replies, "Here!" **qua:** "wherever."

702. **di:** *dei*. **domum:** "house," in the sense of "family" or "race"; the portent of fire had marked Ascanius, Anchises' "grandchild" (*nepotem*), and by implication his descendants as under divine protection.

703. **vestrum hoc augurium:** supply *est*. **vestroque in numine Troia est:** these words do not refer to the actual city of Troy, which was deserted by the gods and all but destroyed. The phrase is highly rhetorical and dramatic: as Anchises utters it, his gaze rests on his son and grandson who are now in themselves "Troy," are obeying the "divine augury" (*vestrum augurium*), and are "relying on divine protection" (*in numine*) to found a new city. Note that the repetition of the adjective *vester* is emphatic.

704. **tibi:** construe closely with *comes*.

dixerat ille, et iam per moenia clarior ignis 705
auditur, propiusque aestus incendia volvunt.
'ergo age, care pater, cervici imponere nostrae;
ipse subibo umeris nec me labor iste gravabit;
quo res cumque cadent, unum et commune periclum,
una salus ambobus erit. mihi parvus Iulus 710
sit comes, et longe servet vestigia coniunx.
vos, famuli, quae dicam animis advertite vestris.
est urbe egressis tumulus templumque vetustum

---

705. **ignis:** i.e. the burning of Troy. **clarior:** this adjective can mean both "brighter" and "louder," and perhaps here refers both to the fire's light and to its crackling.

706. **aestus incendia volvunt:** *aestus* is accusative plural; "the flames roll their fiery flood" (Goold).

707. **ergo age:** "Come, then." This phrase has a conversational tone and is found especially in comedy, though *age* by itself is often used in combination with another imperative. Aeneas begins speaking, though no verb of speech is used, thus suggesting the confusion of the scene. **imponere:** "place yourself on," present passive imperative with middle sense (cf. 383 n.). **cervici...nostrae:** dative of indirect object with the compound verb *imponere* (AG §370).

708. **subibo:** supply *te* (i.e. Anchises); "I will support (you) from below." **umeris:** ablative of means.

709. **quo...cumque:** tmesis for *quocumque*; the clause means "wherever things shall fall" (i.e. "however things turn out"). The metaphor in *cado* is from playing dice. **peric(u)lum:** construe with *ambobus erit* from the next line. **unum...una** (710): note the repetition of this adjective to indicate their shared risks.

710. **ambobus:** dative plural of *ambo*; supply *nobis* (Aeneas and Anchises). **mihi:** cf. *tibi comes* in 704.

711. **sit...servet:** jussive subjunctives. *Servet* = "follow" (cf. 568 n.). **longe:** probably means "behind" (like *pone* at 725) rather then "far off." This word prepares us for Creusa's disappearance at 735-44.

712. **quae dicam:** understand *ea* as the antecedent to this relative clause. **animis advertite:** "pay attention to" (lit. "turn with your minds to"). In this idiomatic phrase, Vergil uses *animis*, though the accusative *animos* is more usual.

713. **est urbe egressis:** "when you go out of the city, there is a..." (lit. "for those who have left the city, there is a..."). *Egressis* is a dative of reference (AG §378.2). **tumulus:** "hill" or "mound," not "tomb," since the temple of Ceres is meant (714). Note the concise and conversational nature of Aeneas' words here.

desertae Cereris, iuxtaque antiqua cupressus
religione patrum multos servata per annos.   715
hanc ex diverso sedem veniemus in unam.
tu, genitor, cape sacra manu patriosque penatis;
me bello e tanto digressum et caede recenti
attrectare nefas, donec me flumine vivo
abluero.'   720
haec fatus latos umeros subiectaque colla
veste super fulvique insternor pelle leonis,

---

714. **desertae:** meaning is unclear. It is probably a transferred epithet, since it is the ancient temple that has been deserted (perhaps because of the war). It might, however, be a reference to Ceres' "desertion" by her daughter Proserpina, who had been abducted by Pluto (Conington). **iuxtaque:** adverb, "and next to it."

715. **religione...servata:** even though the temple has been deserted, superstition (*religione*, cf. 151 n.) still makes people take care of the ancient cypress tree near it. Very old and venerable trees are often regarded with a certain "religious awe." *Religione* is ablative of cause. **multos...per annos:** the *per* is not necessary; a simple accusative of duration would have sufficed. **patrum:** "forefathers."

716. **ex diverso:** "from different directions." The *antiqua cupressus* (714) is a meeting place for the household slaves (*famuli*) to gather by their various routes from the city. *Diverso* contrasts with "one" (*hanc...in unam*). **sedem:** notice the placement of *sedem*: as the central meeting place of Aeneas' family, it lies at the center of the line and is balanced by *hanc* and *unam*, which enclose the line.

717. **tu, genitor, cape...:** another sign of Aeneas' *pietas* toward the gods. Aeneas will not permit himself to handle the *sacra* and *penates*, because his hands are still stained from battle. On the *sacra*, see notes on 293 and 320-1.

718-19. **attrectare nefas:** an impersonal expression; supply *est* with *nefas*, and construe *me* as accusative subject of *attrectare*. **e...digressum...caede recenti:** is literally "coming from fresh bloodshed," but "coming fresh from bloodshed" gives the true emphasis in English. **vivo:** "flowing," "running."

720. **abluero:** future perfect indicative with *donec* ("until"), cf. AG §553 n. 2.

721. **latos umeros:** accusative after *insternor*. **subiecta:** "stooped," "placed under" (from *sub* + *iacio*), so as to be ready to receive Anchises.

722. **veste...fulvique...pelle leonis:** *veste...pelle* are ablatives of means, which in combination represent an example of hendiadys*—"with the covering of a tawny lion" (lit. "with my clothing and hide of a tawny lion"). **super:** adverb, "on top." **insternor:** with middle sense, "I cover my broad shoulders" (cf. 383 n.).

succedoque oneri; dextrae se parvus Iulus
implicuit sequiturque patrem non passibus aequis;
pone subit coniunx.
      ferimur per opaca locorum,   725

723-4. **succedo:** with dative (*oneri*): "I bend my shoulders to" (lit. "move to a position under"). **oneri:** referring to Anchises, whom Aeneas will carry on his shoulders. (Cf. Ovid, *Met.* 13.625, where Anchises is called *venerabile onus*.) **dextrae se...implicuit:** "Iulus grasped my right hand" (lit. "Iulus entwined himself in my right hand"). *Dextrae* (*manui*) is dative after the compound verb *implicuit*. Servius writes, *puerilem expressit timorem, ne manu excidat patris.* **non...aequis:** litotes*; this phrase also emphasizes Iulus' youth, small size, and reliance on his father's protection.

725. **pone:** adverb, "behind"; a largely archaic word, it was also used by Vergil to describe Eurydice (*Georgics* 4.487 *pone sequens*). Cf. 711 *longe* and see 725-95 n. **subit:** here "follows."

725-95. *As they flee the city, Aeneas loses track of Creusa. He frantically rushes back to find her, when suddenly her ghostly form appears, telling him to stop his vain search and to seek the far away land where a happier fate awaits.* Aeneas' loss of Creusa has troubled many readers. It is true that in Vergil's plot Creusa must be gone for Aeneas' affair with Dido and his later engagement to Lavinia to take place. Yet, it is strange that this warrior known for his *pietas* somehow loses track of his wife. The tradition regarding Creusa varied but there were two dominant strands: one (the older) portrayed her leaving Troy with Aeneas (Dionysius of Halicarnassus and Naevius); the other claimed that she was rescued by Aphrodite or by Aphrodite and Cybele (perhaps Stesichorus (the evidence is controversial), Pausanias, and cf. 741 n.). Vergil seemingly follows the second strand but makes it more complicated. He emphasizes that Jupiter and Cybele have detained Creusa on Troy's shores (777-9, 788), but at the same time he underscores Aeneas' negligence concerning his wife. Our understanding of these two details can lead to extremely different interpretations, as Perkell (1981) and Hughes (1997) demonstrate. At the very least, Vergil's treatment underscores Aeneas' human weakenesses and emphasizes the personal losses that he will experience throughout the epic — whether due to his own actions or the exigencies of the gods and fate.

   Aeneas' loss of Creusa resonates with the tale of Orpheus and Eurydice in *Georgics 4*. Indeed, Vergil may even have been drawn to this model in part because the earlier tradition named Aeneas' wife Eurydica, who seems to have acquired the name Creusa during the late Republic, when her identification as a daughter of Priam may also have begun. Aeneas' encounter with Creusa's shade also has important models in Achilles' attempt to embrace Patroclus' shade at *Iliad* 23.99-101 and in Odysseus' attempt to embrace his mother's shade at *Odyssey* 11.206-8. For the larger tradition of and sources for Creusa at the fall of Troy, see Heinze (1915, 1993: 62) and Gantz (1993) 713-16. For interpretation, see Segal (1973-74), Briggs (1979), Perkell (1981), Hughes (1997), Khan (2001), Gale (2003), and R. A. Smith (2005): 77-82.

725. **ferimur:** cf. 337 n. **opaca locorum:** "shadowy places." They pick spots that are "in shadow" and not illuminated by the flames. *Opaca* is the neuter accusative plural adjective used substantively. We might more regularly expect *opacos locos*. (Cf. 235-6 *rotarum lapsus*, and see 332 n.)

et me, quem dudum non ulla iniecta movebant
tela neque adverso glomerati ex agmine Grai,
nunc omnes terrent aurae, sonus excitat omnis
suspensum et pariter comitique onerique timentem.
iamque propinquabam portis omnemque videbar   730
evasisse viam, subito cum creber ad auris
visus adesse pedum sonitus, genitorque per umbram
prospiciens 'nate' exclamat 'fuge, nate; propinquant.
ardentis clipeos atque aera micantia cerno.'
hic mihi nescio quod trepido male numen amicum   735
confusam eripuit mentem. namque avia cursu

726. **dudum:** adverb, "just a little while ago." **movebant:** "move," as in "disturb," "trouble"; subject is *ulla iniecta...tela.*

727. **adverso glomerati ex agmine Grai:** *ex* + ablative here indicates the source or "material" from which the *glomerati Grai* come—"amassed from their opposing ranks." **ex agmine:** Mynors prints *examine,* but this noun is not used of people elsewhere in Vergil.

728. **nunc:** emphatically placed to contrast with *dudum* (726). **omnes...omnis:** note the chiasmus* beginning and ending with *omnis* that emphasizes the overwhelming terror in which they flee. *Omnes...omnis* also contrasts with *non ulla* (726). **terrent:** object is *me* from 726.

729. **suspensum:** "anxious," "unsure," with *me* (726). **comitique onerique:** datives with *timentem* (AG §367c) that refer to Iulus and Anchises respectively.

730. **videbar:** "I thought I had..." Aeneas' uncertainty reflects the darkness and confusion of the flight (cf. 279 n.). *Iamque...evasisse viam* (731) recalls *Georgics* 4.485 (*Iamque pedem referens casus evaserat omnis*), the passage where Orpheus loses Eurydice. Cf. 725-95 n., Putnam (1965) 41-7, and Gale (2003). **portis:** dative with *propinquabam.*

731-2. **evasisse:** "to have passed the road in safety." *Viam* is the direct object of *evasisse,* and *evadere* is used in two senses, partly 1.) "to come to the end of," partly 2.) "to escape," the road being regarded as dangerous. **subito:** adverb. **creber...pedum sonitus:** *creber* grammatically modifies *sonitus,* but in sense it describes *pedum:* "the sound" or "trample of numerous feet." **visus:** supply *est.* As in 730 (see n.), this verb suggests the confusion of the scene.

733. **nate... fuge, nate:** Anchises is now the third person to tell Aeneas to flee — even as he is fleeing! **propinquant:** subject is the implied *Grai.* Note the terseness of Anchises' words.

734. **aera:** here, "bronze swords."

735. **mihi...trepido:** dative of separation (AG §381) after *eripuit.* **nescio quod...numen:** "some divinity." Note the "*-o*" in *nescio* is shortened. **male amicum:** i.e. "unfriendly," modifying *numen.* On *male,* see 23 n.

736. **confusam:** proleptic. **avia:** the adjective *avius* comes from *ab* + *via* and means "out-of-the-way," "trackless." As a neuter substantive, it means "remote paths," as here. **cursu:** lit. "at a run," see 323 n.

dum sequor et nota excedo regione viarum,
heu misero coniunx fatone erepta Creusa
substitit, erravitne via seu lassa resedit,
incertum; nec post oculis est reddita nostris,   740
nec prius amissam respexi animumve reflexi
quam tumulum antiquae Cereris sedemque sacratam
venimus: hic demum collectis omnibus una
defuit, et comites natumque virumque fefellit.
quem non incusavi amens hominumque deorumque,   745
aut quid in eversa vidi crudelius urbe?

---

737. **nota excedo regione viarum:** expands the sense of *avia* (736). **regione:** "direction," the original meaning of the word, which is from *regere* "to direct."

738-9. **heu...resedit:** the disjointed questions vividly mark the upheaval of Aeneas' feelings. **misero:** dative of separation after *erepta*. **seu:** makes *resedit* an alternative to *erravit*; the second question is thus a double one, "did she (either) wander...or sit down?" We would normally expect the first *–ne* after *misero*, effectively the initial word of the question; its placement here, however, gives more emphasis to *fato*. **substitit:** from *subsisto*, "stop in one's path." **via:** ablative of separation with *erravit*.

740. **incertum:** supply *est*. **post:** adverb, "afterwards." **oculis...nostris:** dative.

741. **nec...reflexi:** Aeneas explains that, as they fled the city, he did not look back to Creusa until he had arrived at the appointed destination. At *Alexandra* 1263-4 (a poem transmitted under the name Lycophron, second century BCE), Cassandra prophesies that at Troy's fall Aeneas will show more concern for Anchises and his household gods than for Creusa. **prius:** construe with *quam* (742); "before."

742. **tumulum...sedem:** accusatives of "place to which" with the preposition (*ad*) omitted, as often in poetry (see AG §428g). The temple would stand on "a mound" (*tumulum*). **tumulum antiquae Cereris...:** refers back to the plan of flight Aeneas announced to his *famuli* at 712-16. *Antiquae* describes the temple rather than the goddess. Cf. 713 and n.

743. **hic demum:** "here and here only," "here and not before." **collectis omnibus:** ablative absolute. **una:** "alone," nominative feminine, referring to Creusa. Note the juxtaposition of *omnibus* and *una*.

744. **comites natumque virumque fefellit:** Creusa was lost and so "deceived her companions" (*fefellit* from *fallo*). Aeneas emphasizes that not only he, but also his other companions in flight and his son lost sight of Creusa, though he is the final and thus most emphatic member of this tricolon*.

745. **quem...hominumque deorumque:** *quem* is the interrogative pronoun. Like *amens*, this phrase emphasizes the frantic reaction of Aeneas to losing Creusa. Note that this line is hypermetric: *deorumque* has one too many syllables, but the final *-que* elides with the *aut* of 746. This feature may help convey further Aeneas' frenzy.

746. **crudelius:** neuter accusative of the comparative adjective of *crudelis*, modifying the interrogative pronoun *quid*.

Ascanium Anchisenque patrem Teucrosque penatis
commendo sociis et curva valle recondo;
ipse urbem repeto et cingor fulgentibus armis.
stat casus renovare omnis omnemque reverti   750
per Troiam et rursus caput obiectare periclis.
principio muros obscuraque limina portae,
qua gressum extuleram, repeto et vestigia retro
observata sequor per noctem et lumine lustro:
horror ubique animo, simul ipsa silentia terrent.   755
inde domum, si forte pedem, si forte tulisset,
me refero: inruerant Danai et tectum omne tenebant.
ilicet ignis edax summa ad fastigia vento
volvitur; exsuperant flammae, furit aestus ad auras.
procedo et Priami sedes arcemque reviso: 760

---

747. **Anchisen:** a Greek accusative ending. Note that Aeneas has been carrying Anchises (who holds the *penates*) and grasping Ascanius by the hand.

748. **recondo:** supply *eos* (i.e. Ascanius, Anchises, Penates, *socii*). **curva valle:** supply *in*. Note that the compound words starting with *re-* emphasize that Aeneas is returning to the city to potentially fight again: 749 *repeto*, 750 *renovare*, 750 *reverti*, and also 751 *rursus*.

749. **repeto et cingor:** the actions are in reverse order (hysteron proteron*). *Cingor* is a passive form with middle sense.

750. **stat:** impersonal construction; supply *mihi* ("my purpose is fixed," "I decide...," cf. 660 n.). This construction takes the three infinitives *renovare, reverti,* and *obiectare.*

751. **caput:** here "my life." **periclis:** for *periculis*; dative with the compound verb *obiectare.*

752. **principio:** adverb, "first."

754. **lumine lustro:** *lumine* = "eye"; the phrase means "scan with my eyes."

755. **animo:** this word in the plural usually means "spirit," "courage" (cf. 451, 799), but here it is really equivalent to "heart." There is good authority for *animos* as well, and it is impossible to say whether *animo, simul* or *animos, simul* is original. **terrent:** supply *me* or *animum.*

756. **domum:** *domus* (like *rus*, and names of cities, towns and small islands) does not require a preposition in a "place to which" construction (AG §427.2). Translate with *me refero.* **si forte...si forte...:** this repetition indicates that Aeneas is hopeful but realizes that he will probably not find Creusa. **tulisset:** pluperfect subjunctive in implied indirect discourse; the subject is Creusa. Aeneas would have said "I will go to my house if by chance she will have returned there. This becomes "I returned (*refero* is historic present) to my house if by chance she had...," cf. 94-5 n.

758. **fastigia:** i.e. the top of the house.

et iam porticibus vacuis Iunonis asylo
custodes lecti Phoenix et dirus Vlixes
praedam adservabant. huc undique Troïa gaza
incensis erepta adytis, mensaeque deorum
crateresque auro solidi, captivaque vestis   765
congeritur. pueri et pavidae longo ordine matres
stant circum.
ausus quin etiam voces iactare per umbram
implevi clamore vias, maestusque Creusam
nequiquam ingeminans iterumque iterumque vocavi.   770
quaerenti et tectis urbis sine fine furenti
infelix simulacrum atque ipsius umbra Creusae
visa mihi ante oculos et nota maior imago.

---

761. **porticibus vacuis...asylo:** ablatives of "place in which"; supply *in*.

762. **Phoenix:** the tutor and comrade of Achilles. He was part of the embassy in *Iliad* 9 that attempted to persuade Achilles to return to battle.

763. **praedam:** again underscores the *impietas* of the Greeks, to whom the contents of the temple are now "booty."

764. **mensaeque deorum:** the tables in the temple where offerings were made.

765. **auro solidi:** "solid with gold," i.e. of solid gold.

766. **congeritur:** singular verb, but has as its subjects *gaza, mensae, crateres* and *vestis*. As usual, the number of the verb corresponds to the element of the compound subject that is nearest (here *vestis*).

767. **circum:** adverb, "around."

768. **ausus...umbram:** a participial phrase modifying the subject of the sentence, Aeneas. **quin etiam:** "and furthermore." **voces iactare:** "to fling cries."

769-70. **Creusam...ingeminans:** "repeating the name 'Creusa.'" **iterumque iterumque:** the repetition reinforces that contained in the participle *ingeminans*. This is set against the adverb *nequiquam* ("in vain"), which expresses the futility of the act.

771. **tectis...furenti:** "ranging madly among the houses"; for the syntax of *tectis*, cf. 420-1 n. The manuscripts are split between *furenti* and *ruenti* with Mynors and Hirtzel printing the latter reading. The former reading, however, is supported by other modern editors (e.g. Sabaddini and Geymonat) and perhaps captures better Aeneas' frenzy as he searches for Creusa (cf. 776 n.).

772. **ipsius...Creusae:** take with both *infelix simulacrum* and *umbra*. *Ipsius* is emphatic, since Aeneas has been looking for her but did not expect to find her shade.

773. **nota:** the perfect passive participle of *nosco*; it describes Creusa and is ablative of comparison. Like the gods (cf. 591 n.), the dead are of more than human size. Creusa's words will imply that her status is almost divine. See Khan (2001) 908-9 and 725-95 n.

obstipui, steteruntque comae et vox faucibus haesit.
tum sic adfari et curas his demere dictis: 775
'quid tantum insano iuvat indulgere dolori,
o dulcis coniunx? non haec sine numine divum
eveniunt; nec te hinc comitem asportare Creusam
fas, aut ille sinit superi regnator Olympi.
longa tibi exsilia et vastum maris aequor arandum,   780
et terram Hesperiam venies, ubi Lydius arva

---

774. **steterunt:** note that the second syllable in *steteruntque*, normally long, is here shortened (systole). This line is used twice in the *Aeneid*: here and at 3.48; 4.280 and 12.868 are very close.

775. **adfari...demere:** historical infinitives with Creusa as nominative subject. This line is repeated at 3.153 and 8.35.

776. **quid:** "Why?" **tantum:** adverb, "to such an extent." **insano:** dative of indirect object with the compound verb *indulgere*. Creusa observes Aeneas' loss of control as she attempts to calm him by revealing his fate, just as Venus had done at 594-5. Note the use of spondees in this line and the next.

777. **non...sine numine:** litotes*, "not without the will" is close to "most certainly by the will." Note that Creusa seemingly frees Aeneas from blame by stating that Jupiter himself would not allow her to leave Troy (though perhaps it should be kept in mind that Aeneas is reporting the speech). **haec:** neuter plural, encompassing the fall of Troy, the death and appearance of Creusa, etc. **divum:** for *divorum*.

778. **te:** accusative subject of *asportare*. **hinc:** "from here." **comitem:** "as (your) companion."

779. **fas...:** supply *est*. *Fas* functions here as a synonym for *fata* and describes that immutable "law" which even the gods obey and which the decrees of Jupiter uphold. Both *fas* and *fatum* are etymologically related to *fari* ("speak") (cf. also 3 n.). **aut:** = *nec*. **ille:** applied to Jupiter almost as a title (cf. Plautus, *Mostellaria* 398 *ita ille faxit Iuppiter*). It might be explained as demonstrative, the speaker pointing upward to the sky. However, it also occurs without such effect (cf. 7.110 *sic Iuppiter ille monebat*), a fact suggesting that this usage of the word, though originally demonstrative, had become conventional. We might translate as "the great ruler of Olympus."

780. **longa...exsilia:** plural for singular; supply *erunt*, and construe *tibi* as a dative of possessor. **arandum:** supply *tibi est*, with *tibi* as a dative of agent. The metaphor in *aro* (plowing) for a ship cutting through the water is first employed by Vergil.

781-2. **terram Hesperiam:** sc. *ad. Hesperia* (from Gr. *hesperos*, evening star) means "land to the West," though it is often used as a synonym for Italy. **Lydius...Thybris:** to the north of Rome, the Tiber river flows along the border of Etruria, founded by the Etruscans, a people originally thought to be from Lydia (cf. Herodotus 1.94). Creusa thus provides the most specific information thus far about the location of the land fated to the Trojans, since Hector had only told Aeneas to seek out a new land (294-5). Nonetheless, these details, while perhaps clear to the reader, must be confusing to Aeneas. *Lydius* more literally would

inter opima virum leni fluit agmine Thybris:
illic res laetae regnumque et regia coniunx
parta tibi; lacrimas dilectae pelle Creusae.
non ego Myrmidonum sedes Dolopumve superbas   785
aspiciam aut Grais servitum matribus ibo,
Dardanis et divae Veneris nurus;
sed me magna deum genetrix his detinet oris.
iamque vale et nati serva communis amorem.'

---

identify something in Lydia (not Italy or *Hesperia*), and *Hesperia* is itself vague. See Khan (2001) 907. **arva/ inter opima virum:** "amid rich fields of (plough)men." The diction seems significant: *arva* from *aro* is strictly used for fields carefully cultivated by the plow as opposed to great tracts of land only used for pasture; *opima* indicates that they were kept fertile; *virum* suggests the traditional Roman farmer, owning his own farm (as opposed to estates run by slaves). *Virum* (=*virorum*) goes with *arva*, the phrase meaning "lands worked by men." To take *opima virum* "rich in men" (cf. 22 *dives opum*) is less natural. **leni agmine:** *agmine* means "course," and the phrase is from Ennius, *Annales—quod per amoenam urbem leni fluit agmine flumen*, fr. 171 (Warmington), 163 (Skutsch).

783. **illic:** adverb "there" (in Italy). **res...regnum...regia:** notice the alliteration*; "riches, royalty, and a royal bride." **res laetae:** "happiness" (lit. "happy affairs"). **regia coniunx:** i.e. Lavinia, the daughter of the Latin king Latinus. The Italian war of books 7-12 will be fought over her.

784. **parta:** supply *est*. *Parta* (from *pario*) takes as its compound subject *res...regnum... coniunx*. (Cf. 766 n.). With *tibi, parta* means "is won for you"; the prophecy describes the future as already present. **lacrimas...Creusae:** i.e. tears which the loss of Creusa causes; *Creusae* is objective genitive (cf. 413 n.).

785. **Myrmidonum...Dolopumve:** Thessalian Greeks. See 7 n. **sedes:** as often, "homes."

786. **aut:** here equivalent to *nec*. **servitum:** "to be a slave," a supine with verb of motion (*ibo*) expressing purpose (cf. 114 *scitatum* with n.). This construction is conversational in tone, suited to Creusa's address to Aeneas. **Grais...matribus:** datives with *servitum*.

787. **Dardanis...nurus:** the adjective *Dardanis*, "Trojan," is here used as a noun, "Trojan woman." Dardanus was a forefather of Priam; Creusa, married to Aeneas, was therefore Venus' daughter-in-law (*nurus*). Both words are in apposition to Crĕusa, the speaker of the sentence.

788. **magna deum genetrix:** the "great mother of the gods" is Cybele, who was specially worshipped at Pessinus in Phrygia, but also on Mount Ida and was therefore favorable to the Trojans. Syed (2005) 140 notes: "The introduction of this deity into the Roman pantheon is usually read as asserting Rome's link to Asia Minor through its Trojan origins." Creusa does not explain why this goddess has kept her from leaving Troy, nor does she say that she has died.

789. **serva:** imperative. **communis:** genitive singular, modifying *nati*.

haec ubi dicta dedit, lacrimantem et multa volentem   790
dicere deseruit, tenuisque recessit in auras.
ter conatus ibi collo dare bracchia circum;
ter frustra comprensa manus effugit imago,
par levibus ventis volucrique simillima somno.
sic demum socios consumpta nocte reviso.   795
    Atque hic ingentem comitum adfluxisse novorum
invenio admirans numerum, matresque virosque,
collectam exsilio pubem, miserabile vulgus.
undique convenere animis opibusque parati
in quascumque velim pelago deducere terras.   800

790-4. These lines recall *Odyssey* 11.204-9 (Odysseus with his mother's shade), *Iliad* 23.99-101 (Achilles with Patroclus' shade), and *Georgics* 4.499-502 (Orpheus' loss of Eurydice). Cf. 725-95 n., and see especially Segal (1973-74), Briggs (1979), and Gale (2003).

790. **lacrimantem...volentem:** modifying understood *me* (i.e. Aeneas, who is speaking).

791. **deseruit:** interestingly, Creusa "deserts" Aeneas, perhaps further suggesting that he is not to blame for her failure to leave Troy. Hughes (1997) 421 writes that "with these words, the abandonment motif is fully subverted."

792. **conatus:** supply *sum*. **collo dare bracchia circum:** an elegant variation of the ordinary *circumdare bracchia collo*.

793. **manus:** accusative plural, i.e. Aeneas' hands. **frustra:** construe with *comprensa*.

794. **par...simillima:** both take datives. **volucri...somno:** *volucri* suggests that the ghostly form of Creusa flies away; *somno* stands in for *somnio*, "dream."

796-804. *Aeneas finds his comrades joined by other fugitives, and at dawn he leads them to the mountains.*

796. **hic:** adverb. **ingentem:** modifies *numerum* (797).

797. **matres:** here = *feminas*, which cannot be used in epic meter.

798. **exsilio:** dative of purpose, "for exile"; cf. 1.22 *venturum excidio* "will come for destruction."

799. **convenere:** for *convenerunt*. **animis opibusque parati:** "ready with heart and wealth"; they had made up their minds to follow him and also made preparations for doing so by collecting whatever treasures they could. Some word like *ire* must be supplied after *parati*.

800. **quascumque...terras:** "whatever lands." **velim:** subjunctive in implied indirect discourse. **deducere:** a technical word for founding a colony, lit. "to lead down," i.e. from the mother-city to the place chosen.

iamque iugis summae surgebat Lucifer Idae
ducebatque diem, Danaique obsessa tenebant
limina portarum, nec spes opis ulla dabatur.
cessi et sublato montis genitore petivi."

---

801. **Lucifer:** the morning star (actually Venus in the morning). **Idae:** this is where the shooting star had landed at 696 (see note). The dawn of the new day corresponds to the hope that flight from the city brings to the Trojans. For closural elements as well as intimations of continuation in the final four lines of the book, see Nagle (1983).

803. **nec spes opis ulla:** i.e. Troy was irretrievably lost. *Opis* is objective genitive with *spes*.

804. **sublato...genitore:** ablative absolute. The final picture of Aeneas in book 2 is of him carrying his father Anchises on his shoulders as they flee to the mountains.

Appendix A: Vergil's Meter[1]

Dactylic hexamater was the meter of Greek epic, and beginning with Ennius' *Annales* (second century BCE),[2] it became the meter of Roman epic as well. Its basic rhythm can be felt in the following line from the opening of Longfellow's *Evangeline*:

Thís is the fórest priméval. The múrmuring pínes and the hémlocks

Here five dactyls (búm-ba-ba) are followed by a final disyllabic foot. These metrical units (as with English verse more generally) are created through the use of natural word stress to create patterns of stressed and unstressed syllables. Thus a dactyl in English poetry is a stressed syllable followed by two unstressed syllables (e.g. "Thís is the" and "múrmuring"). Classical Latin meter, however, differs in an important way. Metrical feet are based not on word stress but on the quantity of individual syllables (i.e. whether they are long or short). Thus, in Latin a dactyl contains one long syllable followed by two short ones (– ⏑⏑).

As the name indicates, "dactylic hexameter" literally describes a line that contains six (Gr. *hex*) measures or feet (Gr. *metra*) that are dactylic (– ⏑⏑).[3] In actual practice, however, spondees (– –) could substitute for dactyls within the first four feet,[4] and the line's ending was largely regularized as – ⏑⏑/ –x. The Latin dactylic hexameter can thus be notated as follows:

---

1   For more on Vergil's meter, see Jackson Knight (1944): 232-42, Duckworth (1969): 46-62, Nussbaum (1986), and Ross (2007): 143-52.

2   The early Latin epics by Livius Andronicus and Naevius were composed in Saturnian verse, a meter that is not fully understood.

3   The word "dactyl" comes from the Greek word *dactylos*, "finger." A metrical dactyl with its long and two short syllables resembles the structure of a finger: the bone from the knuckle to the first joint is longer than the two bones leading to the fingertip.

4   More technically the two short syllables of a dactyl are "contracted" into one long; together with the first long syllable, they form a spondee.

$$- \stackrel{\smile\smile}{} / - \stackrel{\smile\smile}{} / - \stackrel{\smile\smile}{} / - \smile\smile / - \times$$

(Here, "/" separates metrical feet; "–" = a long syllable; "‿" = a short syllable; and "x" = an *anceps* ("undecided") syllable, one that is either long or short.)

Very rarely a spondee is used in the fifth foot, in which case the line is called "spondaic."

To *scan* a line (i.e. to identify a line's rhythm and meter), long and short syllables must be identified. A syllable can be *long* in two ways: *by nature*, if it contains a vowel that is inherently long or is a diphthong;[5] or *by position*, if it contains a naturally short vowel followed either by a double consonant (*x* or *z*) or, in most cases, by two consonants.[6] In general, all other syllables are *short*. If, however, a word ending in a vowel, diphthong, or *-m* is followed by a word that begins with a vowel, diphthong, or *h*, the first vowel or diphthong is *elided* (cf. *laeti* in 1.35 below; elided syllables are enclosed in parentheses in the examples below). As a result the two syllables merge and are scanned as one—a phenomenon called *elision*. *Elision* occurs frequently in Vergil.

By applying these rules, we may scan hexameter lines as follows:

mūltă sŭ/pēr Prĭă/mō rŏgĭ/tāns, sŭpĕr / Hēctŏrĕ / mūltă

(*Aen.* 1.750)

prōtrăhĭt / īn mĕdĭ/ōs; quaē / sīnt ĕă / nūmĭnă / dīvŭm

(*Aen.* 2.123)

vēlă dă/bānt laē/t(i) ēt spū/mās sălĭs / aērĕ rŭ/ēbānt

(*Aen.* 1.35)

A long syllable generally takes twice as long to pronounce as a short, and the first syllable of each foot receives a special metrical emphasis known as the *ictus*.

---

5   One can determine if a vowel is long by nature by looking the word up in a dictionary to see if it has a macron over it or by checking inflected endings in a grammar (for example, some endings, like the first and second declension ablative singular (-*a*, -*o*), are always long; others, like the second declension nominative neuter plural (-*a*), are always short).

6   An exception to this general rule: if a short vowel is followed by a mute consonant (*b, c, d, g, p, t*) and a liquid (*l* or *r*), the resulting syllable can be either short or long. Cf. 2.663 where *patris* and *patrem* are short and long respectively: *natum ante ora pătris, pātrem qui obtruncat ad aras*. It should also be noted that *h* is a breathing, not a consonant; it therefore does not help make a vowel long by position.

The flow of a line is affected not only by its rhythm but also by the placement of word breaks. A word break between metrical feet is called a *diaeresis*:[7]

ēt iăcĭt. / ārrēc/tāē mēn/tēs stŭpĕ/făctăquĕ / cōrdă   (*Aen.* 5.643)

Here, diaereses occurs after *iacit* and after *stupefactaque*[8]; the former helps reinforce the syntactic pause after *iacit*. A word break within a metrical foot is called a *caesura*. When a caesura falls after the first syllable of a foot, it is called "strong" (as after the first *super* in 1.750 above); if it falls after the second syllable in a dactylic foot, it is called "weak" (as after the first *multa* in 1.750). The most important caesura in any given line often coincides with a sense break and is called the *main* or *principal caesura*.[9] It most frequently falls in the third foot, but also occurs not uncommonly in the second or fourth (or sometimes both). The slight pause implied in the main caesura helps shape the movement of each verse by breaking it into two (or more) parts. Here are the first seven lines of the *Aeneid*, scanned and with the principal caesurae marked ("||"):

ārmă vĭ/rūmquĕ că/nō, || Trō/iāē quī / prīmŭs ăb / ōrīs

Ītălĭ/ām fā/tō prŏfŭ/gūs || Lā/vīniăquĕ / vēnĭt

lītŏră, / mūlt(um) īl(le) / ēt tēr/rīs || iāc/tātŭs ĕt / āltō

vī sŭpĕ/rūm, || sāē/vāē mĕmŏ/rēm Iū/nōnĭs ŏb / īrăm,

mūltă quŏ/qu(e) ēt bēl/lō pās/sūs, || dūm / cōndĕrĕt / ūrbĕm

īnfēr/rētquĕ dĕ/ōs Lătĭ/ō, || gĕnŭs / ūndĕ Lă/tīnŭm

Ālbā/nīquĕ pă/trēs || āt/qu(e) āltāē / mōēnĭă / Rōmāē.

(Note that in line 2, *Laviniaque* is pronounced as four [not five] syllables, as if the second "*i*" were a consonant.)

---

7   When a *diaeresis* occurs just before the fifth foot, it is often called a *bucolic diaeresis* because this type of diaeresis was used frequently in pastoral poetry: e.g. *nos patriam fugimus: tu, Tityre,* || *lentus in umbra* (*Ecl.* 1.4).

8   In the combinations *qu, gu, su* (e.g. *–que, sanguis, suesco*), note that the *u* is consonantal but that the combinations themselves count as a single consonant for the purpose of scansion.

9   Readers may differ on where (or even if) there is a main caesura in a given line.

In addition to metrical length, words also have a natural accent,[10] which may coincide or clash with the metrical stress (*ictus*), which falls on the first long syllable of each foot. Coincidence of word accent and metrical stress produces fluidity in the verse; clashing of word accent and metrical stress creates tension. For example:

$$\overset{x}{}\quad \overset{x}{} \quad \overset{/}{} \quad \overset{x}{} \quad \overset{/}{} \quad \overset{/}{}$$

īnfān/dūm, rē/**gī**năˏ, **iŭ**/bēs rěnŏ/**vā**rě dŏ/**lō**rěm   (*Aen.* 2.3)

(Naturally accented syllables are in boldface; "/" = ictus that coincides with word accent; "x" = ictus that clashes with word accent.)

In this line, there are several clashes in the first four feet (wherein the word accent generally does not coincide with the verse accent), followed by co-incidence in the final two feet.[11] In creating such clashes, the placement of caesurae can be particularly important. For example, "if a word of two or more syllables ends after the first long of a foot (that is, producing a strong caesura), there will be a clash between accent and *ictus* in that foot," because the final syllable of such words is not accented.[12] The strong caesurae in 2.3 (above) and in 2.108, 199 (below) display this principle well.

One of Vergil's artistic feats was to manage the sequence of clash and coincidence of ictus and word accent in such a way as to achieve a rhythmically varied and pleasing line. In general we find that Vergilian hexameters are characterized by the clash of *ictus* and word accent in the first four feet and by the coincidence of *ictus* and word accent in the last two feet,[13] which results in a pleasing resolution of stress at line end.

$$\overset{/}{}\quad \overset{x}{} \quad \overset{x}{} \quad \overset{x}{} \quad \overset{/}{} \quad \overset{/}{}$$

Saepě **fŭ**gām **Dă**năī **Trō**iā cŭpĭērě rělīctā   (2.108)

---

10   Disyllabic words have their accent on their initial syllable: *cáris, dábant, mólis*. If, however, words are three syllables or longer, the word accent falls: on the penultima (second to last syllable), if it is long (*ruébant, iactátos*) but on the antepenultima (the syllable preceding the penultima), if the penultima is short (*géntibus, mária, pópulum*).

11   Classical Latin speakers would presumably have pronounced the word accents in reading lines, while still maintaining the basic rhythm of hexameter. Otherwise, the ictus would have transformed the basic sound of the word.

12   Ross (2007): 146. For word accentuation, see n. 10 (above).

13   Vergil sometimes avoids such resolution for special effect, though he does so rarely. For example, in the following line, a clash between ictus and word accent occurs in the final foot: *sternitur/ exani/misque tre/mens pro/cumbit hu/mi bos* (5.481).

     /   x   x   x   /   /
Hīc ălĭūd **mā**iūs **mĭ**sĕrīs **mūltō**quĕ trĕ**mēn**dŭm (2.199)

This rhythmical innovation constituted an advance over Vergil's predecessors, who could write such lines as, e.g., Ennius' *spársis/ hástis/ lóngis/ cámpus/ spléndet et/ hórret*, which exhibits a coincidence of *ictus* and word accent throughout the entire line.

Appendix B: Stylistic Terms

Vergil's skillful use of language is a defining element of his artistry. He often employs rhetorical figures and stylistic devices to reinforce the content of his poetry. Careful attention should therefore be paid both to what Vergil says and to how he says it. The following list defines many of the stylistic terms and features that are encountered in studying Vergil with examples drawn primarily from Book 2. For discussion of these examples, see the relevant commentary notes. For more information on the terms, see Lanham (1991) and Brogan (1994). Fuller information on Vergilian style can be found in Jackson Knight (1944): 225-341, Camps (1969): 60-74, and especially O'Hara (1997). Stylistic analyses of Vergilian passages are presented in Horsfall (1995): 237-48 and Hardie (1998): 102-14.

Alliteration: the repetition of the initial consonant sound in neighboring words. E.g., *Hic aliud maius miseris multoque tremendum* (2.199). *Alliteration* is often used to create *onomatopoeia*, and occurs frequently with *assonance* and *consonance*. Cf. also 2.9, 87, 207, 209, 245, 273, 303, 313, 418-19, 498.

Anaphora (Gr. "bringing back"): the repetition of a word at the beginning of consecutive sentences or clauses. E.g., *"vos aeterni ignes, et non violabile vestrum/ testor numen," ait, "vos arae ensesque nefandi"* (2.154-5). Cf. 2.108-10, 218, 501.

Anastrophe (Gr. "turning back"): the inversion of normal word order, usually involving prepositions and their objects. E.g., *hic Hecuba et natae nequiquam altaria circum* (2.515). Cf. 2.564. *Anastrophe* is a type of *hyperbaton* (see below).

Aposiopesis (Gr. "becoming silent"): the abrupt stopping of a sentence or a thought. E.g., *nec requievit enim, donec Calchante ministro –/ sed quid ego haec autem nequiquam ingrato revolvo* (2.100-1). Here Sinon artfully cuts short his train of thought at a powerful moment.

Apostrophe (Gr. "turning away"): a sudden shift of address to a figure (or idea), absent or present. E.g., *nec te tua plurima, Panthu,/ labentem pietas nec Apollinis infula texit* (2. 429-30). Here, as Aeneas describes those fallen in battle, he suddenly addresses one of them (Panthus) by name. Cf. also 2.56, 160, 431, 432.

121

Assonance (Lat. "answer with the same sound"): the repetition of vowel sounds in neighboring words or phrases. E.g., *moriamur et in medi(a) arma ruamus* (2.353). See also *alliteration* and *consonance*.

Asyndeton (Gr. "unconnected"): the omission of connectives between words, phrases, or sentences. In the following example, Venus reveals to Aeneas the causes behind Troy's fall: *non tibi Tyndaridis facies invisa Lacaenae/ culpatusve Paris, divum inclementia, divum,/ has evertit opes sternitque a culmine Troiam* (2.601-3). There is no connective between *cupatusve Paris* and *divum inclementia*. In addition, this particular instance of *asyndeton* implies contrast: "It is not the hated face of Helen…but the cruelty of the gods that overturns…" Such "adversative" asyndeton is not uncommon. Cf. 2.27-8, 85 (adversative), 183-4, 663.

Chiasmus (Gr. "crossing"): an arrangement of words whereby parallel constructions are expressed in reverse word order. E.g., *Fracti bello fatisque repulsi* (2.13). Cf. 2.167, 281, 636, 728. The word "chiasmus" is derived from the Greek letter "chi" because if the parallel constructions are split in half and placed one over the other, an X is formed when the syntactically related words are connected.

fracti   bello

X

fatisque   repulsi

Consonance (Lat. "concord"): the repetition of consonant sounds in neighboring words or phrases. E.g., *praecipitat suadentque cadentia sidera somnos* (2.9). Note the use of *d* and *t* sounds in this line.

Dicolon Abundans: see **Theme and Variation**.

Ellipsis (Gr. "leaving out"): the omission of a syntactically necessary word or words, the meaning of which must be inferred. E.g., *Laocoon ardens summa decurrit ab arce,/ et procul "o miseri…"* (2.41-2). A verb of speaking must be understood with *et procul*. Cf. 2.287, 473.

Enallage (Gr. "interchange"): a distortion in normal word order, whereby a word, instead of modifying the word to which it belongs in sense, modifies another grammatically. E.g., *virgineas ausi divae contingere vittas* (2.168). Here *virgineas* describes *divae* (Pallas Athena) in sense, but it grammatically modifies *vittas*. *Enallage* is also called "transferred epithet." Cf. 2.508, 576.

End-stopped lines: see **Enjambment**.

Enjambment (Fr. "crossing over," "spanning"): the continuation of the sense or syntactic unit from one line to the next. E.g., *"Cuncta equidem tibi, rex, fuerit* *quodcumque, fatebor/ vera," inquit...* (2.77-8). Enjambed words are often followed by some kind of pause (here a comma) that adds emphasis. Cf. 2.79-80, 481, 505, 591. Lines without enjambment are called *end-stopped*.

Epanalepsis (Gr. "taking up again"): the repetition of a syntactically unnecessary word or phrase from a preceding line. E.g., *ad caelum tendens ardentia lumina frustra,/ lumina, nam teneras arcebant vincula palmas* (2.405-6). Here Cassandra is being dragged away with her hands bound from Pallas' temple. Cf. 2.602.

Golden Line and Variations: in dactylic hexameter, an artful arrangement of two substantive/adjective phrases with a verb in between. It usually takes the form of ABCab, where Aa and Bb are both adjective-noun phrases, while C is a verb. E.g.,

A   B   C   a   b
egressi optata potiuntur Troes harena   (1.172)

The variation ABCba is often called a *silver line*. E.g.,

A   B   C   b   a
aeternumque adytis effert penetralibus ignem   (2.297)

Hendiadys (Gr. "one through two"): the expression of one idea through two terms joined by a conjunction. E.g., *sanguine placastis ventos et virgine caesa* (2.116). Here *sanguine...et virgine caesa* essentially means "with the blood of a slaughtered maiden." Cf. 2.265, 296, 319, 413, 534.

Hyperbaton (Gr. "transposed"): a distortion of normal word order. E.g., *ecce autem gemini a Tenedo tranquilla per alta/ (horresco referens) immensis orbibus angues* (2.203-4). Note the deliberate (and suspenseful) separation of *angues* from *gemini*. *Hyperbaton* is also used to create artful arrangements of words, such as *golden lines* and *synchysis*. Cf. 2.422.

Hyperbole (Gr. "excess"): exaggeration. E.g., *clamores simul horrendos ad sidera tollit* (2.222). Cf. 2.488.

Hypotaxis: see **Parataxis.**

Hysteron Proteron (Gr. "later as earlier"): the reversal of the chronological order of events. E.g., *moriamur et in media arma ruamus* (2.353). This line is traditionally considered an example of *hysteron proteron*, but see 2.353 n. Cf. 2.258-9, 547.

Interlocking word order: see **synchysis.**

Interpretatio: see **Theme and Variation.**

Irony (Gr. "dissembling"): saying one thing to imply its opposite. E.g., *ipse manu mortem inveniam; miserebitur hostis,/ exuviasque petet* (2.645-6). Here, Anchises really means the opposite of *miserebitur.* Cf. 2.645 n.

Litotes (Gr. "simplicity"): the description of something by negating its opposite. E.g., *haud ignota loquor* (2.91). "Things not unknown" = "things (well) known." Cf. 2.154, 171.

Metaphor (Gr. "transference"): the application of a word or phrase from one field of meaning to another, thereby suggesting new meanings. E.g., *scandit fatalis machina muros/ feta armis* (2.237-8). Here, the wooden horse (*machina*) is described as "pregnant" (*feta*).

Metonymy (Gr. "change of name"): the substitution of one word for another somehow closely related. E.g., *si Pergama dextra/ defendi possent, etiam hac defensa fuissent* (2.291-2). Here Hector says that Troy could not be protected even by his own "valor" (lit. *dextra* = "right hand"). Cf. 2.238, 301, 311, 312, 335, 618. *Synecdoche* is a type of *metonymy.*

Onomatopoeia (Gr. "making of a word" or "name"): the use or formation of words that imitate natural sounds. E.g., *fit sonitus spumante salo* (2.209). Here the alliteration of *s* imitates the sound of the sea. *Onomatopoeia* often involves other devices such as *alliteration, assonance,* and *consonance.* Cf. 2.207.

Oxymoron (Gr. "pointedly foolish"): the juxtaposition of seemingly contradictory words. E.g., *festina lente* (Gr. *speude bradeos,* Suetonius, *Augustus* 25.4). Cf. 2.518.

Parataxis (Gr. "placing side by side"): the sequential ordering of independent clauses (as opposed to *hypotaxis,* the subordination of one clause to another). A famous example is Caesar's *veni, vidi, vici.* An example from *Aeneid* 2: *vix positum castris simulacrum: arsere coruscae/ luminibus flammae arrectis...* (2.172-3). Though the two halves of the sentence are independent, in sense one is subordinated to the other: "scarcely had the image been placed..., when glittering flames blazed..." Vergil leaves it to the reader to sense such logical relationships. *Parataxis* is particularly characteristic of Vergil and epic more generally. Cf. 2.692.

Paronomasia (Gr. "slight alteration of name"): a wordplay or pun. E.g., *tu ne qua parentis/ iussa time neu praeceptis parere recusa* (2.606-7). The noun *părens* ("parent") is seemingly associated with the verb *pārere* ("to obey"), though the two words are not etymologically related. Cf. 2.7, 44, 470, 552.

Pleonasm (Gr. "excess"): redundancy, especially for the sake of emphasis. E.g., *Primus ibi ante omnis magna comitante caterva* (2.40). Here *primus* and *ante omnis* are essentially equivalent in meaning; the use of both emphasizes Laocoon's stature.

Polyptoton (Gr. "in many cases"): the repetition of a word in its inflected cases. E.g., *hos cape fatorum comites, his moenia quare/ magna...* (2.294-5). *Polyptoton* is a type of *anaphora* that often occurs with *asyndeton*, as in this example. Cf. 2.294, 325, 483-4.

Polysyndeton (Gr. "much-connected"): the repetition or excessive use of conjunctions. E.g., *coniugiumque domumque patris natosque videbit* (2.579).

Prolepsis (Gr. "anticipation"): the use of a word or phrase that anticipates a later event. E.g., *pars stupet innuptae donum exitiale Minervae* (2.31). Here Aeneas' use of *exitiale* looks forward to the destruction that the *donum* (i.e. the wooden horse) will eventually cause Troy. Cf. 2.195, 669, 736.

Rhetorical question: a question that is posed not to receive an answer but for some other purpose or effect. E.g., *o miseri, quae tanta insania, cives?* (2.42). Here, Laocoon questions how the Trojans could trust the Greeks and the wooden horse. Cf. also 2.43-4, 69-70.

Simile (Lat. "similar"): a figurative comparison between two different things. It is an important component of epic style. E.g., *qualis mugitus, fugit cum saucius aram/ taurus et incertam excussit cervice securim* (2. 223-4). In the process of performing a sacrifice, Laocoon is attacked by twin serpents. His groaning is compared to that of a bull, who in the midst of being sacrificed, flees the altar. Cf. 2.304-8, 355-8, 379-81, 416-19, 471-5, 496-9, 626-31.

Synchysis (Gr. "mingling," "confusion"): an arrangement of two phrases (here Aa and Bb) that interweave their members in an ABab pattern. It is also called *interlocking word order.* E.g.,

<pre>
    A   B   a   b
mixtoque undantem pulvere fumum   (2.609)
</pre>

Here the *synchysis* may be seen to mimic the mingling of dust and smoke that is described. Cf. 2.173, 213-14, 479, 609.

Synecdoche (Gr. "understanding one thing with another"): a type of metonymy that uses the part for the whole (or the reverse). E.g., *ultro Asiam magno Pelopea ad moenia bello/ venturam* (2.193-4). Here "the walls of Pelops' city" are used to represent Greece as a whole. Cf. 2.298, 478.

Theme and Variation: the restatement of an initial phrase in different language. E.g., *sed si tantus amor casus cognoscere nostros/ et breviter Troiae supremum*

audire laborem (2.10-11). *Theme and variation* is also called *interpretatio* and *dicolon abundans*. Cf. 2.389, 399, 409.

Transferred Epithet: see **Enallage.**

Tricolon (Gr. "having three limbs"): the grouping of three parallel clauses or phrases. When the third element is the longest, the resulting *tricolon* is called *abundans, crescens,* or *crescendo.* E.g., *squalentem barbam et concretos sanguine crinis/ vulneraque illa gerens, quae circum plurima muros/ accepit patrios* (2.277-8). In this description of Hector, the participle *gerens* governs three accusative phrases in increasing length (i.e. *tricolon crescendo*): *squalentem barbam, concretos sanguine crinis,* and *vulneraque illa... quae plurima muros accepit patrios.* Cf. 2.277, 296-7, 320, 369, 414-15, 507-8, 511, 571-3, 744.

Zeugma (Gr. "yoking"): the governing of two words by one verb or adjective, which is strictly appropriate for just one of them. E.g., *inclusos Danaos et...laxat claustra* (2.258-9). Cf. 2.320-1, 378, 654.

Works Cited

Adler, E. (2003) *Vergil's Empire: Political Thought in the Aeneid*. Lanham, MD.

Allen, G. (2000) *Intertextuality*. London.

Anderson, W.S. (2005) *The Art of the Aeneid*. Second edition. Wauconda, IL.

Armstrong, D., Fish, J., Johnston, P. A., and Skinner, M. (eds.) (2004) *Vergil, Philodemus, and the Augustans*. Austin.

Austin, R. G. (ed.) (1964) *P. Vergili Maronis Aeneidos Liber Secundus*. Oxford.

Bandera, C. (1981) "Sacrificial levels in Virgil's *Aeneid*," *Arethusa* 14: 217-39.

Barchiesi, A. (1984) *La traccia del modello: effetti omerici nella narrazione virgiliana*. Pisa.

_____(1998) "The statue of Athena at Troy and Carthage," in *Style and Tradition: Studies in Honor of Wendell Clausen*, eds. P. Knox and C. Foss. Stuttgart and Leipzig: 130-40.

Bowie, A. M. (1990) "The death of Priam: allegory and history in the *Aeneid*," *Classical Quarterly* 40: 470-81.

Briggs, W. W., Jr. (1979) "Eurydice, Venus and Creusa: a note on structure in Virgil," *Vergilius* 25: 43-4.

_____(1981) "Virgil and the Hellenistic Epic," *Aufstieg und Niedergand der römischen Welt* 2.31.2: 948-84.

Brogan, T. V. F. (ed.) (1994) *The New Princeton Handbook of Poetic Terms*. Princeton.

Cairns, F. (1989) *Virgil's Augustan Epic*. Cambridge.

Camps, W. A. (1969) *An Introduction to Virgil's Aeneid*. Oxford.

Clausen, W. (1987) *Virgil's Aeneid and the Tradition of Hellenistic Poetry*. Berkeley, CA.

_____(1994) *A Commentary on Virgil, Eclogues*. Oxford.

_____(2002) *Virgil's Aeneid: Decorum, Allusion, and Ideology*. Munich and Leipzig.

Coleman, R. (1977) *Virgil: Eclogues*. Cambridge.

_____(1982) "The gods in the *Aeneid*," *Greece and Rome* 29: 143-68.

Conington, J., and Nettleship, H. (eds.) (1858-83) *The Works of Virgil*. Three volumes. London.

Conte, G. B. (1986) *The Rhetoric of Imitation: Genre and Poetic Memory in Virgil and Other Latin Poets*, tr. C. Segal. Ithaca, NY.

_____(1999) "The Virgilian paradox: an epic of drama and sentiment," *Proceedings of the Cambridge Philological Society* 45: 17-42.

Crook, J. (1996) "Political history: 30 B.C. to A.D. 14," in *The Augustan Empire: 43 B.C. – A.D. 69. The Cambridge Ancient History*, vol. X. Second edition, eds. A. Bowman, E. Champlin, and A. Lintott. Cambridge: 70-112.

Della Corte, F. (ed.) (1984-91) *Enciclopedia Virgiliana*. Six volumes. Rome.

Duckworth, G. (1969) *Vergil and Classical Hexameter Poetry: A Study in Metrical Variety*. Ann Arbor.

Edmunds, L. (2001) *Intertextuality and the Reading of Roman Poetry*. Baltimore.

Egan, R. B. (1996) "A reading of the Helen-Venus episode in *Aeneid* 2," *Echos du monde classique* 40: 379-95.

Eliot, T. S. (1957) *On Poetry and Poets*. London.

Fagles, R. (1990) *Homer: Iliad*. New York.

Farrell, J. (1991) *Vergil's Georgics and the Traditions of Ancient Epic: The Art of Allusion in Literary History*. Oxford.

_____(1997) "The Virgilian intertext," in *The Cambridge Companion to Virgil*, ed. C. Martindale. Cambridge: 222-38.

_____(2005) "The Augustan Period: 40 BC-AD 14," in *A Companion to Latin Literature*, ed. S. J. Harrison. Oxford: 44-57.

Feeney, D. (1991) *The Gods in Epic: Poets and Critics of the Classical Tradition*. Oxford.

Fowler, D. P. (1997) "On the shoulders of giants: intertextuality and classical studies," *Materiali e discussioni per l'analisi dei testi classici* 39: 13-34.

Frangoulidis, S. A. (1992) "Duplicity and gift-offerings in Vergil's *Aeneid* 1 and 2," *Vergilius* 38: 26-37.

Gale, M. (2000) *Virgil on the Nature of Things: The Georgics, Lucretius and the Didactic Tradition*. Cambridge.

_____(2003) "Poetry and the backward glance in Virgil's *Georgics* and *Aeneid*," *Transactions of the American Philological Association* 133: 323-52.

Galinsky, K. (1988) "The anger of Aeneas," *American Journal of Philology* 109: 321-48.

_____(1996) *Augustan Culture: An Interpretive Introduction*. Princeton.

_____(2003) "Greek and Roman drama and the *Aeneid*," in *Myth, History, and Culture in Republican Rome: Studies in Honour of T. P. Wiseman*, eds. D. Braund and C. Gill. Exeter: 275-94.

_____(ed.) (2005) *The Cambridge Companion to the Age of Augustus*. Cambridge.

Gantz, T. (1993) *Early Greek Myth: A Guide to Literary and Artistic Sources*. Two volumes. Baltimore.

Gardiner, J. (1987) "Virgil, *Aeneid* 2.349-50," *The Classical Quarterly* 37: 454-7.

George, E. V. (1974) *Aeneid VIII and the Aitia of Callimachus*. Leiden.

Geymonat, M. (ed.) (1973) *P. Vergili Maronis opera. Post Remigium Sabbadini et Aloisium Castiglioni recensuit Marius Geymonat*. Paravia.

Goold, G. P. (1970) "Servius and the Helen Episode," *Harvard Studies in Classical Philology* 74: 101-68. Reprinted in *Oxford Readings in Vergil's Aeneid*, ed. S. J. Harrison (1990). Oxford: 60-126.

_____(ed.) (1999) *Virgil*. Two volumes. Cambridge, MA.

Gransden, K. W. (1990) "The Fall of Troy," in McAuslan and Walcott (eds.) (1990): 121-33.

Gurval, R. A. (1995) *Actium and Augustus*. Ann Arbor.

Hardie, P. R. (1984) "The sacrifice of Iphigeneia: an example of 'distribution' of a Lucretian theme in Virgil," *Classical Quarterly* 34: 406-12.

_____(1986) *Virgil's Aeneid: Cosmos and Imperium*. Oxford.

_____(1991) "The *Aeneid* and the *Oresteia*," *Proceedings of the Virgil Society* 20: 29-45

_____(1993) *The Epic Successors of Virgil*. Cambridge.

_____(1997) "Virgil and tragedy," in *The Cambridge Companion to Virgil*, ed. C. Martindale. Cambridge: 312-26.

_____(1998) *Virgil*. New Surveys in the Classics 28. Oxford.

_____(ed.) (1999) *Virgil: Critical Assessments of Classical Authors*. Four volumes. London.

Harries, B. (1989) "Back to the horse: symbol and narrative in *Aeneid* 2," *Liverpool Classical Monthly* 14: 136-41.

Harrison, E. L. (1990) "Divine action in *Aeneid*, book two," reprint of *Phoenix* 24 (1970): 320-32, in *Oxford Readings in Vergil's Aeneid*, ed. S. J. Harrison (1990). Oxford: 46-59.

Harrison, S. J. (ed.) (1990) *Oxford Readings in Vergil's Aeneid*. Oxford.

_____(ed.) (2005) *A Companion to Latin Literature*. Oxford.

Heinze, R. (1915) *Vergils epische Technik*. Third edition. Leipzig and Berlin.

_____(1993) *Virgil's Epic Technique*, tr. H. Harvey, D. Harvey, and F. Robertson. Berkeley, CA.

Hershkowitz, D. (1998) *The Madness of Epic: Reading Insanity from Homer to Statius*. Oxford.

Heyworth, S. (2005) "Pastoral," in *A Companion to Latin Literature*, ed. S. J. Harrison. Oxford: 148-58.

Hexter, R. (1990) "What was the Trojan horse made of?: interpreting Vergil's *Aeneid*," *The Yale Journal of Criticism* 3: 109-31.

Hinds, S. (1998) *Allusion and Intertext: Dynamics of Appropriation in Roman Poetry*. Cambridge.

Hirtzel, F. A. (ed.) (1900) *P. Vergili Maronis Opera*. Oxford.

Horsfall, N. (1995) *A Companion to the Study of Virgil*. Leiden.

_____(2006) *Virgil, Aeneid 3: A Commentary*. Leiden.

Hughes, L. (1997) "Vergil's Creusa and *Iliad* 6," *Mnemosyne* 50: 401-23.

Jackson Knight, W. F. (1944) *Roman Vergil*. London.

Jocelyn, H. D. (ed.) (1969) *The Tragedies of Ennius: The Fragments*. Cambridge.

Johnson, W. R. (1976) *Darkness Visible: A Study of Vergil's Aeneid*. Berkeley.

_____(1999) "*Dis aliter visum*: self-telling and theodicy in *Aeneid* 2," in *Reading Vergil's Aeneid: An Interpretive Guide*, ed. C. Perkell. Norman, OK: 50-63.

Johnston, P. A. (1980) *Vergil's Agricultural Golden Age: A Study of the Georgics*. Leiden.

Jones, A. H. M. (1970) *Augustus*. London.

Jones, J. W. (1965) "Trojan legend: who is Sinon?," *Classical Journal* 61: 122-8.

_____(1970) "The Trojan horse: *timeo Danaos et dona ferentis*," *Classical Journal* 65: 241-7.

Kennedy, D. (1992) "'Augustan' and 'Anti-Augustan': reflections on terms of reference" in *Roman Poetry and Propaganda in the Age of Augustus*, ed. A. Powell. Bristol: 26-58.

Kenney, E. J. (1979) "*Iudicium transferendi*: Virgil, *Aeneid* 2.469-505 and its antecedents," in *Creative Imitation and Latin Literature*, eds. D. West and A. J. Woodman. Cambridge: 103-20.

Khan, A. (2001) "Exile and the kingdom: Creusa's revelations and Aeneas' departure from Troy," *Latomus* 60: 906-15.

Knauer, G. N. (1964a) *Die Aeneis und Homer: Studien zur poetischen Technik Vergils mit Listen der Homerzitate in der Aeneis*. Göttingen.

_____(1964b) "Vergil's *Aeneid* and Homer," *Greek, Roman and Byzantine Studies* 5: 61-84. Reprinted in *Oxford Readings in Vergil's Aeneid*, ed. S. J. Harrison (1990). Oxford: 390-412.

Knox, B. M. W. (1950) "The serpent and the flame: the imagery of the second book of the *Aeneid*," *American Journal of Philology* 71: 379-400.

Lanham, R. A. (1991) *A Handlist of Rhetorical Terms*. Second edition. Berkeley, CA.

Lloyd-Jones, H. (ed.) (1994-96) *Sophocles*. Three volumes. Cambridge, MA.

Lombardo, S. (1997) *Homer: Iliad*. Indianapolis, IN.

_____(2005) *Virgil: Aeneid*. Indianapolis, IN.

Lynch, J. P. (1980) "Laocoön and Sinon: Virgil, *Aeneid* 2.40-198," *Greece and Rome* 27: 170-9.

Lyne, R. O. A. M. (1987) *Further Voices in Vergil's Aeneid*. Oxford.

McAuslan, I., and Walcot, P. (eds.) (1990) *Virgil*. Greece and Rome Studies. Oxford.

Mack, S. (1980) "Virgil, *Aeneid* 2.250-2," *The Classical Quarterly* 30: 153-8.

Mahoney, A. (ed.) (2001) *Allen and Greenough's New Latin Grammar*. Newburyport, MA.

Manuwald, B. (1985) "*Improvisi aderunt*: zur Sinon-Szene in Vergils *Aeneis* (2.57-198)," *Hermes* 113: 183-208.

Martindale, C. (1993) "Descent into Hell: reading ambiguity, or Virgil and the critics," *Proceedings of the Virgil Society* 21: 111-50.

_____(ed.) (1997) *The Cambridge Companion to Virgil*. Cambridge.

Molyneux, J. H. (1986) "Sinon's narrative in *Aeneid* II," *Latomus* 45: 873-7.

Moskalew, W. (1990) "Myrmidons, Dolopes, and Danaans: wordplays in *Aeneid* 2," *Classical Quarterly* 40: 275-9.

Murgia, C. (1971) "More on the Helen episode," *Classical Antiquity* 4: 203-17.

_____(2003) "The date of the Helen episode," *Harvard Studies in Classical Philology* 101: 405-26.

Mynors, R. A. B. (ed.) (1969) *P. Vergili Maronis Opera*. Oxford.

_____(ed.) (1990) *Virgil: Georgics*. Oxford.

Nagle, B. R. (1983) "Open-ended closure in *Aeneid* 2," in *Classical World* 76: 257-63.

Nappa, C. (2005) *Reading After Actium: Vergil's Georgics, Octavian, and Rome*. Ann Arbor.

Nelis, D. (2001) *Vergil's Aeneid and the Argonautica of Apollonius Rhodius*. Leeds.

Nussbaum, G. B. (1986) *Vergil's Meter: A Practical Guide for Reading Latin Hexameter Poetry*. Bristol.

O'Hara, J. J. (1990) *Death and the Optimistic Prophecy in Vergil's Aeneid*. Princeton.

_____(1996) *True Names: Vergil and the Alexandrian Tradition of Aetiological Wordplay*. Ann Arbor.

_____(1997) "Virgil's style," in *The Cambridge Companion to Virgil*, ed. C. Martindale. Cambridge: 241-58.

_____(2007) *Inconsistency in Roman Epic: Studies in Catullus, Lucretius, Vergil, Ovid and Lucan*. Cambridge.

Otis, B. (1964) *Virgil: A Study in Civilized Poetry*. Oxford.

Page, T. E. (ed.) (1889) *P. Vergili Maronis Aeneidos Lib. II*. London.

_____(ed.) (1894, 1900) *Virgil: Aeneid*. Two volumes. London.

Panoussi, V. (2002) "Vergil's Ajax: allusion, tragedy, and heroic identity in the *Aeneid*," *Classical Antiquity* 21: 95-134.

Pavlock, B. (1985) "Epic and tragedy in Vergil's Nisus and Euryalus episode," *Transactions of the American Philological Association* 115: 207-24.

Pelling, C. (1996) "The Triumviral period," in *The Augustan Empire: 43 B.C. – A.D. 69. The Cambridge Ancient History*, vol. X. Second edition, eds. A. Bowman, E. Champlin, and A. Lintott. Cambridge: 1-69.

Perkell, C. (1981) "On Creusa, Dido, and the quality of victory in Virgil's *Aeneid*," *Women's Studies* 8 (1981): 201-23.

_____(1989) *The Poet's Truth: A Study of the Poet in Virgil's Georgics*. Berkeley.

_____(1994) "Ambiguity and irony: the last resort?," *Helios* 21: 63-74.

_____ (ed.) (1999) *Reading Vergil's Aeneid: An Interpretive Guide*. Norman, OK.

Petrini, M. (1997) *The Child and the Hero: Coming of Age in Catullus and Vergil*. Ann Arbor.

Pöschl, V. (1950) *Die Dichtkunst Vergils: Bild und Symbol in der Aeneis*. Innsbruck.

_____(1962) *The Art of Vergil: Image and Symbol in the Aeneid*, tr. G. Seligson. Ann Arbor.

Powell, A. (ed.) (1992) *Roman Poetry and Propoganda in the Age of Augustus*. London.

Putnam, M. (1965) *The Poetry of the Aeneid*. Cambridge, MA.

_____(1979) *Virgil's Poem of the Earth: Studies in the Georgics*. Princeton.

_____(1993) "The languages of Horace, *Odes* 1.24," *Classical Journal* 88.2: 123-35.

_____(1995) *Virgil's Aeneid: Interpretation and Influence*. Chapel Hill.

Quint, D. (1993) *Epic and Empire*. Princeton.

Reckford, K. J. (1981) "Helen in *Aeneid* II and VI," *Arethusa* 14: 85-99.

Reed, J. D. (2007) *Virgil's Gaze*. Princeton.

Renehan, R. (1973) "Pseudo-Vergil's *ultrix flamma*: a problem in linguistic probabilities," *Classical Philology* 68: 197-202.

Ross, D. O. (1987) *Virgil's Elements: Physics and Poetry in the Georgics*. Princeton.

_____(1998) "Images of fallen Troy in the *Aeneid*," in *Style and Tradition: Studies in Honor of Wendell Clausen*, eds. P. Knox and C. Foss. Stuttgart and Leipzig: 121-9.

_____(2007) *Virgil's Aeneid: A Reader's Guide*. Oxford.

Rossi, A. (2002) "The fall of Troy: between tradition and genre," in *Clio and the Poets: Augustan Poetry and the Traditions of Ancient Historiography*, eds. D. S. Levene and D. P. Nelis. Leiden: 231-51.

_____(2004) *Contexts of War: Manipulations of Genre in Virgilian Battle Narrative*. Ann Arbor.

Rowell, H. T. (1966) "The ancient evidence of the Helen episode in *Aeneid* II," in *The Classical Tradition: Literary and Historical Studies in Honor of Harry Caplan*, ed. L. Wallach. Ithaca, NY: 210-21.

Scullard, H. H. (1982) *From the Gracchi to Nero: A History of Rome from 133 B.C. to A.D. 68*. Fifth edition. London.

Segal, C. P. (1973-74) "'Like winds and winged dream': a note on Virgil's development," *Classical Journal* 69: 97-101.

Shotter, D. (2005) *Augustus Caesar*. Second edition. London.

Sklenár, R. (1990) "The death of Priam: *Aeneid* 2.506-558," *Hermes* 118: 67-75.

Skutsch, O. (ed.) (1985) *The Annals of Q. Ennius*. Oxford.

Smith, R. A. (2005) *The Primacy of Vision in Virgil's Aeneid*. Austin.

Smith, R.M. (1999) "Deception and sacrifice in *Aeneid* 2.1-249," *American Journal of Philology* 120 (1999): 503-23.

Southern, P. (1998) *Augustus*. New York.

Spence, S. (1999) "The polyvalence of Pallas in the *Aeneid*," *Arethusa* 32: 149-63.

Stahl, H.-P. (ed.) (1998) *Vergil's Aeneid: Augustan Epic and Political Context*. London.

Syed, Y. (2005) *Vergil's Aeneid and the Roman Self: Subject and Nation in Literary Discourse*. Ann Arbor.

Syme, R. (1939) *The Roman Revolution*. Oxford.

Thomas, R. (1986) "Virgil's *Georgics* and the art of reference," *Harvard Studies in Classical Philology* 90: 171-98.

_____(1988) *Virgil: Georgics*. Two volumes. Cambridge.

_____(1999) *Reading Virgil and His Texts: Studies in Intertextuality*. Ann Arbor.

_____(2001) *Virgil and the Augustan Reception*. Cambridge.

Tracy, S. V. (1987) "Laocoon's guilt," *American Journal of Philology* 108: 451-4.

Van Sickle, J. (1992) *A Reading of Virgil's Messianic Eclogue*. New York.

Vernant, J.-P. and Vidal-Naquet, P. (1988) *Myth and Tragedy in Ancient Greece*, tr. J. Lloyd. New York.

Wallace-Hadrill, A. (1993) *Augustan Rome*. London.

Warmington, E. H. (1935-40) *Remains of Old Latin*. Four volumes. Cambridge, MA.

West, M. L. (ed.) (2003) *Greek Epic Fragments from the Seventh to Fifth Centuries BC*. Cambridge, MA.

White, P. (1993) *Promised Verse: Poets in the Society of Augustan Rome*. Cambridge, MA.

_____(2005) "Poets in the new milieu: realigning," in *The Cambridge Companion to the Age of Augustus*, ed. K. Galinsky. Cambridge: 321-39.

Wigodsky, M. (1972) *Vergil and Early Latin Poetry*. Wiesbaden.

Wilkinson, L. P. (1963) *Golden Latin Artistry*. Cambridge.

_____(1969) *The Georgics of Virgil: A Critical Survey*. Cambridge.

Williams, G. W. (1983) *Technique and Ideas in the Aeneid*. New Haven and London.

Williams, R. D. (1972-73) *Virgil: Aeneid*. Two volumes. London.

Wlosok, A. (1976) "Vergils Didotragödie: ein Beitrag zum Problem des Tragischen in der *Aeneis*," in *Studien zum antiken Epos*, eds. H. Görgemanns and E. A. Schmidt. Meisenheim: 228-50.

_____(1999) "The Dido tragedy in Virgil: a contribution to the question of the tragic in the *Aeneid*," transl. of Wlosok (1976), in *Virgil: Critical Assessments of Classical Authors*, vol. 4, ed. P. Hardie. London: 158-81.

West, D. and Woodman, A. J. (eds.) (1979) *Creative Imitation and Latin Literature*. Cambridge.

Wright, M.R. (1997) "'*Ferox uirtus*': anger in Virgil's "Aeneid," in *The Passions in Roman Thought and Literature*, eds. S. M. Braund and C. Gill. Cambridge: 169-84.

Wyatt, W. (ed.) *Homer: Iliad*. Two volumes. Cambridge, MA.

Zanker, P. (1988) *The Power of Images in the Age of Augustus*, tr. A. Shapiro. Ann Arbor.

List of Abbreviations

abl.	= ablative
acc.	= accusative
adj.	= adjective
adv.	= adverb
cf.	= *confer*, i.e. compare
comp.	= comparative
conj.	= conjunction
dat.	= dative
dep.	= deponent
f.	= feminine
gen.	= genitive
i.e.	= *id est*, that is
indecl.	= indeclinable
indef.	= indefinite
interj.	= interjection
intr.	= intransitive
interrog.	= interrogative
m.	= masculine
n.	= neuter
nom.	= nominative
num.	= numeral
opp.	= opposed
part.	= participle
pass.	= passive
perf.	= perfect
pers.	= personal
pl.	= plural
poss.	= possessive
prep.	= preposition
pron.	= pronoun
rel.	= relative
sc.	= *scilicet*, i.e. understand, supply
sing.	= singular
subst.	= substantive
superl.	= superlative
tr.	= transitive
v.	= verb
viz.	= *videlicet*, namely

Vocabulary

(In general, macrons are placed only over long vowels in a metrically indeterminate position, as in the *Oxford Latin Dictionary*.)

A

ā, ab, prep. with abl. *from*; *by* (with pass. verbs)

abdō, -ere, -didī, -ditum, v. tr. *put away; hide;* of sword, *bury, plunge;* 553

abeō, -īre, -īvī or -iī, -itum, v. intr. *go away, go forth, depart*

abiēs, -etis, f. *fir*

abluō, -ere, -luī, -lūtum, v. tr. *wash off, purify*

abnegō, -āre, -āvī, -ātum, v. tr. *refuse*

abstineō, -ēre, -tinuī, -tentum, v. tr. and intr. *hold away; refrain*

absum, abesse, āfuī, v. intr. *am away, absent*

ac, see **atque**

Acamās, -antis, m. a Greek hero, 262

accīdō, -ere, -cīdī, -cīsum, v. tr. *cut at, hack*

accingō, -ere, -cinxī, -cinctum, v. tr. *gird on;* v. intr., 235, *gird themselves;* middle sense, **ferrō accingor,** 671, *I gird myself with my sword*

accipiō, -ere, -cēpī, -ceptum, v. tr. *receive, welcome; hear*

accommodō, -āre, -āvī, -ātum, v. tr. *fit to, fasten to, adapt*

ācer, ācris, ācre, adj. *sharp, fierce* comp. **ācrior,** superl. **ācerrimus**

acernus, -a, -um, adj. *of maple wood, maple*

Achāicus, -a, -um, adj. *Achaean,* hence generally *Greek,* 462

Achillēs, -is and **-ī,** m. son of Peleus and Thetis, the bravest and greatest of the Greek warriors at Troy; he slew Hector, 29, 197, etc.

Achīvī, -ōrum and **-um,** m. *Greeks,* 45, etc.

aciēs, -ēī, f., *edge; line of battle; battle*

ad, prep. with acc. *to, towards; at*

addō, -ere, -didī, -ditum, v. tr. *add, join to*

adeō, adv. *to such an extent;* giving emphasis, *indeed,* 567

adflīgō, -ere, -flīxī, -flīctum, v. tr. *strike down, crush*

adflīctus, -a, -um, part. of **adflīgō,** as adj. *shattered, ruined; disheartened*

adflō, -āre, -āvī, -ātum, v. tr. *breathe upon*

adfluō, -ere, -fluxī, v. intr. *flow to, flow together, throng*

[adfor], -fārī, -fātus sum, v. dep. tr. *speak to; bid farewell to,* 644

adglomerō, -āre, -āvī, -ātum, v. tr. *join to; crowd together*

adgredior, -ī, -gressus sum, v. dep.
tr. *advance to, approach, attack,
undertake*

adhūc, adv. *as yet, still*

aditus, -ūs, m. *entrance, approach*

admīror, -ārī, -ātus sum, v. dep. tr.
admire, am surprised at, wonder

adōrō, -āre, -āvī, -ātum, v. tr. *pray to,
entreat*

adsentiō, -īre, -sensī, -sensum, v. intr.
assent, approve

adservō, -āre, -āvī, -ātum, v. tr. *guard
closely; closely cling to*

adstō, -āre, -stitī, v. intr. *stand by,
stand*

adsum, -esse, -fuī, v. intr. *am present,
am at hand, am here,* 182; *appear,*
271

adversus, -a, -um, adj. *turned toward,
opposing, hostile*

advertō, -ere, -vertī, -versum, v. tr. and
intr. *turn towards, regard*

adytum, -ī, n. *the innermost shrine of a
temple, sanctuary*

aedēs, -is, f. in sing. *temple*; in pl.
house; halls, 487

aedificō, -āre, -āvī, -ātum, v. tr. *build*

aeger, -gra, -grum, adj. *sick, weary,
fainting*

Aenēās, -ae, m. *Aeneas,* 2

aēnus, -a, -um, adj. *of bronze or copper*

aequaevus, -a, -um, adj. *of like age*

aequō, -āre, -āvī, -ātum, v. tr. *make
equal, equal*

aequor, -oris, n. *level surface, expanse
of sea, sea*

aequus, -a, -um, adj. *level; equal, fair.*
As subst. **aequum,** *justice,* 427

aerātus, -a, -um, adj. *of bronze or
copper*

aes, aeris, n. *bronze or copper*

aestus, -ūs, m. *heat; fiery flood,* 706;
fiery glow, 759

aetās, -ātis, f. *time of life, age*

aeternus, -a, -um, adj. *everlasting,
eternal*

aethēr, -eris, acc. **era,** m. *the bright
upper air, ether, sky, heaven,
firmament*

aevum, -ī, n. *age, time.* **integer aevī
sanguis,** 638, *strength unimpaired
by age*

ager, agrī, m. *field*

agger, -eris, m. *bank, mound, barrier*

agitātor, -ōris, m. *driver*

agitō, -āre, -āvī, -ātum, v. tr. *keep
moving; pursue, hunt; ponder*

agmen, -inis, n. *course, stream,* 782;
*host on the march, band; ranks;
advance,* 212

agnōscō, -ere, -nōvī, -nitum, v. tr.
recognize

agō, -ere, ēgī, āctum, v. tr. *drive, move;
goad on,* 128; *bring up, advance,*
441; *lead.* **age,** *come now,* 707

agricola, -ae, m. *farmer*

Aiāx, -ācis, m. *Ajax,* 414

āiō, v. defective *say*; third pers. sing. **ait**

aliquī, -qua, -quod, indef. pron. adj.
some, any

aliquis, -qua, -quid, indef. pron. subst.
any one, some one

aliter, adv. *otherwise*

alius, -a, -ud, adj. *another, other*; **aliī...
aliī,** *some...others*

almus, -a, -um, adj. *nurturing, kindly*

altāria, -ium, n. pl. *altar*

alter, -tera, -terum, adj. *one of two,
another, a second*; **alter...alter,** *the
one...the other*

altus, -a, -um, adj. *lofty, deep; stately,*
448; **altum,** as n. subst., *the deep
sea*

alvus, -ī, f. *belly*

ambiguus, -a, -um, adj. *uncertain; doubtful; of double meaning*, 99

ambō, -ae, ō, adj. *both*

āmens, -entis, adj. *out of one's mind, mad, distracted*

amīcus, -a, -um, adj. *friendly*

amīcus, -ī, m. *friend*

āmittō, -ere, -mīsī, -missum, v. tr. *let go, lose*

amnis, -is, m. *stream, river*

amor, -ōris, m. *love, longing, desire*

amplector, -ī, -plexus sum, v. dep. tr. *embrace*

amplus, -a, -um, adj. *spacious*

an, conj. *whether, or*

Anchīsēs, -ae, m. *Anchises*, father of Aeneas, 300, 597, 687, 747

Androgeōs, -geī or -geō, m. a Greek, 371, 382, 392

Andromachē, -ēs, f. wife of Hector, 456

anguis, -is, m. and f. *snake*

angustus, -a, -um, adj. *narrow;* angusta viārum, 332, *the narrow (places) of the streets*

anima, -ae, f. *breath, life*

animus, -ī, m. *mind, thought, heart;* in pl. gen. *high spirits, spirit, courage; mood, temper*, 73

annus, -ī, m. *year*

ante, adv. and prep. with acc. *before*

antīquuus, -a, -um, adj. *old; ancient*

aperiō, -īre, -uī, -ertum, v. tr. *open*

apex, -icis, m. *point, top; tip of a flame*, 682

Apollō, -inis, m. the god of divination; identified with Phoebus, the sun-god, brother of Diana, 121, 430

appāreō, -ēre, -pāruī, -pāritum, v. intr. *appear*

aptō, -āre, -āvī, -ātum, v. tr. *fit, fit on*

apud, prep. with acc. *with, among*

āra, -ae, f. *altar*

arbor, -oris, f. *tree*

arceō, -ēre, -uī, v. tr. *confine*

ardens, -entis, adj. *on fire, eager, fiery, flashing*

ardeō, -ēre, arsī, v. intr. *am on fire; blaze forth*, 172; *burn with eagerness, am eager*

arduus, -a, -um, adj. *lofty, towering high; rearing his head*, 475

Argīvus, -a, -um, adj. *Argive, of Argos*, 254, etc.

Argolicus, -a, -um, adj. *connected with Argos, Argive, Greek*, 56, etc.

Argos, n. sing, only in nom. and acc., also Argī, -ōrum, 178, m. pl. capital town of the Argolis in the Peloponnese, 95, 326

ariēs, -etis m. *ram; battering-ram*

arma, -ōrum, n. pl. *arms*

armentum, -ī, n. *herd*

armiger, -ī, m. *armor-bearer*

armipotens, -entis, adj., *powerful in arms*

armō, -āre, -āvī, -ātum, v. tr. *arm;* armātus, as subst. *an armed man*, 328

arō, -āre, -āvī, -ātum, v. tr. *plow*

arrigō, -ere, -rexī, rectum, v. tr. *life, raise up, rear; uplift eyes*, 173; *prick up ears*, 303

ars, artis, f. *art, skill, cunning*

artifex, -icis, m. and f. *cunning workman, contriver, schemer*

artus, -ūs, m. gen. in pl. *joint, limb*

artus, -a, -um, adj. *close-fitting, tight*

arvum, -ī, n. *plowed land, field*

arx, arcis, f. *place of defense*, 322; *citadel, height*

Ascanius, -ī, m. son of Aeneas and Creusa, also called Iulus, 598, 652, 666, 747

ascendō, -ere, -scendī, -scensum, v.
intr. and tr. *climb, go up to*
ascensus, -ūs, m. *climbing, ascent*
Asia, -ae, f. *Asia Minor*, 193, 557
asper, -era, -erum, adj. *rough, wild,*
fierce, cruel. asprīs, 379 by syncope
aspiciō, -spicere, -spexī, -spectum, v.
tr. *look on, see*
aspīrō, -āre, -āvī, -ātum, v. intr. with
dat. *breathe upon; favor*, 385
asportō, -āre, -āvī, -ātum, v. tr. *carry*
away
ast, see at
astrum, -ī, n. *star*
Astyanax, -actis, m. son of Hector and
Andromache, 457
asȳlum, -ī, n. *place of refuge, sanctuary*
at, ast, conj. *but*
āter, ātra, ātrum, adj. *black, gloomy*
atque, ac, conj. *and*
Atrīdēs, -ae, m. patronymic, *son*
of Atreus: the Atridae were
Agamemnon and Menelaus,
leaders of the Greeks against Troy,
104, 415, 500
ātrium, -ī, n. *entrance room, hall*: in pl.
halls, rooms
attollō, -ere, v. tr. *lift up, raise up, rear*
attrectō, -āre, -āvī, -ātum, v. tr.
handle, touch
auctor, -ōris, m. *author, originator*
audeō, -ēre, ausus sum, v. semi-dep.
tr. *dare.* audeō in + acc., 347, *am*
bold for
audiō, -īre, -īvī or -iī, -ītum, v. tr. *hear;*
heed, 346
augurium, -ī, n. *omen by the utterance*
of birds; augury, omen
aura, -ae, f. *air, breeze.* ad aurās, 699,
to heaven; ferre sub aurās, 158,
divulge
aurātus, -a, -um, adj. *gilded*

aureus, -a, -um, adj. *golden*
auris, -is, f. *ear*
aurum, -ī, n. *gold*
Auster, -trī, m. *the South wind; wind*
ausum, -ī, n. *daring deed*
aut, conj. *or.* aut...aut, *either...or*
autem, conj. *but, however.* sed...autem,
but indeed
Automedōn, -ontis, m. charioteer of
Achilles, 477
auxilium, -ī, n. *help, aid, assistance*
āvehō, -ere, -vexī, -vectum, v. tr. *carry*
away; āvectōs, 43, *have sailed away*
āvellō, -ere, -vellī or -vulsī, -vulsum, v.
tr. *tear away*
āversus, -a, -um, adj. *turned away,*
averse, 170
āvertō, -ere, -vertī, -versum, v. tr. *turn*
away
āvius, -a, -um, adj. *pathless*; n. pl. āvia,
736, *remote paths*
avus, -ī, m. *grandfather; ancestor*
axis, -is, m. *axle, axis; the axis of*
heaven; height of heaven, 512

B

barba, -ae, f. *beard*
barbaricus, -a, -um, adj. *barbaric* (Gr.
barbaros = one who speaks an
unknown tongue)
Bēlīdēs, -ae, m. patronymic,
descendant of Belus, i.e. Palamedes,
82
bellum, -ī, n., *war*
bīgae, -ārum, f. pl. *two-horse chariot*
bipatens, -entis, adj. *doubly open*; of
gates, *with both halves open, wide*
open, 330
bipennis, -is, f. *double axe*
bis, adv. *twice*
bōs, bovis, m. and f. *ox, cow*
bracchium, -ī, n. *arm*

breviter, adv. *shortly, briefly*
brūma, -ae, f. *the shortest day, winter*

C

cadō, -ere, cecidī cāsum, v. intr. *fall;* of star, *set*
caecus, -a, -um, adj. *blind; dark,* 19; *secret, hidden*
caedēs, -is, f. *slaughter, carnage*
caedō, -ere, cecīdī, caesum, v. tr. *cause to fall; cut; slay*
caelicola, -ae, m. and f. *one who dwells in heaven; heavenly being*
caelum, -ī, n. *heaven, sky*
caerulus, -a, -um, adj. *dark blue*
Calchās, -antis, m. the chief prophet of the Greeks, 100, 122, 176, 182, 185
cālīgō, -inis, f. *thick darkness*
cālīgō, -āre, v. intr. *am dark, misty*
campus, -ī, m. *plain, field*
canō, -ere, cecinī, cantum, v. tr. *sing, chant;* of prophetic utterance, *declare, prophesy,* 176 n.; *divine,* 124
capiō, -ere, cēpī, captum, v. tr. *catch, seize, take; take prisoner*
captīvus, -a, -um, adj. *taken prisoner, captive, plundered*
captus, -a, -um, part. of **capiō,** as adj. *captive, prisoner,* as subst. **captus, -ī,** m. *a prisoner*
capulus, -ī, m. *handle, hilt of sword*
caput, -itis, n. *head; life,* 751; *top*
Capys, -yos, m. name of a Trojan, 35
cardō, -inis, m. *hinge, pivot, socket*
careō, -ēre, -uī, -itum, v. intr. with abl. *am without, free from*
carīna, -ae, f. *keel; ship*
cārus, -a, -um, adj. *dear, loved*
Cassandra, -ae, f. daughter of Priam inspired by Apollo, but doomed by him always to prophesy truly and never to be believed, 246, 343, 404

cassus, -a, -um, adj. with abl. *deprived of*
castra, -ōrum, n. pl. *camp*
cāsus, -ūs, m. *fall; accident, hazard, chance; disaster,* 10
caterva, -ae, f. *crowd*
catulus, -ī, m. *a young dog; cub*
causa, -ae, f. *cause, reason*
caverna, -ae, f. *cavern; hollow,* 19
cavō, -āre, -āvī, -ātum, v. tr. *make hollow*
cavus, -a, -um, adj. *hollow; enfolding,* 360; *vaulted,* 487
cēdō, -ere cessī, cessum, v. intr. *go away, yield, retire*
celsus, -a, -um, adj. *lofty*
centum, num. adj. indecl. *hundred*
Cerēs, -eris, f. goddess of agriculture, 714, 742
cernō, -ere, crēvī, crētum, v. tr. *distinguish* with the eyes, *see*
certātim, adv. *with emulation, eagerly*
certō, -āre, -āvī, -ātum, v. intr. *contend, strive*
certus, -a, -um, adj. *sure, fixed; unswerving,* 212
cervīx, -īcis, f. *neck*
cessō, -āre, -āvī, -ātum, v. intr. *cease*
[cēterus], -a, -um, adj. rare in sing. not in nom. m. *the other, the rest*
ceu, adv. *as, just as; as if*
cieō, -ēre, cīvī, citum, v. tr. *set in motion, rouse, stir up*
cingō, -ere, cinxī, cinctum, v. tr. *put around; gird.* In mid. sense *gird on* arms, *don,* 511, 521, 749
cinis, -eris, m. *ashes*
circum, adv. and prep. with acc. *around*
circumdō, -are, -dedī, -datum, v. tr. *place round, put around, fling around.* Tmesis 218, 792

circumerrō, -āre, -āvī, -ātum, v. tr.
wander around; range around, 599

circumfundō, -ere, -fūdī, -fūsum, v.
tr. *pour round.* In middle sense
circumfundimur, 383, *we pour
around, surround;* **circumfūsa,** 64,
crowded around

**circumspiciō, -spicere, -spexī,
-spectum,** v. intr. and tr. *look
round; look round on*

circumstō, -āre, stetī, v. intr. *stand
round*

circumvolō, -āre, -āvī, -ātum, v. intr.
and tr. *fly* or *hover around*

cīvis, -is, m. and f. *citizen*

clādēs, -is, f. *disaster*

clāmor, -ōris, m. *shout; clamor*

clangor, -ōris, m. *cry; blaring* of
trumpets

clārescō, -ere, clāruī, inceptive, v. intr.
grow clear

clārus, -a, -um, adj. *clear, bright*

classis, -is, f. *fleet*

claustrum, -ī, n. *bar*

clipeus, -ī, m. *round shield*

coepī, -isse, coeptum, v. defective tr.
begin

cognoscō, -ere, -nōvī, -nitum,
inceptive v. tr. *begin to recognize,
learn*

cōgō, -ere, coēgī, coactum, v. tr. *drive
together, compel.* **coactīs,** 196,
forced or *false tears*

colligō, -ere, -lēgī, -lectum, v. tr.
gather together

collum, -ī, n. *neck*

coluber, -brī, m. *serpent, snake*

columba, -ae, f. *dove*

coma, -ae, f. *hair;* of trees, *foliage, leafy
head,* 629

comans, -antis, adj. *hairy; crested*

comes, -itis, m. and f. *comrade;*
predicative, 181, *to accompany
them*

comitō, -āre, -āvī, -ātum, v. tr.
accompany, 580

comitor, ārī, -ātus sum, v. dep. tr.
accompany

commendō, -āre, -āvī, -ātum, v. tr.
entrust to

commūnis, -e, adj. *shared; common*

compāgēs, -is, f. *fastening; joint, seam;
timbers*

compellō, -āre, -āvī, -ātum, v. tr.
address

complector, -ī, -plexus sum, v. dep. tr.
embrace, clasp, enfold

compleō, -ēre, -plēvī, -plētum, v. tr.
fill up

compositō, adv. *by agreement*

comprendō or **comprehendō, -ere,
-endī, -ensum,** v. tr. *grasp; grasp
with the mind, comprehend*

comprimō, -ere, -pressī, -pressum, v.
tr. *check, restrain*

concēdō, -ere, -cessī, -cessum, v. intr.
withdraw from, leave; withdraw to,
523

concidō, -ere, -cidī, v. intr. *fall down*

concilium, -ī, n. *assembly, council*

conclāmō, -āre, -āvī, -ātum, v. intr.
shout together; cry

concrētus, -a, -um, adj. *grown together,
matted*

concurrō, -ere, -currī, -cursum, v.
intr. *run together*

concutiō, -ere, -cussī, -cussum, v. tr.
shake vigorously

condensus, -a, -um, adj. *very thick;
huddled together,* 517

condō, -ere, -didī, -ditum, v. tr. *put
together, hide.* **conduntur,** 401, in
middle sense, *hide themselves*

confertus, -a, -um, adj. *closely packed*
confīgō, -ere, -fīxī, -fixum, v. tr. *pierce*
confiteor, -ērī, -fessus sum, v. dep. tr.
   confess, acknowledge; reveal, 591
conflīgō, -ere, -flixī, -flictum, v. intr.
   clash together, 417; *join battle*
confundō, -ere, -fūdī, -fūsum, v. tr.
   pour together, confuse
confūsus, -a, -um, part. of **confundo**
   as adj. *confused, perplexed*
congemō, -ere, -uī, v. intr. *groan deeply*
congerō, -ere, -gessī, -gestum, v. tr.
   heap together
congredior, -ī, -gressus sum, v. dep.
   intr. *come together; fight*
cōniciō, -ere, -iēcī, -iectum, v. tr. *hurl
   strongly*
coniugium, -ī, n. *marriage; husband*
coniunx, coniugis, m. and f. *one
   joined; husband, wife*
cōnor, ārī, -ātus sum, v. dep. intr. and
   tr. *endeavor, attempt*
consanguinitās, -ātis, f. *blood
   relationship*
conscius, -a, -um, adj. *knowing with
   someone else, allied; conscious of,
   knowing,* 141; *conscious of guilt,* 99,
   with gen.
consequor, -ī, -secūtus sum, v. tr.
   follow
conserō, -ere, -seruī, -sertum, v. tr.
   join; **cons. proelium,** *engage in
   battle*
consīdō, -ere, -sēdī, -sessum, v. intr.
   settle down, sink down
consilium, -ī, n. *counsel, plan*
consistō, -ere, -stitī, -stitum, v. intr.
   stand still
conspectus, -ūs, m. *a gazing, regarding;*
   in conspectū, 21, *in sight;*
   conspectū in mediō, 67, *in the
   midst of our sight*

consūmō, -ere, -sumpsī, -sumptum, v.
   tr. *consume, spend*
contexō, -ere, -texuī, -textum, v. tr.
   weave together
conticescō, -ere, -uī, v. intr. *become
   silent*
contineō, -ēre, -tinuī, -tentum, v. tr.
   check, hold back
contingō, -ere, tigī, -tactum, v. tr.
   *touch, reach; lay hands on, touch
   and pollute; strike,* 649
contorqueō, -ēre, -torsī, -tortum, v. tr.
   throw vigorously
contrā, adv. *on the other side* or *hand;*
   prep. with acc., *against*
contrārius, -a, -um, adj. *opposite*
convellō, -ere, -vellī, rarely **-vulsī,**
   -vulsum, v. tr. *pluck violently, rend
   away, tear down*
conveniō, -īre, -vēnī, -ventum, v. intr.
   come together, flock together; v. tr.
   meet
convertō, -ere, -vertī, -versum, v. tr.
   turn, turn around; change, 73;
   direct, 191
convolvō, -ere, -volvī, -volūtum, v. tr.
   roll together
cōpia, -ae, f. *abundance;* of troops,
   forces
cōram, adv. *in public; face to face*
Coroebus, -ī, m. suitor of Cassandra,
   341, 386, etc.
corpus, -oris, n. *body; dead body,
   corpse,* 365
corripiō, -ere, -ripuī, -reptum, v. tr.
   snatch eagerly, seize
coruscus, -a, -um, adj. *vibrating;
   flashing, glittering*
costa, -ae, f. *rib*
crātēr, ēris, m. *mixing-bowl*
crēber, -bra, -brum, adj. *frequent,
   repeated*

crēdō, -ere, -didī, ditum, v. intr. with dat. *trust, believe*

crescō, -ere, crēvī, crētum, v. intr. *grow;* **crētus** as adj. *born, sprung,* 74

Creūsa, -ae, f. wife of Aeneas, 562, etc.

crīmen, -inis, n. *charge; crime,* 65

crīnis, -is, m. *hair;* pl. *locks*

crūdēlis, -e, adj. **crūdēlior, crūdēlissimus,** *cruel*

cruentus, -a, -um, adj. *bloody*

culmen, -inis, n. *height, summit; roof;* **tōta culmina,** 446, *roof covering*

culpa, -ae, f. *fault*

culpō, -āre, -āvī, -ātum, v. tr. *blame, hold guilty*

cum, conj. *when, since*

cum, prep. with abl. *with, together with;* always suffixed to the personal pronouns **mē, tē, sē, nōbīs, vōbīs,** e.g. **mēcum**

cumulus, -ī, m. *heap*

cunctus, -a, -um, adj. *all together, all*

cumque, see **quōcumque**

cupīdō, -inis, f. *desire*

cupiō, -ere, -īvī or **-iī, -ītum,** v. tr. *desire*

cupressus, -ī. f. *cypress*

cūr, adv. *why?*

cūra, -ae, f. *care, anxiety, trouble*

cūrō, -āre, -āvī, -ātum, v. tr. *care for, regard*

currō, -ere, cucurrī, cursum, v. intr. *run, hurry*

cursus, -ūs, m. *running, course:* **cursū sequor,** 736, *I hurriedly pursue*

curvus, -a, -um, adj. *bent, curved, curving, winding*

cuspis, -idis, f. *spear*

custōs, -ōdis, m. *guardian, guard*

D

Danaī, -ōrum or **-um,** m. *the Greeks,* so called from Danaus, an old king of Argos, 5, etc.

Dardania, -ae, f. *Dardania,* the land of Dardanus, ancestor of the Trojans; so *Troy,* 325

Dardanidae, -ārum, m. patronymic, *children of Dardanus, Trojans,* 59, 72, 242, 445

Dardanis, -idis, f. *Trojan woman,* 787

Dardanius, -a, -um, *connected with Dardanus; Trojan,* 582

Dardanus, -a, -um, adj. *Dardan, Trojan,* 618

dē, prep. with abl. *from, down from; derived from, of,* 78

dea, -ae, f. *goddess*

dēbeō, -ēre, -uī, -itum, v. tr. *owe;* **dēbitus,** *due*

decem, num. adj. indecl. *ten*

decōrus, -a, -um, adj. *graceful, elegant*

dēcurrō, -ere, -currī or **-cucurrī, -cursum,** v. intr. *run down*

decus, -oris, n. *ornament, honor*

dēdūcō, -ere, -dūxī, -ductum, v. tr. *lead down, lead from, conduct,* technical word for founding a colony, 800

dēfendō, -ere, -fendī, -fensum, v. tr. *strike away; defend*

dēfensor, -ōris, m. *defender*

dēfetiscor, -ī, -fessus sum, v. dep. intr. *become weary;* **dēfessus,** *weary*

dēficiō, -ere, -fēcī, -fectum, v. intr. *fail, flag, cease*

dēgener, -eris, adj. *unworthy of the race, degenerate*

deinde (rarely as trisyllable **deïnde**) adv. *thereafter, then*

Dēiphobus, -ī, m. son of Priam, 310

dēlābor, -ī, lapsus sum, v. dep. intr. *slip
down; fall into,* 377

dēligō, -ere, -lēgī, -lectum, v. tr. *choose*

dēlitescō, -ere, -lituī, v. intr. *hide
myself, lie hidden*

dēlūbrum, -ī, n. *shrine, temple*

dēmens, -tis, adj. *out of one's mind,
mad*

dēmittō, -ere, -mīsī, -missum, v. tr.
send down, lower

dēmō, -ere, dempsī, demptum, v. tr.
take away

dēmoror, -ārī, -ātus sum, v. dep. tr.
keep waiting, delay

dēmum, adv., *at last.* Emphasizing
word, hīc dēmum, 743 *here and
here only;* so sīc dēmum, 795

dēnique, adv. *at last; in this last
extremity,* 70

densus, -a, -um, adj. *thick*

dēpascor, -ī, -pastus sum, v. dep. tr.
feed on

dēpōnō, -ere, -posuī, -positum, v. tr.
lay down, lay aside, drop

dēscendō, -ere, -scendī, -scensum, v.
intr. *go down, descend*

dēserō, -ere, -seruī, -sertum, v. tr.
desert, forsake

dēstinō, -āre, -āvī, -ātum, v. tr. *set
apart, mark out*

dēsuescō, -ere, -suēvī, -suētum, v. tr.
render unaccustomed; dēsuētus,
unaccustomed

dēsum, -esse, -fuī, v. intr. *am wanting,
am away, am missing*

dēsuper, adv. *from above*

dētineō, -ēre, -uī, -tentum, v. tr.
detain, hold back

deus, -ī, m. *god;* gen. pl. deum or
deōrum; dī and dīs are often used
for deī and deīs

dēvolvō, -ere, -vī, -volūtum, v. tr. *roll
down*

dexter, -tera, -terum, and -tra, -trum,
adj. *on the right hand; favorable,
propitious*

dextera, or dextra, -ae, f. *the right
hand; deeds of right hand (=valor),*
291.

dīcō, -ere, dīxī, dictum, v. tr. *say,
speak; call name*

dictum, -ī, n. *word*

diēs, -ēī, m. (in sing. often fem.) *day;
time*

diffugiō, -ere, -fūgī, -fugitum, v. intr.
flee in different directions

dīgerō, -ere, -gessī, -gestum, v. tr.
distribute; arrange, i.e. *explain,* 182

dignus, -a, -um, adj. *worthy, deserved*

dīgredior, -ī, -gressus sum, v. dep. intr.
depart, come from

dīlectus, -a, -um, adj. *chosen, dear*

dīripiō, -ere, -ripuī, -reptum, v. tr. *tear
asunder; plunder*

dīrus, -a, -um, adj. *fearful, terrible,
dread, monstrous*

discēdō, -ere, -cessī, -cessum, v. intr.
depart

discō, -ere, didicī, v. tr. *learn*

discors, -cordis, adj. *differing,
disagreeing*

disiciō, -ere, -iēcī, -iectum, v. tr. *dash
apart, destroy*

diū, adv. *for a long time*

dīva, -ae, f. *goddess*

dīvellō, -ere, -vellī, -vulsum, v. tr. *tear
away or apart*

dīversus, -a, -um, adj. *different; in
different directions:* ex dīversō,
716, *from different directions*

dīves, -itis, adj. *rich*

dīvidō, -ere, -vīsī, -vīsum, v. tr. *divide;
cut a way through, breach,* 234

dīvīnus, -a, -um, adj. *divine*
dīvus, -ī, m. *deity, god*; gen. pl. often **dīvum**
dō, dare, dedī, datum, v. tr. *give, grant, afford; utter words,* 790; *make, cause,* 310, 482; *let drop,* 566; **vēla d.,** 136, *set sail;* **poenās d.,** 366, *pay the penalty;* **sonitum d.,** 243, *crash;* **ruīnam dedit,** 310, *has fallen in ruin;* **datī...circum,** see **circumdō**
Dolopes, -um, m. a Thessalian people, who came to Troy with Phoenix, 7, 29, 415, 785
dolor, -ōris, m. *grief, sorrow*
dolus, -ī, m. *guile, treachery, treason;* pl. *wiles,* 62
dominor, -ārī, -ātus sum, v. dep. intr. *hold sway*
domō, -āre, -uī, itum, v. tr. *tame, subdue*
domus, -ūs, f. *house, home, palace*
dōnec, conj. *until*
dōnum, -ī, n. *gift*
Dōricus, -a, -um, adj. *connected with the Dorians,* an ancient Greek race, *Greek,* 27
dracō, -ōnis, m. *serpent*
dubius, -a, -um, adj. *doubtful*
dūcō, -ere, duxī, ductum, v. tr. *draw, lead, guide, draw out, prolong; trail,* 694
ductor, -ōris, m. *leader*
dūdum, adv. *a while ago, lately*
dulcis, -e, adj. *sweet, darling*
dum, conj. *while; until*
duo, -ae, -o num. adj. *two*
dūrus, -a, -um, adj. *hard, cruel*
dux, ducis, m. *leader*
Dymās, -antis, m. father of Hecuba, 340, 394, 428

E

ecce, interj. *lo! behold!*
edax, -ācis, adj. *consuming, devouring*
ēdisserō, -ere, -seruī, -sertum, v. tr. *speak, relate at length,* 149
ēdūcō, -ere, -dūxī, -ductum, v. tr. *draw out; raise up;* **ēductum sub astra,** 461, *rising high to the stars*
efferō, efferre, extulī, ēlātum, v. tr. *bear forth, raise; bring forth,* 297
effigiēs, -ēī, f. *image*
effor, -fārī, -fātus sum, v. dep. tr. *speak out, utter*
effugiō, -ere, -fūgī, v. tr. and intr. *flee from, escape*
effugium, -ī, n. *escape*
effulgeō, -ēre, -fulsī, v. intr. *shine forth, flash forth*
effundō, -ere, -fūdī, -fūsum, v. tr. *pour forth, shed*
egeō, -ēre, -uī, v. intr. *am needy;* with abl. *am in need of, need*
ego, meī, pers. pron. *I*
ēgredior, -gredī, -gressus sum, v. intr. *go out; go out from, quit*
ei, interj. with dat., *alas!*
ēlābor, -ī, -lapsus sum, v. intr. *slip out, escape from*
ēmicō, -āre, -micuī, -micātum, v. intr. *flash forth*
ēmoveō, -ēre, -mōvī, -mōtum, v. tr. *move out; wrench from, upheave*
enim, conj. *for; indeed.* **nec enim,** 100, *for indeed...not;* **sed enim,** 164 *but indeed*
ensis, -is, m. *sword*
eō, īre, īvī or **iī, itum,** v. intr. *go; trickle,* 174
Eōus, -a, -um, adj. *eastern,* 417
Epēos, -ī, m. the inventor of the wooden horse, 264

Ēpytus, -ī, m. a Trojan, 340

equidem, adv. *indeed, truly*

equus, -ī, m. *horse*

ergō, adv. *therefore*

Erīnys, -yos, f. *Fury,* 337, 573

ēripiō, -ere, -uī, reptum, v. tr. *snatch away, tear from; rob of,* 736; *save, rescue; remove;* **ēripe fugam,** 619, *quickly take flight*

errō, -āre, -āvī, -ātum, v. intr. *wander, roam*

error, -ōris, m. *wandering; mistake; deception, trick* 48

ērubescō, -ere, -uī, v. incept. intr. and tr. *begin to grow red; feel shame about; blush for,* i.e. *respected,* 542

ēruō, -ere, ēruī, ērutum, v. tr. *tear or dig out; overthrow, uproot*

et, conj. *and;* adv, *even, also,* **et** or **que...et,** *both...and*

etiam, conj. *also, even*

etsī, conj, *even if, although*

Eurus, -ī, m. *East wind,* 418

Eurypylus, -ī, m. a Greek, 114

ēvādō, -ere, -vāsī, -vāsum, v. intr. and tr. *go up, climb up, ascend; go out, pass beyond; emerge,* 531; *come to end of; escape, pass in safety,* 731

ēveniō, -īre, -vēnī, -ventum, v. intr. *turn out, come to pass, happen*

ēvertō, -ere, -vertī, -versum, v. tr. *overthrow*

ēvincō, -ere, -vīcī, -victum, v. tr. *conquer completely, overpower, overmaster*

ex or **ē,** prep. with abl. *out of, from*

exardescō, -ere, -arsī, -arsum, v. intr. *blaze up, kindle*

excēdō, -ere, -cessī, -cessum, v. intr. *leave, depart; swerve from,* 737

excidium, -ī, n. *destruction; sack of city,* 643

excidō, -ere, -cidī, v. intr. *fall out or from*

excīdō, -ere, -cīdī, -cīsum, v. tr. *cut off, destroy; cut out,* 481

excitō, -āre, -āvī, -ātum, v. tr. *arouse, startle*

exclāmō, -āre, -āvī, -ātum, v. intr. *cry out*

excutiō, -ere, -cussī, -cussum, v. tr. *shake out, shake free, dash from;* **excutior somnō,** 302, middle sense, *I shake myself free from sleep*

exeō, -īre, -iī or **-īvī, -itum,** v. intr. *go out, go forth*

exercitus, -ūs, m. *army*

exhālō, -āre, -āvī, -ātum, v. tr. *breathe out*

exigō, -ere, -ēgī, -actum, v. tr. *drive out*

exitiālis, -e, adj. *ruinous*

exitium, -ī, n. *ruin, destruction*

exitus, -ūs, m. *departure, end, death*

exoptō, -āre, -āvī, -ātum, v. tr. *greatly desire, long for*

exorior, -īrī, -ortus sum, v. dep. intr. *rise out or up*

expediō, -īre, -īvī or **-iī, ītum,** v. tr. *extricate, set free;* **expedior,** 633, *I escape*

expendō, -ere, -pendī, -pensum, v. tr. *weigh out; pay, pay the penalty of,* 229

experior, -īrī, -pertus sum, v. dep. tr. *try, test, experience*

expleō, -ēre, -plēvī, -plētum, v. tr. *fill up, fill*

explicō, -āre, -uī and **-āvī, -itum** and **-ātum,** v. tr. *unfold*

exprōmō, -ere, -prompsī, -promptum, v. tr. *bring forth; utter,* 280

exsanguis, -e, adj. *bloodless, pale*

exscindō, -ere, -scidī, -scissum, v. tr. *cut out, extirpate; raze,* 177

exsilium, -ī, n. *banishment, exile*
exspectō, -āre, -āvī, -ātum, v. tr. *look for eagerly*
exstinguō, -ere, -stinxī, -stinctum, v. tr. *extinguish; kill*
exsultō, -āre, -āvī, -ātum, v. intr. *leap up; rejoice, exult*
exsuperō, -āre, -āvī, -ātum, v. tr. and intr. *conquer; mount above; tower high*
extemplō, adv. *immediately*
extrā, prep. with acc. *outside; beyond*
extrēmus, -a, -um, superl. adj. *outmost; utmost.* **extrema,** 349, *desperate acts;* **extrēmā morte,** 447, *in death's extremity;* **flamma extrēma,** 431, *the funeral fire*
exuō, -ere, -uī, -ūtum, v. tr. *strip off.* **exūtīs vinclīs,** 153, *unfettered*
exuviae, -ārum, f. *things stripped off; spoils,* 275, 646; *skin of snake,* 473

F

fabricātor, -ōris, m. *builder*
fabricō, -āre, -āvī, -ātum, v. tr. *make, construct*
faciēs, -ēī, f. *face; appearance;* pl. 622, *shapes, forms*
facilis, -e, adj. *easy; light to bear,* 646
faciō, -ere, fēcī, factum, v. tr. *do; make; cause.* Passive **fīō, fierī, factus sum,** *am made; become*
factum, -ī, n. *deed*
fallō, -ere, fefellī, falsum, v. tr. *deceive; give the slip to; escape the notice of*
falsus, -a, -um, adj. *false*
fāma, -ae, f. *report, rumor, renown*
famulus, -ī, m. *attendant, servant*
fās, n. indecl. *divine law; what is lawful.* **fās est,** *heaven permits one to, one may*

fastīgium, -ī, n. *gable roof, roof, battlement*
fātālis, -e, adj. *fated; fateful*
fateor, -ērī, fassus sum, v. dep. tr. *confess*
fātum, -ī, n. *that which is spoken; oracle; fate, destiny*
for, fārī, fātus sum, v. defective *speak, say, tell, talk*
faucēs, -ium, f. pl. *throat; jaws*
fax, facis, f. *torch*
fēmineus, -a, -um, adj. *having to do with a woman*
fenestra, -ae, f. *window, opening*
feriō, -īre, v. tr. *strike*
ferō, ferre, tulī, lātum, v. tr. *bear, bring, carry; carry off; snatch, seize,* 600; *endure, see with patience,* 131; *relate, say,* 161, 230; **f. pedem,** 756, *make one's way;* **f. oculōs,** 570, *cast a glance;* **rapiuntque feruntque,** 374, *plunder and pillage;* **f. sub aurās,** 158, *divulge;* **quid ferat,** 75, *what is his purpose.* **feror,** *am carried, rush, go on*
ferrum, -ī, n. *iron; sword*
ferus, -a, -um, adj. *wild, fierce, wrathful.* As subst. *wild beast; the beast,* 51
fessus, -a, -um, adj. *weary*
festīnō, -āre, -āvī, -ātum, v. intr. *hasten, hurry*
festus, -a, -um, adj. *festal*
fētus, -a, -um, adj. *pregnant, filled with*
fictus, -a, -um, adj. *feigned, false*
fīdens, -entis, pres. part. of **fīdō** as adj. *confident*
fidēs, -ēī, f. *faith; promise; pledge,* 143; *what causes belief,* i.e. *proof,* 309; *honor, protection,* 541 n.

fīdō, -ere, fīsus sum, v. intr. with dat. *have confidence in, trust*; with gen. 61

fīdūcia, -ae, f. *confidence, reliance, trust*

fīdus, -a, -um, adj. *faithful; sure,* 281; *trustworthy, safe,* 400; *to be trusted,* 377; **male f.** 23, *treacherous*

fīgō, -ere, fixī, fixum, v. tr. *fix; fasten, plant kisses on,* 490; **fixus,** as adj. *firm, unshaken, resolved*

fingō, -ere, finxī, fictum, v. tr. *shape, mold, form*

fīnis, -is, m. and f. *end.* **sine fīne,** 771, *unceasingly*

fīō, see **faciō**

firmō, -āre, -āvī, -ātum, v. tr. *make strong, confirm*

firmus, -a, -um, adj. *strong, firm*

fixus, see **fīgō**

flāgitō, -āre, -āvī, -ātum, v. tr. *keep asking for, demand*

flagrō, -āre, -āvī, -ātum, v. intr. *burn, blaze*

flamma, -ae, f. *flame; fire, fury,* 587; pl. *fire signal,* 256

flectō, -ere, flexī, flexum, v. tr. *bend, turn, influence*

fleō, -ēre, -ēvī, -ētum, v. intr. *weep*

flētus, -ūs, m. *weeping, tears*

fluctus, -ūs, m. *wave; tide,* 206

flūmen, -inis, n. *river, stream*

fluō, -ere, fluxī, fluxum, v. intr. *flow, ebb away*

foedō, -āre, -āvī, -ātum, v. tr. *defile, pollute*

fons, fontis, m. *fountain*; pl. *water,* 686

foris, -is, f. *door*; pl. *doors, entrance*

formīdō, -inis, f. *fear, dread, panic*

fors, f. *chance,* only used in nom. and abl. **fors et,** 139 *perhaps.* **forte,** *by chance, as it happened.* **si forte,** 756 *if by chance, in the hope that possibly*

forsitan, adv. *perhaps*

fortis, -e, adj. *bold, brave.* **fortior, fortissimus**

fortūna, -ae, f. *fortune; chance of safety,* 656

fragor, -ōris, m. *breaking, crash*

frangō, -ere, frēgī, fractum, v. tr. *break, crush*

fremitus, -ūs, m. *roaring, roar*

fretum, -ī, n. *strait, foam* of the sea, *sea*

frīgidus, -a, -um, adj. *cold*

frons, frondis, f. *branch, foliage*

frustrā, adv. *in vain*

frux, frūgis, f. mostly in pl. **frūgēs,** *fruit of the earth, corn.* **salsae frūgēs,** 133

fuga, -ae, f. *flight, retreat*

fugiō, -ere, fūgī, v. intr. and tr. *flee, flee from, escape*

fulgeō, -ēre (or **fulgō, -ere**), **fulsī,** v. intr. *gleam, shine*

fulmen, -inis, n. *thunderbolt*

fulvus, -a, -um, adj. *yellow, tawny*

fūmō, -āre, -āvī, v. intr. *smoke, reek*

fūmus, -i. m. *smoke*

fundāmentum, -ī, n. *foundation*

fundō, -ere, fūdī, fūsum, v. tr. *pour, pour forth; spread out light,* 683; *rout,* 421; *spread out;* **fūsī,** 252, *lying at their ease*

fundus, -i. m. *bottom, depth*

fūnis, -is, m. *rope*

fūnus, -eris, n. *funeral, death*: pl. *carnage,* 361

furiō, -āre, -āvī, -ātum, v. tr. *make furious, enrage, madden;* **furiātus,** *maddened, frenzied*

furō, -ere, -uī, v. intr. *rave, rage, rush madly,* 771; **furens,** *mad,* 499; *inspired,* 345
furor, -ōris, m. *rage, madness, frenzy*
furtim, adv. *by stealth*
futūrus, -a, -um, fut. part. of **sum,** as adj. *to come, future*

G

galea, -ae, f. *helmet*
gaudeō, -ēre, gāvīsus sum, v. intr. *rejoice; delight to*
gaza, -ae, f. *treasure*
gelidus, -a, -um, adj. *cold, icy*
geminus, -a, -um, adj. *twin-born, twin; two,* 203
gemitus, -ūs, m. *groan, roar; pitiful cry,* 73, etc.
gener, -erī, m. *son-in-law*
genetrix, -īcis, f. *mother*
genitor, -ōris, m. *father*
gens, -tis, f. *family, race*
genus, -eris, n. *race, descent, kin, kind*
gerō, -ere, gessī, gestum, v. tr. *bear, carry, wear; enjoy,* 90
glomerō, -āre, -āvī, -ātum, v. tr. *form into a ball; gather together, assemble*
glōria, -ae, f. *glory*
Gorgō or **Gorgōn, -onis,** f. *a Gorgon,* creatures with serpent locks and the power of turning beholders into stone; the head of one of them, Medusa, was fixed by Pallas on her shield, 616
gradus, -ūs, m. *step; step* or *rung* of ladder, 443
Graecus, -a, -um, adj. *Greek*
Graius, -a, -um, adj. *Greeks,* 148, 157, etc.
grāmen, -inis, n. *grass;* pl. *herbage*

grātēs, only in nom. and acc. f. pl. *thanks*
grātus, -a, -um, adj. *pleasing, welcome;* comp. **grātior, grātissimus**
gravis, -e, adj. *heavy*
graviter, adv. *heavily*
gravō, -āre, -āvī, -ātum, v. tr. *make heavy, burden*
gressus, -ūs, m. *step*
gurges, -itis, m. *whirlpool; violent torrent,* 497

H

habeō, -ēre, -uī, -itum, v. tr. *have; hold, regard*
haereō, -ēre, haesī, haesum, v. intr. *cling, cling to, stick to, remain steadfast* or *unmoved*
hasta, -ae, f. *spear*
haud, adv. *not at all; not*
hauriō, -īre, hausī, haustum, v. tr. *drink up; draw (blood), devour,* 600
hebetō, -āre, -āvī, -ātum, v. tr. *make dull, dull*
Hector, -oris, m. *son of Priam, bravest of the Trojans, slain by Achilles,* 270, 275, 282, 522
Hectoreus, -a, -um, adj. *of Hector,* 543
Hecuba, -ae, f. *wife of Priam,* 501, 515
Hesperius, -a, -um, adj. *western,* and so *Italian* when contrasted with Greece or Asia, 781
heu, interj. *alas!*
hīc, adv. *here; hereupon*
hic, haec, hoc (or **hōc**), dem. adj. and pron. *this*
hiems, hiemis, f. *winter, storm*
hinc, adv. *hence, from this place; from this cause; hereupon; from this time, henceforth*
hodiē, adv. *today*
homō, -inis, m. *man*

horrendus, -a, -um, gerundive from **horreō** as adj. *horrible, dreadful*

horreō, -ēre, horruī, v. intr. *shudder*

horrescō, -ere, horruī, v. intr. *begin to shudder*

horror, -ōris, m. *shuddering, horror, dread,* 559; **armōrum h.** 301, *the alarm of battle*

hortor, -ārī, -ātus sum, v. dep. tr. *encourage, exhort, advise, urge*

hostia, -ae, f. *sacrificial victim*

hostis, -is, m. *stranger, enemy*

hūc, adv. *hither, to this place, into this place, here*

humus, -ī, f. *ground;* **humī** is the locative case used adverbially, *on the ground*

Hypanis, -is, m., name of a Trojan, 340, 428

I

iaceō, -ēre, -uī, -itum, v. intr. *lie, am prostrate*

iactō, -āre, -āvī, -ātum, v. tr. *keep throwing, fling; utter wildly,* 588

iactūra, -ae, f. *flinging away, loss*

iaculor, -ārī, -ātus sum, v. dep. tr. *fling, hurl*

iam, adv. *already, now; by now, at last; soon,* 662; with negatives, *any longer*

iamdūdum, adv. *already some time since, long ago*

iamprīdem, adv. *for a long time now*

iānua, -ae, f. *gate, door*

ibi, adv. *there, then*

ictus, -ūs, m. *stroke, blow;* **sine ictū,** 544, *without wounding, ineffectually*

Īda, -ae, f. a mountain close to Troy, 801

Īdaeus, -a, -um, adj. *of Mount Ida, Idaean,* 696

ignārus, -a, -um, adj. *not knowing, ignorant; ignorant of,* with gen.

ignis, -is, m. *fire; lightning,* 649

ignōtus, -a, -um, adj. *unkown*

Īliacus, -a, -um, adj. *belonging to Ilium,* 117, 431

Īlias, -adis, f. *Trojan woman,* 580

īlicet, adv. *forthwith, immediately*

Īlium, -ī, n. poetic name for *Troy,* 241, 325, 625

ille, illa, illud, dem. pron. *that; that famous; that man, woman, thing; he, she, it*

illīc, adv. *in that place, there*

imāgō, -inis, f. *phantom; form; mental image, thought, vision,* 560

imbellis, -e, adj. *unwarlike*

immānis, -e, adj. *huge, vast, awful, monstrous*

immemor, -oris, adj. *unmindful*

immensus, -a, -um, adj. *immeasurable, boundless, monstrous*

immisceō, -ēre, -uī, -mixtum, v. tr. *intermingle*

immittō, -ere, -mīsī, -missum, v. tr. *send against, let loose*

impellō, -ere, -pulī, -pulsum, v. tr. *drive on, urge, push forward*

imperium, -ī, n. *military command; empire*

impetus, -ūs, m. *onset, attack*

impius, -a, -um, adj. *unholy*

impleō, -ēre, -ēvī, -ētum, v. tr. *fill up, fill*

implicō, -āre, -āvi or **-uī, -ātum** or **-itum,** v. tr. *entwine*

impōnō, -ere, -posuī, -positum, v. tr. *place on, set to*

improbus, -a, -um, adj. *excessive, immoderate; reckless* hunger, 356; *shameless,* 80

imprōvidus, -a, -um, adj. *unforeseeing*

imprōvīsus, -a, -um, adj. *unforeseen, sudden*

īmus, -a, -um, adj. used as superl. of **inferus,** *lowest, bottom of; inmost,* **per īma ossa,** 120, *through his very bones;* **ex īmō,** 625, *from its foundations*

in, prep. with acc. *towards, into, against, among;* with abl. *in, on, amid; in the case of,* 390, 541

incendium, -ī, n. *burning, fire, blaze, conflagration*

incendō, -ere, -cendī, -censum, v. tr. *kindle, fire*

inceptum, -ī, n. *beginning; design, purpose*

incertus, -a, -um, adj. *not sure, doubtful, unstable, fickle; ill aimed,* 224

incidō, -ere, -cidī, -cāsum, v. intr. *fall on*

incipiō, -ere, -cēpī, -ceptum, v. tr. and intr. *begin*

inclēmentia, -ae, f. *lack of pity, cruelty*

inclūdō, -ere, -clūsī, -clūsum, v. tr. *shut in*

inclutus, -a, -um, adj. *famous*

incolumis, -e, adj. *safe, unharmed*

incomitātus, -a, -um, adj. *unaccompanied*

incumbō, -ere, -cubuī, -cubitum, v. intr. with dat. *lean upon; add fresh weight to,* 653; **inc. pelagō,** 205, *skim over the sea*

incurrō, -ere, -currī (or **-cucurrī**), **-cursum,** v. intr. *run into or against; fall upon,* 409

incūsō, -āre, -āvī, -ātum, v. tr. *bring charge against, accuse*

inde, adv. *from that place or time, then, from there*

indicium, -ī, n. *information, charge*

indignor, ārī, -ātus sum, v. intr. and tr. *am wrathful; be idignant over*

indignus, -a, -um, adj. *unworthy; cruel,* 285

indomitus, -a, -um, adj. *unrestrained, unchecked, uncontrolled*

indulgeō, -ēre, dulsī, dultum, v. intr. with dat. *yield to, indulge in*

induō, -ere, -duī, -dūtum, v. tr. *don, put on.* Mid. **induitur,** 393, *he puts on;* **indūtus,** 275, *having put on*

inēluctābilis, -e, adj. *not to be struggled out of, inevitable*

inermis, -e, adj. *unarmed*

iners, -ertis, adj. *inactive; motionless, lifeless*

infandus, -a, -um, adj. *unspeakable; awful, monstrous; too grievous to tell,* 3

infēlīx, -īcis, adj. *unhappy, luckless, ill starred*

infensus, -a, -um, adj. *hostile*

infestus, -a, -um, adj. *unsafe, dangerous; hostile*

infula, -ae, f. *headband, fillet,* 430

ingeminō, -āre, -āvī, -ātum, v. tr. *redouble, repeat*

ingens, -entis, adj. *huge*

ingrātus, -a, -um, adj. *unpleasant, ungrateful*

ingruō, -ere, -gruī, v. intr. *rush on, bear down (on), roll onward,* 301

iniciō, -ere, -iēcī, -iectum, v. tr. *fling on, throw into, fling at*

inimīcus, -a, -um, adj. *unfriendly, hostile*

inīquus, -a, -um, adj. *unfavorable*

inlābor, -lābī, -lapsus, v. dep. intr. *glide into*

inlūdō, -ere, -lūsī, -lūsum, v. intr. and tr. *make fun of, mock at, insult*

innoxius, -a, -um, adj. *harmless*

innuptus, -a, -um, adj. *unmarried, unwedded,* 31

inquam, v. defective, *say*

inritus, -a, -um, adj. *vain, useless*

inruō, -ere, -uī, v. intr. *rush on* or *into*

insānia, -ae, f. *madness*

insānus, -a, -um, adj. *not healthy, mad, frantic*

inscius, -a, -um, adj. *ignorant; in dazed ignorance,* 307

insequor, -ī, -secūtus sum, v. dep. tr. *follow after, pursue*

insertō, -āre, -āvī, -ātum, v. tr. *insert, put into*

insideō, -ēre, -sēdī, -sessum, v. intr. and tr. *am seated in; take possession of, occupy*

insidiae, -ārum, f. pl. *ambush, plot, snare, fraud*

insigne, -is, n. *ornament, mark of distinction; badge,* 389

insinuō, -āre, -āvī, -ātum, v. tr. and intr. *twine, wind into, penetrate, creep*

insonō, -āre, -uī, -itum, v. intr. *sound within, echo*

insons, -sontis, adj. *guiltless*

inspiciō, -ere, -spexī, -spectum, v. tr. *look into; spy into,* 47

instar, n. indecl. *image, likeness;* with gen. 15

instaurō, -āre, -āvī, -ātum, v. tr. *repair, renew*

insternō, -ere, -strāvī, -strātum, v. tr. *lay upon; cover over.* In mid. sense, 722

instō, -āre, -stitī, v. intr. *press on;* with inf. *strive eagerly to*

instruō, -ere, -struxī, -structum, v. tr. *build up, equip, furnish;* **instructīs nāvibus,** 254, *with ships arrayed for battle*

insula, -ae, f. *island*

insultō, -āre, -āvī, -ātum, v. intr. *leap upon; taunt*

insuper, adv. *in addition*

integer, -gra, -grum, adj. *untouched; undamaged, unmarred, sound*

intemerātus, -a, -um, adj. *unviolated; inviolable,* 143

intendō, -ere, -tendī, -tensum or **-tentum,** v. tr. *stretch or direct towards; draw tightly,* 237

intentus, -a, um adj. *stretched toward, eager, intent*

inter, prep. with acc. *among, between*

interclūdō, -ere, -clūsī, -clūsum, v. tr. *hinder, prevent*

intereā, adv. *meanwhile*

interior, ius, comp. adj. *inner*

intexō, -ere, -texuī, -textum, v. tr. *weave in, interlace*

intonō, -āre, -uī, v. intr. *thunder;* **intonat** impersonally, *it thunders*

intorqueō, -ēre, -torsī, -tortum, v. tr. *hurl against*

intrā, prep. with acc. *within*

intus, adv. *from within, within*

inultus, -a, -um, adj. *unavenged*

inūtilis, -e, adj. *useless*

invādō, -ere, -vāsī, -vāsum, v. intr. and tr. *go against, rush upon, attack*

inveniō, -īre, -vēnī, -ventum, v. tr. *come upon, find*

inventor, -ōris, m. *discoverer, contriver*

invidia, -ae, f. *envy*

invīsus, -a, -um, (1) part. of **invideō,** *hated, hateful.* (2) adj. *unseen*

invītus, -a, -um, adj. *unwilling, against one's will*

involvō, -ere, -volvī, -volūtum, v. tr. *enroll, enwrap*

Īphitus, -ī, m. a Trojan, 435

ipse, -a, -um, pron. *himself, herself, itself; very*

īra, -ae, f. *anger, wrath; angry longing,* 575

is, ea, id, demonstr. pron. *that; he, she, it*

iste, -a, -ud, pron. dem. *that, that of yours,* 661

ita, adv. *in this way, thus, so*

iter, itineris, n. *road, journey, way*

iterum, adv. *a second time, again*

Ithacus, -a, -um, adj. *belonging to Ithaca,* an island in the Ionian sea, the home of Ulysses, 104, etc.

iuba, -ae, f. *crest, mane, plume*

iubeō, -ēre, iussī, iussum, v. tr. *bid, command*

iugum, -ī, n. *that which joins; yoke; mountain ridge*

Iūlus, -ī, m. son of Aeneas, 563, etc.

iunctūra, -ae, f. *joint, joinings*

iungō, -ere, iunxī, iunctum, v. tr. *join, unite*

Iūnō, -ōnis, f. queen of heaven, wife of Jupiter, the bitter enemy of Troy, 612, 761

Iūppiter, Iovis, m. *Iupiter,* the greatest of the gods; 326, 689, *the god of the clear sky, heaven, the sky*

iūs, iūris, n. *right; human law*

iussum, -ī, n. *command*

[iussus, -ūs,] m., only in abl.sing. *command*

iustus, -a, -um, adj. *just, righteous*

iuvenālis, -e, adj. *youthful*

iuvenis, -is, m. and f. originally adj. *young,* then used as subst. *youth, young man*

iuventa, -ae, f. *youth*

iuventūs, -ūtis, f. *youth; body of young men*

iuvō, -āre, iūvī, iūtum, v. tr. *assist;* **iuvat,** impersonally, *it delights, is a pleasure to, is my joy to*

iuxtā, adv. and prep. with acc. *next, close to, near*

L

lābēs, -is, f. *slipping, downfall;* **mali l.** 97, *slip towards destruction*

labō, -āre, -āvī, -ātum, v. intr. *totter, reel;* **labans,** *weak, yielding,* 463

labor, -ōris, m. *labor; distress, toil, agony;* pl. *sufferings, troubles.* In 306 *things produced by labor*

lābor, -ī, lapsus sum, v. dep. intr. *glide, glide past, slip, fall down*

Lacaena, -ae, f. *Spartan woman,* 601

lacrima, -ae, f. *tear*

lacrimō, -āre, -āvī, -ātum, v. intr. *weep*

lacus, -ūs, m. *lake; marsh,* 135

laedō, -ere, laesī, laesum, v. tr. *hurt, injure; outrage,* 231

laetus, -a, -um, adj. *glad; joyous, prosperous, rich; bounteous,* 306 n.

laevus, -a, -um, *left, on the left hand;* **intonuit laevum,** 693 *it thundered on the left; foolish, misled; unfavorable, misleading, perverse,* 54; **laeva, -ae,** f. (sc. **manus**) *left hand*

lambō, -ere, -ī, v. tr. *lick*

lāmentābilis, -e, adj. *to be lamented*

Lāocoōn, -ontis, m. priest of Apollo, 41, 201, 213, 230

lapsō, -āre, v. intr. *slip, stumble*

lapsus, -ūs, m. *gliding;* **rotārum l.** 236, *smooth gliding wheels*

largus, -a, -um, adj. *plentiful, abundant*

Lārisaeus, -a, -um, adj. *connected with Larissa, a town in Thesaly,* 197

lassus, -a, -um, adj. *faint, weary*

lātē, adv. *far and wide*

latebra, -ae, f. (rare in sing.) *lurking-place, retreat*

lateō, -ēre, -uī, v. intr. *lie hid, lurk*

latus, -eris, n. *side*

lātus, -a, -um, adj. *broad*

laudō, -āre, -āvī, -ātum, v. tr. *praise*

laurus, -ī and **-ūs,** f. *laurel*

laus, laudis, f. *praise, renown*

laxō, -āre, -āvī, -ātum, v. intr. *loosen, release*

legō, -ere, lēgī, lectum, v. tr. *pick, choose; gather up; pass over surface of, skim,* 208

lēnis, -e, adj. *gentle, smooth, calm*

leō, -ōnis, m. *lion*

lētum, -ī, n. *death*

levis, -e, adj. *light, fickle; flickering*

levō, -āre, -āvī, -ātum, v. tr. *make light; ease, relieve; remove*

lex, lēgis, f. *law*

lignum, -ī, n. *wood*

ligō, -āre, -āvī, -ātum, v. tr. *bind*

līmen, -inis, n. *threshold, door*

līmes, -itis, m. *boundary; path*

līmōsus, -a, -um, adj. *muddy*

lingua, -ae, f. *tongue*

linquō, -ere, līquī, v. tr. *leave*

litō, -āre, -āvī, -ātum, v. intr. *make a sacrifice with favorable results, receive favorable omens*

lītus, -oris, n. *shore*

locō, -āre, -āvī, -ātum, v. tr. *place*

locus, -ī, m. (pl.: **loci,** m. and **loca,** n.) *place, position, room*

longaevus, -a, -um, adj. *of great age, aged*

longē, adv. *afar, at a distance*

longus, -a, -um, adj. *long*

loquor, -ī, locūtus sum, v. dep. tr. *speak; speak of*

lōrum, -ī, n. *thong, rein*

lūbricus, -a, -um, adj. *slippery*

Lūcifer, -erī, m. *the morning star,* 801

luctus, -ūs, m. *grief, lamentation, cry of grief*

lūgeō, -ēre, luxī, luctum, v. intr. and tr. *bewail, lament*

lūmen, -inis, n. *light; eye*

lūna, -ae, f. *moon;* **per lunam,** 340, *in the moonlight*

lupus, -ī, m. *wolf*

lustrō, -āre, -āvī, -ātum, v. tr. *go round; traverse; survey, scan,* 754

lux, lūcis, f. *light; day,* 668; *sheen, reflection,* 470

Lӯdius, -a, -um, adj. *connected with Lydia, a district on the W. coast of Asia Minor,* 781

M

Machāon, -onis, a Greek, son of Aesculapius, famous as a surgeon, 263

māchina, -ae, f. *machine, engine*

mactō, -āre, -āvī, -ātum, v. tr. *slay, sacrifice*

maestus, -a, -um, adj. *sad;* comp. **maestior;** superl. **maestissimus**

magis, comp. adv. *more*

magnus, -a, -um, adj. *great, mighty; loud,* **magnō,** 104, *at a high price;* comp. **māior;** sup. **maximus**

male, adv. *badly;* **m. fida,** 23, *treacherous;* **m. amicus,** 735 *unfriendly*

malum, -i. n. *evil; trouble, destruction,* 97

malus, -a, -um, adj. *bad; baneful, poisonous,* 471; comp. **pēior;** sup. **pessimus**

maneō, -ēre, mansī, mansum, v. intr. and tr. *remain, last.* **prōmissīs m.** 160, *abide by your promise.* With acc. 194, *await, be in store for*

manica, -ae, f. *handcuff; fetter*

manifestus, -a, -um, adj. *palpable, clear, plain*

manus, -ūs, f. *hand; handful; band, troop*

mare, -is, n. *sea*

Mars, Martis, m. god of War; hence *war,* 335, 440

māter, mātris, f. *mother*

mēcum, for **cum mē,** *with me; to myself,* 93

medius, -a, -um, adj. *middle, midst of* **medium,** 218, *his waist*

melior, -ius adj. used as comp. of **bonus,** *better*

meminī, -isse, v. defective tr. *remember*

memorābilis, -e, adj. *deserving to be related, memorable*

memorō, -āre, -āvī, -ātum, v. tr. *relate, tell, say*

mendax, -ācis, adj. *lying*

Menelāus, -ī, m. son of Atreus, brother of Agamemnon, husband of Helen, 264

mens, mentis, f. *mind, soul, thought*

mensa, -ae, f. *table*

mentior, -īrī, -ītus sum, v. dep. intr. *lie; falsely state*

mercor, -ārī, -ātus sum, v. dep. tr. *buy, purchase*

mereō, -ēre, -uī, -itum, also as dep. **mereor, -ērī, meritus sum,** v. intr. and tr. *deserve, merit*

metus, -ūs, m. *fear*

meus, -a, -um, poss. adj. *my:* **meī,** *my people, kin,* etc.

micō, -āre, -uī, v. intr. *move quickly to and fro; flicker,* 475

mīles, -itis, m. *soldier; body of soldiers, soldiery*

mille, num. adj. indecl. *one thousand;* in pl., neut. declinable subst. **mīlia** *thousands*

Minerva, -ae, goddess of wisdom; identified with the goddess Pallas, who aided the Greeks in the Trojan wars, 31, 189, 404

minister, -trī, m. *attendant; aider, abettor*

ministra, -ae, f. *female attendant, servant*

minor, -ārī, -ātus sum, v. dep. intr. and tr. *overhang; threaten*

mīrābilis, -e, adj. *wonderful*

mīror, -ārī, -ātus sum, v. dep. intr. and tr. *admire; wonder at*

misceō, -ēre, -uī, mixtum, v. tr. *mingle, confound;* **incendia m.** 329, *spreads fire and confusion;* **miscentur moenia luctū,** 298 n. *the city is thrown into confusion*

miser, -era, -erum, adj. superl. **miserrimus,** *wretched, unhappy*

miserābilis, -e, adj. *pitiable, wretched*

misereor, -ērī, -itus sum, v. dep. intr. with gen. *pity*

miserescō, -ere, v. intr. *feel pity*

mittō, -ere, mīsī, missum, v. tr. *send*

modo, adv. *only*

moenia, -ium, n. pl. *walls, a fortress; city buildings,* opp. to **mūrus,** 234

mōlēs, -is, f. *mass, huge mass; monster,* 185; *bank,* 497; *pile*

mōlior, -īrī, -ītus sum, v. dep. tr.
perform with toil, undertake;
fugam m., 109, take flight
mollis, -e, adj. *soft*
moneō, -ēre, -uī, -itum, v. tr. *warn,
advise*
mons, -tis, m. *mountain*
monstrō, -āre, -āvī, -ātum, v. tr. *show*
monstrum, -ī, n. *omen; prodigy,
monster*
montānus, -a, -um, adj. *belonging to a
mountain*
mora, -ae, f. *delay*
morior, -ī, mortuus sum, v. dep. intr.
die
moror, -ārī, -ātus sum, v. dep. tr.
and intr. *delay; linger; heed, pay
attention to*, 287
mors, -tis, f. *death*
morsus, -ūs, m. *bite*
mortālis, -e, adj. *mortal, human*; as
subst. *a mortal*
moveō, -ēre, mōvī, mōtum, v. tr. *move;
arouse, stir*, 96
mucrō, -ōnis, m. *point, edge; blade*, 449
mūgitus, -ūs, m. *bellowing*
multō, adv. *by much, far*
multus, -a, -um, adj. *much, many a*; in
pl. *many*
mūrus, -ī, m. *wall, city wall*, opp. to
moenia, 234
mūtō, -āre, -āvī, -ātum, v. tr. *change;
exchange*
Mycēnae, -ārum, f. the royal city of
Agamemnon in Argolis, 25, 180,
331, 577
Mygdonidēs, -ae, m. patronymic, *son
of Mygdon*, viz. Coroebus, 342
Myrmidonēs, -um, m. a people of
Thessaly and the subjects of
Achilles, 7, 252, 785

N

nam, namque, conj. *for*
narrō, -āre, -āvī, -ātum, v. tr. *tell,
relate*
nascor, -ī, nātus sum, v. dep. intr. *am
born.* nate deā, 289, *goddess born*
nātus, -ī, m. *son*; nāta, -ae, f. *daughter*;
nātī, *children*
nāvis, -is, f. *ship*
nē, adv. with imperative, *not, do not*;
conj. with subj. *lest, that not.* nēve
(neu)…nēve (neu)…, *neither…nor*
-ne, interrog. enclitic particle; mēne,
657
nebula, -ae, f. *mist*
nec, see neque
nefandus, -a, -um, adj. *unutterable;
impious*
nefās, n. indecl. *that which divine law
forbids; guilt; sacrilege, impiety; a
guilty creature*, 585
negō, -āre, -āvī, -ātum, v. tr. *say no,
deny*
Neoptolemus, -ī, m. son of Achilles,
also called Pyrrhus, 263, 500, 549
nepōs, -ōtis, m. *grandson, descendant*
Neptūnius, -a, -um, adj. *connected
with Neptune*
Neptūnus, -ī, m. the god of the sea,
201, 610
neque or nec, conj. *neither*; neque…
neque, *neither…nor.* neque enim,
for indeed…not
nēquīquam, adv. *in vain, idly*
Nēreūs, -eī and -eōs, a sea-god, 419
nesciō, -īre, -īvī or -iī, -scītum, v. tr.
not to know. nesciō quod, 735,
used as adj. *I know not what,
some…*
neu or nēve, see nē
nex, necis, f. *murder, death*

nī or **nisi,** conj. *unless*

nihil or **nīl,** indecl. *nothing, nought*; as adv. *in no way*

nimbus, -ī, m. *rain-cloud, storm cloud, dark cloud*

nitidus, -a, -um, adj., *shining, bright, glistening*

nītor, -ī, nīsus or **nixus sum,** v. dep. intr. *strive; climb* with effort; *force one's way,* 443; **nītens,** 380, *pressing down, stepping*

nōdus, -ī, m. *knot*

nōmen, -inis, n. *name; reputation*

nōn, adv. *not*

nōs, pl. of **ego,** *we*

noscō, -ere, nōvī, nōtum, 3. v. tr. *learn*; in perf. *know*

noster, -tra, -trum, adj. *our*; **nostrī,** as subst. *those of our side, our friends,* etc.

nōtus, -a, -um, adj. *well-known, familiar*; **sic nōtus Vlixēs,** 44, *Is Ulysses known to us in this way?*; superl. **nōtissimus,** 21 **(noscō); nōtā** 773

Notus, -ī, m. *South wind,* 417

novus, -a, -um, adj. *new, fresh, strange*

nox, noctis, f. *night*

nūbēs, -is, f. *cloud*

nūdus, -a, -um, adj. *naked, bare, uncovered*

nullus, -a, -um, adj. *not any, no, none*

nūmen, -inis, n. *a nod; divine will, divine purpose,* 123; *divine power, majesty, power; diety*

numerus, -ī, m. *number*

numquam, adv. *never*; as emphatic negative, 670

nunc, adv. *now*

nuntius, -ī, m. *messenger, message*

nurus, -ūs, f. *daughter-in-law*

nusquam, adv. *nowhere*

nūtō, -āre, -āvī, -ātum, v. intr. *nod, sway to and fro*

O

Ō, interj. *O!*

ob, prep. with acc. *on account of*

obdūcō, -ere, -duxī, -ductum, v. tr. *draw over, cover*

obiectō, -āre, -āvī, -ātum, v. tr. *fling to, expose*

obiciō, -ere, -iēcī, -iectum, v. tr. *fling to; present against,* 444

oblātus, see **offerō**

oblīviscor, -ī, oblītus sum, v. dep. tr. *forget*

obruō, -ere, -uī, -utum, v. tr. *overwhelm*

obscūrus, -a, -um, adj. *dim, dark, hidden*

observō, -āre, -āvī, -ātum, v. tr. *watch, observe, mark*

obsideō, -ēre, -sēdī, -sessum, v. tr. *sit down against; beseige; am stationed at,* 450

obstipescō, -ere, -stipuī, v. intr. *become amazed, confounded, stand amazed*

obtegō, -ere, -texī, -tectum, v. tr. *cover over, hide*

obtruncō, -āre, -āvī, -ātum, v. tr. *cut to pieces, butcher*

occāsus, -ūs, m. *fall, destruction*

occidō, -ere, -cidī, -cāsum, v. intr. *fall down, perish*

occultō, -āre, -āvī, -ātum, v. tr. *conceal*

occumbō, -ere, -cubuī, -cubitum, v. intr. *fall down*; with dat. *yield to; meet,* 62

Ōceanus, -ī, m. *ocean*

oculus, -ī, m. *eye*

ōdī, ōdisse, v. defective tr. *hate*

odium, -ī, n. *hate*

offerō, offerre, obtulī, oblātum, v.
tr. *put before, present*; **sē offert,**
371, *comes to meet us*; **oblātī,** 340,
appeared
Olympus, -ī, m. a mountain in
Thessaly, the seat of the gods;
heaven, 779
ōmen, -inis, n. *omen, sign*
omnipotens, -entis, adj. *omnipotent,*
almighty
omnis, -e, adj. *all, whole*
onus, -eris, n. *burden*
opācus, -a, -um, adj. *shady*; **opāca**
locōrum, 725, *those spots that were*
in shadow
opīmus, -a, -um, adj. *rich*
oppōnō, -ere, -posuī, -positum, v. tr.
place opposite, expose to; **oppositī,**
333, *facing all comers, hostile*;
oppositās, 497, *opposing*
ops, opis, f. *aid, help, power*; in pl.
opēs, *wealth, resources*
optō, -āre, -āvī, -ātum, v. tr. *desire*
opus, -eris, n. *work*
ōra, -ae, f. *shore, coast*
ōrāculum, -ī, n. *oracle*
orbis, -is, m. *round, circuit, circle; coil,*
204
Orcus, -ī, m. *the lower world*
ordior, īrī, orsus sum. v. dep. tr. and
intr. *begin*
ordō, -inis, m. *order, row, rank*; **ūnō**
ordine, 102, *in one rank*, i.e. *alike*
orior, īrī, ortus sum, v. dep. intr. *arise,*
rise
ornus, -ī, f. *mountain ash*
ōrō, -āre, -āvī, -ātum, v. tr. *pray,*
entreat
ōs, ōris, n. *mouth; face, lips; opening,*
482
os, ossis, n. *bone*
osculum, -ī, n. *kiss*

ostendō, -ere, -tendī, -tensum and
-tentum, v. tr. *show*
Othryadēs, -ae, m. patronymic, *son of*
Othrys, viz. Panthus, 319, 336

P

Palamēdēs, -is, m. king of Euboea; lost
his life through the treachery of
Ulysses, 82
Palladium, -ī, n. *The Palladium,*
an image of Pallas supposed to
have fallen from heaven. On its
preservation depended the safety
of Troy, 166, 183
Pallas, -adis, f. Greek name for
Minerva, the goddess of war and
wisdom, 15, 163, 615
palma, -ae, f. *palm* of the hand
palūs, -ūdis, f. *marsh*
pandō, -ere, pandī, pansum and
passum, v. tr. *open, unfold, open*
out; **passīs crīnibus,** 403, *with*
dishevelled hair
Panthūs, voc. **-thū,** a Trojan,
nephew of Hecuba and father of
Euphorbus, 318, etc.
pār, paris, adj. *equal, like*
parcō, -ere, pepercī, v. intr. with dat.
spare; cease
parens, -tis, m. and f. *parent*
pāreō, -ēre, -uī, -itum, v. intr. with dat.
obey
pariēs, -etis m. *wall* of house
pariō, -ere, peperī, partum, v. tr.
produce; procure, gain, win
Paris, -idis, m. son of Priam; carried
off Helen and so caused the Trojan
war, 602
pariter, adv. *equally, alike; side by side,*
205
parma, -ae, f. small round *shield*

parō, -āre, -āvī, -ātum, v. tr. *make ready, prepare.* **parātus,** 799, *ready*
pars, -tis, f. *part*; often = *some,* 31, etc.
parvus, -a, -um, adj. *small; comp.* **minor;** superl. **minimus**
pascor, pāsci, pāstus sum, v. dep. *feed, feed on,*
passim, adv. *everywhere, scattered*
passus, -ūs, m. *pace, step*
passus, part. (1) of **pandō,** see above; (2) of **patior,** see below
pastor, -ōris, m. *shepherd*
patefaciō, -ere, -fēcī, -factum, v. tr. *make open, open*
pateō, -ēre, -uī, v. intr. *am open*
pater, patris, m. *father.* **pater,** *the Father,* i.e. Jupiter, 617
patescō, -ere, patuī, v. inceptive intr. *begin to be open or obvious*
patior, patī, passus sum, v. dep. tr. *suffer, endure*
patria, -ae, f. *fatherland, homeland*
patrius, -a, -um, adj. *belonging to one's father or fatherland, father's, native*
paulātim, adv. *little by little*
pauper, -eris, adj. *poor*
pavidus, -a, -um, adj. *terrified*
pavitō, -āre, -āvī, -ātum, v. intr. *am in great fear*
pavor, -ōris, m. *fear, panic*
pectus, -oris, n. *breast, heart*
pelagus, -ī, n. *sea*
Pelasgī, -ōrum, m. the oldest inhabitants of Greece, hence simply *Greeks,* 83; **Pelasgus, -a, -um,** adj. *Greek,* 106, 152
Peliās, -ae, m. companion of Aeneas, 435, 436
Pēlīdēs, -ae, m. patronymic, *son of Peleus,* 548 (= Achilles) or *descendant of Peleus,* 263 (= Pyrrhus)

pellax, -ācis, adj. *deceitful, seductive*
pellis, -is, f. *skin, hide*
pellō, -ere, pepulī, pulsum, v. tr. *drive away*
Pelopēus, -a, -um, adj. *belonging to Pelops* an ancient king of Elis after whom all southern Greece was called Peloponnesus, *Greek,* 193
penātēs, -ium, m. *gods of the household,* 293, 514, 717, 747
pendeō, -ēre, pependī, v. intr. *hang*
Pēneleus, -ī, m. a Greek, 425
penetrāle, -is, n. *inmost place, shrine;* pl. *chambers,* 484; **adytīs penetrālibus,** 297, as adj.
penitus, adv. *from within; utterly*
per, prep. with acc. *through, throughout, over, down, among, during;* **per superōs,** 141, *by the gods above;* **per lūnam,** 340, *in the moonlight*
pereō, -īre, -īvī or **-iī, -itum,** v. intr. *perish, die*
pererrō, -āre, -āvī, -ātum, v. tr. *wander over*
perfundō, -ere, -fūdī, -fūsum, v. tr. *soak, steep*
Pergama, -ōrum, n. the citadel of Troy, hence *Troy,* 177, 291, 375, 556, 571
perīculum or **perīclum, -ī,** n. *danger*
Periphās, -antis, m. a companion of Pyrrhus, 476
periūrus, -a, -um, adj. *forsworn*
perrumpō, -ere, -rūpī, -ruptum, v. tr. *break through*
persolvō, -ere, -solvī, -solūtum, v. tr. *pay in full*
perstō, -āre, -stitī, -stātum, v. intr. *persist, continue*
perveniō, -īre, -vēnī, -ventum, v. intr. *come to, reach*

pervius, -a, -um, adj. *providing a way through*; **p. usus**, 453, *a passage*
pēs, pedis, m. *foot*
petō, -ere, -īvī or -iī, ītum, v. tr. *seek, make for*
phalanx, -angis, f. *phalanx; dense mass of troops*
Phoebus, -ī, m. *poetical name of Apollo*, lit. *the radiant one*, 114, 319
Phoenix, -īcis, m. *a companion of Achilles*, 762
Phryges, -um, m. *inhabitants of Asia Minor in the district near Troy*, 191, 344
Phrygius, -a, -um, adj. *Phrygian*, 68, 276, 580
pietās, -ātis, f. *dutiful affection, piety, regard; regard of gods* for men, 536
pīneus, -a, -um, adj. *of pine*
piō, -āre, -āvī, -ātum, v. tr. *expiate*
placeō, -ēre, -uī, -itum, v. intr. with dat. *please*; **placet** impersonally, *it is pleasing to; it is resolved*, 659
plācō, -āre, -āvī, -ātum, v. tr. *appease, pacify*
plangor, -ōris, m. *beating of the breast, mourning*
plūrimus, -a, -um, superl. adj. *very much, great*; in pl. *very many*
poena, -ae, f. *punishment, vengeance*; **poenās dare**, *pay the penalty, suffer punishment*, etc.
Polītēs, -ae, m. *a son of Priam*, 526
polus, -ī, m. *the pole, heaven*
pōne, adv. *behind*
pōnō, -ere, posuī, positum, v. tr. *put, place; put aside*; **positum**, 644, intr. *laid out* for burial
pontus, -ī, m. *sea*
populus, -ī, m. *people, nation*
porta, -ae, f. *gate*

porticus, -ūs, f. *arcade, colonnade, cloisters*
portō, -āre, -āvī, -ātum, v. tr. *carry*
poscō, -ere, poposcī, v. tr. *demand, cry for*
possum, posse, potuī, v. irreg. intr. *am able, can*
post, prep. with acc. *after, behind*; adv. *afterwards*
postis, -is, f. *post*; pl. *doors*, 442; *gate*, 454
postquam, conj. *after*
potens, -entis, adj. *powerful, mighty*
praeceps, -cipitis, adj. *headforemost, headlong; driven headlong home*; as subst. *precipice*; **in praecipitī**, 460, *on a sheer edge*
praeceptum, -ī, n. *precept, instruction, warning*
praecipitō, -āre, -āvī, -ātum, v. intr. and tr. *fall* or *throw headlong, hurry downwards*, 9; *urge on*, 317
praecipuē, adv. *especially*
praecordia, -ōrum, n. *heart, breast*
praeda, -ae, f. *booty, spoil*
praemetuō, -ere, v. tr. *fear beforehand*. Rare word, 573
praemium, -ī, n. *reward*
[prec-], defective noun f., nom. and gen. sing. not found, **precem** and **precī**, rare, **prece** and pl. com., *prayer*
prehendō or prendō, -ere, -dī, -sum, v. tr. *seize, lay hold of, occupy*
premō, -ere, pressī, pressum, v. tr. *press; strike down, trample on*, 380; *pin, pierce*, 530
prensō, -āre, -āvī, -ātum, v. tr. *grasp strongly*
[prex, precis,] f., see [prec-]

Priamēius, -a, -um, adj. *of Priam;*
     P. virgō, 403, *the maiden, P.'s*
     daughter
Priamus, -ī, m. king of Troy during the
     siege, 22, etc.
prīdem, adv. *long ago;* **iam p.** *now for a*
     long time
prīmum, adv. *first, firstly*
prīmus, -a, -um, adj. *first, earliest; in*
     the lead, 613; **in līmine prīmō,**
     485, *on the very threshold*
principium, -ī, n. *beginning;* **principiō,**
     used as adv. *first,* 752
prius, adv. *sooner, before, first*
priusquam, or as two words **prius...**
     quam, conj. *before, till*
prō, prep. with abl. *for, in the place of,*
     before
prōcēdō, -ere, -cessī, -cessum, v. intr.
     advance
procul, adv. *at a distance, from afar*
prōcumbō, -ere, -cubuī, -cubitum, v.
     intr. *sink forwards, down, fall flat*
prōditiō, -ōnis, f. *a bringing forward;*
     betrayal; charge of treason, 83
prōdō, -ere, -didī, -ditum, v. tr. *put*
     forward; betray
prōdūcō, -ere, -duxī, -ductum, v. tr.
     lead forward, prolong
proelium, -ī, n. *battle*
prōlābor, -ī, -lapsus sum, v. dep. intr.
     glide forwards, sink down
prōmissum, -ī, n. *promise*
prōmittō, -ere, -mīsī, -missum, v. tr.
     promise
prōmō, -ere, prompsī, promptum, v.
     tr. *bring forth* or *out*
propinquō, -āre, -āvī, -ātum, v. intr.
     with dat. *approach*
propinquus, -a, -um, adj. *near; akin:*
     allied
propior, -ius, comp. adj. *nearer*

propius, comp. adv. *nearer*
prōsequor, -ī, -secūtus sum, v. dep.
     tr. and intr. *accompany, escort; go*
     forwards, continue speaking, 107
prospiciō, -ere, -spexī, -spectum, v.
     intr. *look forward*
prōtegō, -ere, -texī, -tectum, v. tr. *put*
     in front as a cover; protect
prōtinus, adv. *immediately*
prōtrahō, -ere, -traxī, -tractum, v. tr.
     drag forth
prōvehō, -ere, -vexī, -vectum, v. tr.
     carry forward; in pass. *sail to,*
     proceed to, 24
proximus, -a, -um, superl. adj. *nearest*
pūbēs, -is, f. *youth, body of youths*
puella, -ae, f. *girl, maiden*
puer, -erī, m. *boy, youth, young man*
pugna, -ae, f. *fight*
pulcher, -chra, -chrum, adj. *beautiful,*
     glorious
pulvis, -eris, m. *dust*
puppis, -is, f. *stern, ship*
pūrus, -a, -um, adj. *pure, bright*
putō, -āre, -āvī, -ātum, v. tr. *think*
Pyrrhus, -ī, son of Achilles, 469, etc.

Q

quā, adv. *by what way; where; wherever*
quaerō, -ere, quaesīvī, quaesītum,
     v. tr. *seek, search, enquire about,*
     question; gain, win
quālis, -e, adj. interrog. *of what sort;*
     rel. *of such a sort as*
quam, adv. *how, as;* conj. **prius...**
     quam, *before,* **post...quam,** *after,*
     etc.
quamquam, conj. *although*
quandō, adv. and conj. *when; because,*
     since
quantum, adv. *how much, how*

quantus, -a, -um, adj. *how great; as great as*

quater, num. adv. *four times*

quatiō, -ere, –, quassum, v. tr. *shake*

-que, conj. enclitic, *and;* **-que...-que** or **et,** *both...and*

quī, quae, quod, rel. pron. *who, which.* **ex quō,** 648, etc. *from the day,* or *time when,* i.e. *since*

quī, quae (or **qua**), **quod,** indef. adj. *any, some.* **nesciō quod,** see **nesciō**

quī, quae, quod, interrog. adj. *what? which?*

quia, conj. *because*

quīcumque, quaecumque, quodcumque, indef. rel. pron. and adj. *whoever, whatever*

quid, interrog. adv. *why?*

quidem, adv. *indeed*

quiēs, -ētis, f. *rest, repose, slumber*

quīn, conj. *but that;* to corroborate with or without **etiam,** *moreover*

quīnī, -ae, -a, distrib. num. adj. *five each, five*

quīnquāgintā, num. adj. *fifty*

quis, quid, interrog. pron. *who? what?*

quis, quae (or **qua**), **quid,** indef. pron. *any one, any.*

quisquam, quicquam (quidquam), indef. pron. *anyone, anything*

quisque, quaeque, quidque (quicque) or **quodque,** indef. pron. and adj. *each*

quisquis, quidquid (quicquid), indef. pron. *whoever, whatever*

quō, interrog. and rel. adv. *to where, for what purpose,* 150

quōcumque, adv. *wherever; howsoever;* **quō...cumque,** tmesis, 709

quod, conj. (1) *because;* (2) introd. substantival sentence, *that, the fact that,* 664

quod, used as adverb, *as to which, therefore,* 141

quōnam, adv. *whither?*

quondam, adv. *once, formerly; at times*

quoque, conj. *also, too*

quot, num. adj. indecl. *how many, as many as*

R

rabiēs, no gen. or dat. **rabiem, rabiē,** *rage*

rapidus, -a, -um, adj, *hurrying, rapid, swift, whirling*

rapiō, -ere, -uī, raptum, v. tr. *seize, snatch, take, plunder*

raptō, -āre, -āvī, -ātum, v. tr. *snatch violently, drag*

raptor, -ōris, m. *plunderer*

ratiō, -ōnis, f. *reason, cause*

raucus, -a, -um, adj. *hoarse; hollow sounding; echoing,* 545

recēdō, -ere, -cessī, -cessum, v. intr. *withdraw; retire, depart*

recens, -entis, adj. *fresh*

recipiō, -ere, -cēpī, -ceptum, v. tr. *take back, recover, admit, take in*

recondō, -ere, -didī, -ditum, v. tr. *hide far back, conceal*

recūsō, -āre, -āvī, -ātum, v. tr. *refuse*

recutiō, -ere, -cussī, -cussum, v. tr. *strike backwards* or *back.* **uterō recussō,** 52, *because its womb was made to vibrate*

reddō, -ere, reddidī, redditum, v. tr. *give back, restore; pay as due,* 537; *answer,* 323

redeō, -īre, īvī or **-iī, -itum,** v. intr. *return*

reditus, -ūs, m. *return*

redūcō, -ere, -duxī, -ductum, v. tr. *lead back, bring back*

referō, -ferre, rettulī, relātum, v. tr. *carry or take back; relate.* **mē ref.** 757, *I return;* pass. 169, *recede*

reflectō, -ere, -flexī, -flexum, v. tr. *bend back; cast behind,* 741

refugiō, -ere, -fūgī, v. intr. and tr. *flee back, shrink, start back; recoil from,* 380, with acc.

refulgeō, -ēre, -fulsī, v. intr. *shine out,* 590

rēgīna, -ae, f. *queen*

regiō, -ōnis, f. *direction,* 737; *district*

rēgius, -a, -um, adj. *royal*

regnātor, -ōris, m. *ruler*

regnum, -ī, n. *kingdom; royalty, princely place; power*

rēligiō, -ōnis, f. *religion, piety; object of religious awe; sacred offering,* 151

rēligiōsus, -a, -um, adj. *holy, sacred*

relinquō, -ere, -līquī, -lictum, v. tr. *leave behind, abandon, leave*

relūceō, -ēre, -luxī, *flash, gleam back*

remeō, -āre, -āvī, -ātum, v. intr. *return*

remētior, -īrī, -mensus sum, v. dep. tr. *measure back, retrace*

remittō, -ere, -mīsī, -missum, v. tr. *send back*

renovō, -āre, -āvī, -ātum, v. tr. *renew, try again*

reor, rērī, ratus sum, v. dep. intr. *think*

repellō, -ere, reppulī, repulsum, v. tr. *drive back; baffle, rebuff,* 13

rependō, -ere, -pendī, -pensum, v. tr. *weigh* or *pay back*

repente, adv. *suddenly*

repetō, -ere, -īvī or **-iī, -ītum,** v. tr. *reseek*

repleō, -ēre, -plēvī, -plētum, v. tr. *fill*

reportō, -āre, -āvī, -ātum, v. tr. *carry back*

reposcō, -ere, v. tr. *claim in return; demand*

reprimō, -ere, -pressī, -pressum, v. tr. *keep back, restrain*

requiescō, -ere, -quiēvī, -quiētum, v. intr. *rest*

requīrō, -ere, -quīsīvī, -quīsītum, v. tr. *seek to know, ask*

rēs, reī, f. *thing; affair; tale,* 196; **rēs laetae,** 783, *happy affairs, riches;* **rēs summa,** 322, *the main battle*

resideō, -ēre, -sēdī, v. intr. *sit down, stay behind*

resistō, -ere, -stitī, v. intr. *resist, withstand*

resolvō, -ere, -solvī, -solūtum, v. tr. *unloose, break, reveal*

respiciō, -ere, -spexī, -spectum, v. tr. *look back for or at*

responsum, -ī, n. *reply, answer*

restinguō, -ere, -stinxī, -stinctum, v. tr. *put out*

restō, -āre, -stitī, v. intr. *remain, am left*

retrō, adv. *backwards*

revertor, -ī, -versus sum, v. dep. intr. *return*

revinciō, -īre, -vinxī, -vinctum, v. tr. *bind back*

revīsō, -ere, v. tr. *revisit, seek again*

revolvō, -ere, -volvī, -volūtum, v. tr. *roll back; retrace tale,* 101

rex, rēgis, m. *king, prince*

Rhīpeus, -eos, m. comrade of Aeneas, 339, 394, 426

rōbur, -oris, n. *oak-wood, oak; strength*

rogō, -āre, -āvī, -ātum, v. tr. *ask*

roseus, -a, -um, adj. *rosy*

rota, -ae, f. *wheel*

ruīna, -ae, f. *downfall, ruin;* **trahit ruīnam,** 465, 631, *has come crashing down*

rumpō, -ere, rūpī, ruptum, v. tr. *break; cause to break forth; burst*

ruō, -ere, -uī, v. intr. *fall; rush; hurry,* 250

rursus, adv. *back again; anew*

S

sacer, -cra, -crum, adj. *holy, sacred;* **sacrum, -ī,** n. as subst. *sacred rite,* 132; *hymns,* 239; *sacred objects,* 293

sacerdōs, -ōtis, m. *priest*

sacrō, -āre, -āvī, -ātum, v. tr. *make holy, hallow;*

saepe, adv. *often*

saeviō, -īre, -iī, -ītum, v. intr. *am fierce, wrathful, rage*

saevus, -a, -um, adj. *fierce, cruel; horrible*

salsus, -a, -um, adj. *salty;* **salsae fruges,** 133

saltus, -ūs, m. *leap*

salum, -ī, n. *brine, sea*

salūs, -ūtis, f. *safety*

sanctus, -a, -um, adj. *holy, sacred*

sanguineus, -a, -um, adj. *bloody, blood-red*

sanguis, -inis, m. *blood; life,* 72; *stock,* 74; *vigor,* **integer aevī sanguis,** 639, *strength unimpaired by age*

saniēs, -ēī, f. *gore*

sat, see **satis**

sata, -ōrum, n. pl. *sown things, crops*

satiō, -āre, -āvī, -ātum, v. tr. *satisfy*

satis, or **sat,** indecl. adj. and adv. *enough, sufficient, sufficiently*

satus, part. of **serō**

saucius, -a, -um, adj. *wounded*

saxum, -ī, n. *rock, stone*

Scaeus, -a, -um, adj. applied to the *left* or western gate of Troy, 612

scālae, -ārum, f. *steps, ladder*

scandō, -ere, v. tr. *climb, mount*

scelerātus, -a, -um, adj. *guilty; wicked,* 576 n.

scelus, -eris, n. *guilt, crime*

scīlicet, adv. *one may know, doubtless, of course*

scindō, -ere, scidī, scissum, v. tr. *cleave, tear, rend, divide*

scītor, -ārī, -ātus sum, v. dep. tr. *seek to know; enquire of; consult,* 114

Scȳrius, -a, -um, adj. *belonging to Scyros* one of the Sporades near Euboea and birthplace of Pyrrhus, 477

sē, suī, reflex. pron. *himself, herself, itself, themselves*

secō, -āre, -uī, sectum, v. tr. *cut.*

sēcum, for **cum sē**

sēcrētus, -a, -um, adj. *separate, remote, hidden, retired*

secundus, -a, -um, adj. *following; favorable,* **vīrēs secundās,** 617, *strength for victory*

secūris, -is, f. *ax*

secus, adv. *otherwise*

sed, conj. *but;* **sed enim,** *but indeed,* 164

sedeō, -ēre, sēdī, sessum, v. intr. *sit;* **sedet hoc animō,** 660, *is fixed, firm*

sēdēs, -is, f. *seat, position;* pl. *place,* 465; *home,* 642; *palace,* 437, 760; *temple,* 232

seges, -etis f. *cornfield; corn crop*

segnitiēs, -ēī, f. *slowness*

semper, adv. *always, ever*

senex, senis, adj. *old,* comp. **senior**

sententia, -ae, f. *opinion, judgement*

sentiō, -īre, sensī, sensum, v. tr. *perceive*

sentis, -is, m. *thorn*

sepeliō, -īre, -īvī or **-iī, sepultum,** v. tr. *bury*

septem, num. adj. *seven*

sepulcrum, -ī, n. *tomb, burial place*

sequor, -ī, secūtus sum, v. dep. intr. and tr. *follow*

serēnus, -a, -um, adj. *clear, bright, fair*

serō, -ere, sēvī, satum, v. tr. *sow;* **satus,** *born, sprung from,* 540

serpens, -entis, m. and f. *serpent*

serpō, -ere, serpsī, v. intr. *creep*

sērus, -a, -um, adj. *late*

serviō, -īre, -īvī or **-iī, -ītum,** v. intr. with dat. *am a servant, serve*

servō, -āre, -āvī, -ātum, v. tr. *keep, preserve, guard; keep close to, follow;* **servans, -antis,** as adj. with gen. *observant of;* superl. **servantissimus,** 427

sēsē, strengthened form of **se,** *himself,* etc.

seu, see **sī**

sī, conj. *if;* **sīve (seu)...sīve (seu),** *whether...or*

sībilus, -a, -um, adj. *hissing*

sīc, adv. *in this way, so, thus*

siccus, -a, -um, adj. *dry; thirsty,* 358

sīdus, -eris, n. *star, constellation*

Sīgēus, -a, -um, adj. *Sigean, connected with Sigeum,* a promontory in the Troad, 312

signō, -āre, -āvī, -ātum, v. tr. *mark, distinguish, point out*

signum, -ī, n. *sign*

silentium, -ī, n. *silence*

sileō, -ēre, -uī, v. intr. *am silent*

silva, -ae, f. *wood*

similis, -e, adj. *like;* sup. **simillimus**

simul, adv. *at the same time, together*

simulācrum, -ī, n. *image, phantom*

simulō, -āre, -āvī, -ātum, v. tr. *imitate, pretend*

sīn, conj. *but if*

sine, prep. with abl. *without*

sinister, -tra, -trum, adj. *left, on the left hand;* as subst. **sinistra, -ae,** f. *the left hand*

sinō, -ere, sīvī, situm, v. tr. *permit, allow*

Sinōn, -ōnis, m. a Greek, 79, 195, 259, 329

sinuō, -āre, -āvī, -ātum, v. tr. *make to bend, curve; winds,* 208

sinus, -ūs, f. *bay, gulf*

sistō, -ere, stitī, statum, v. tr. *place, set*

sīve, see **sī**

socer, -erī, m. *father-in-law;* **socerōs,** 457, *father-* and *mother-in-law*

socius, -ī, m. *companion, comrade;* as adj. **socius, -a, -um,** *confederate, united, allied, friendly*

sōl, sōlis, m. *the sun*

soleō, -ēre, solitus sum, v. intr. *am accustomed*

solidus, -a, -um, adj. *solid, whole, firm*

sollemnis, -e, adj. *customary; religious, solemn*

solum, -ī, n. *ground*

solvō, -ere, solvī, solūtum, v. tr. *release, shake free*

sōlus, -a, -um, adj. *alone*

somnus, -ī, m. *sleep; vision of the night,* 794

sonitus, -ūs, m. *sound, loud crash,* 466; *sound of feet,* 732

sonō, -āre, -uī, -itum, v. intr. *sound*

sonus, -ī, m. *sound; speech*

sopor, -ōris, m. *sleep*

sors, sortis, f. *lot; fate*

sortior, -īrī, -ītus sum, v. dep. intr. and tr. *draw lots; choose by lot, select,* 18

spargō, -ere, sparsī, sparsum, v. tr. *scatter, spread about; sow*

Sparta, -ae, f. the chief city of Laconia and residence of Menelaus, 577

speciēs, -ēī, f. *appearance, sight*

spērō, -āre, -āvī, -ātum, v. tr. *hope,*
hope for, look forward to, expect,
dream, 658

spēs, -eī, f. *hope, expectation*

spīra, -ae, f. *coil*

spissus, -a, -um, adj. *thick*

spolium, -ī, n. *spoil*

sponsa, -ae, f. *betrothed; bride*

spūmeus, -a, -um, adj. *foaming*

spūmō, -āre, -āvī, -ātum, v. intr. *foam*

squāleō, -ēre, -uī, v. intr. *am rough,*
stiff

squāmeus, -a, -um, adj. *scaly*

stabulum, -ī, n. *stall, stable*

statiō, -ōnis, f. *halting-place;*
anchorage, 23

statuō, -ere, statuī, statūtum, v. tr. *set*
up, establish, build, construct

stella, -ae, f. *star*

sternō, -ere, strāvī, strātum, v. tr.
stretch out, lay low, devastate; pass.
are strewn, scattered, 364

Sthenelus, -ī, m. a Greek, charioteer of
Diomede, 261

stō, -āre, stetī, statum, v. intr. *stand,*
stand firm; stat, 750, *I am resolved*

strīdō, -ere (also strīdeō, -ēre), dī, v.
intr. *creak, grate; crash,* 418

stringō, -ere, strinxī, strictum, v. tr. of
a sword *unsheath, draw*

struō, -ere, struxī, structum, v. tr.
build; devise, contrive, 60

studium, -ī, n. *inclination, eagerness;*
pl. *factions,* 39

stupeō, -ēre, -uī, v. intr. and tr. *am*
amazed; am amazed at, 31

stuppeus, -a, -um, adj. *flaxen*

suādeō, -ēre, suāsī, suāsum, v. tr.
advise, counsel

sub, prep. with acc. *to, beneath,*
towards. ferre sub aurās, 158,
divulge; with abl. *under; under the*
shelter of, 188; *on a charge,* 83

subeō, -īre, -īvī or -iī, -itum, v.
intr. and tr. *go under, come up,*
approach, enter, rise up before one's
mind, 560; *come up to help,* 216,
467; *seize,* 575; *follows,* 725; subībō
umerīs, 708, *I will support you on*
my shoulders

subiciō, -ere, -iēcī, -iectum, v. tr. *place*
under, subiecta, 721, *stooped*

subitō, adv. *suddenly*

subitus, -a, -um, adj. *sudden*

sublābor, -ī, -lapsus sum, v. dep.
intr. *slip down, glide away; sink*
backward, 169

subsistō, -ere, -stitī, v. intr. *stand still,*
halt; stick, 243

succēdō, -ere, -cessī, -cessum, v. intr.
with dat. *go below,* or *towards;*
press up to, 478; suc. onerī, 723, *I*
go under, support

successus, -ūs, m. *success*

succurrō, -ere, -currī, -cursum, v. intr.
run up to, aid, succor; occur to the
mind, 317

sūdō, -āre, -āvī, -ātum, v. intr. *sweat,*
reek

sūdor, -ōris, m. *sweat*

sufferō, -ferre, sustulī, sublātum, v. tr.
and intr. *bear up; bear up against,*
withstand

sufficiō, -ere, -fēcī, -fectum, v. tr.
supply; suffuse

sulcus, -ī, m. *furrow*

sulphur, -uris, n. *brimstone, sulphur*

sum, esse, fuī, futūrus, v. intr. *to*
be, am, fuerit quodcumque, 77,
whatever the result

summus, -a, -um, superl. adj. *highest,*
last, topmost, top of, see superus

sūmō, -ere, sumpsī, sumptum, v. tr.
take; exact penalty

super, prep. with abl. *over; on the top of; concerning;* with acc. *over;* as adv. *in addition, besides,* 71, 348; *above:* **satis superque,** 642, *enough and more than enough;* **super... eram,** 567, by tmesis, **supersum**

superbus, -a, -um, adj. *arrogant, proud*

superō, -āre, -āvī, -ātum, v. tr. and intr. *rise above, tower above; survive; am superior, vanquish; pass over, climb*

supersum, -esse, -fuī, v. intr. *remain over; survive:* **super...eram,** 567, by tmesis

superus, -a, -um, adj. *that is above;* superl. **suprēmus,** *last,* and **summus,** *highest;* **superī, -ōrum,** *those above; the gods above,* 141, 659

supplex, -icis, adj. *suppliant*

suprēmus, -a, -um, superl.; see **superus,** *highest, last;* **suprēmum congemuit,** 630, *it has groaned one last time*

surgō, -ere, surrexī, surrectum, v. intr. *rise*

suscitō, -āre, -āvī, -ātum, v. tr. *stir up, arouse*

suspectus, -a, -um, adj. *suspected*

suspensus, -a, -um, adj. *doubtful,* 114; *anxious, unsure,* 729

suus, -a, -um, possess. adj. *his own, her own, its own, their own*

T

tabulātum, -ī, n. *floor or story*

taceō, -ēre, -uī, -itum, v. intr. *am silent, keep silence*

tacitus, -a, -um, adj. *silent, peaceful*

tactus, -ūs, m. *touching, touch*

tālis, -e, adj. *of such kind, such*

tam, adv. *so*

tamen, adv. *nevertheless, yet*

tandem, adv. *at length*

tantum, adv. *so much, to such an extent,* 776; *only*

tantus, -a, -um, adj. *so great*

tardus, -a, -um, adj. *slow*

taurus, -ī, m. *bull*

tectum, -ī, n. *roof; house, hall*

tēcum, for **cum tē,** *with you*

tegō, -ere, texī, tectum, v. tr. *cover, conceal; shield,* protect, 430; **sī qua tegunt,** 159, *whatever they conceal;* **teguntur,** 227, mid. *conceal themselves;* **tectus,** 126 *shut up in tent*

tellūs, -ūris, f. *the earth; country*

tēlum, -ī, n. *weapon, dart*

temperō, -āre, -āvī, -ātum, v. tr. and intr. *check; refrain*

tempestās, -ātis, f. *storm*

templum, -ī, n. *temple*

temptō, -āre, -āvī, -ātum, v. tr. *try, attempt, probe, explore*

tempus, -oris, n. (1) *time, hour,* (2) in pl. *the temples of the head*

tendō, -ere, tetendī, tentum or **tensum,** v. tr. and intr. *stretch; direct one's course, make for; strive* or *struggle to,* 220; *pitch a tent,* 29

tenebrae, -ārum, f. pl. *darkness, gloom*

Tenedos, -ī, f. an island four miles from the coast of Troad, 21, 203, 255

teneō, -ēre, -uī, tentum, v. tr. *hold, hold fast, restrain, cling to, keep, hem in, reach*

tener, -era, -erum, adj. *tender*

tenuis, -e, adj. *thin*

tenus, prep. with abl. placed after noun, *as far as*

ter, num. adv. *three times, thrice*

terebrō, -āre, -āvī, -ātum, v. tr. *bore through*

tergum, -ī, n. *back*: simply *body, frame*, 231 **ā tergō,** 455, *in the rear*

terra, -ae, f. *dry land, land, earth*

terreō, -ēre, -uī, -itum, v. tr. *terrify*

testor, -ārī, -ātus sum, v. dep. tr. *call to witness*

testūdō, -inis, f. *tortoise; covering* of shields, 441

Teucer, -crī, m. ancient king of Troy, son-in-law of Dardanus, hence **Teucrī, -ōrum,** *Trojans*; as adj. **Teucrōs penātīs,** 747

Teucria, -ae, f. *land of Troy,* 26

texō, -ere, texuī, textum, v. tr. *weave*

thalamus, -ī, m. *(marriage) chamber*

Thessandrus, -ī, m. a Greek, 261

Thoās, -antis, m. a Greek

Thybris, -idis, m. an old name for the river *Tiber,* 782

Thymoetēs, -ae, m., a Trojan, 32

timeō, -ēre, -uī, v. tr. *fear*

tollō, -ere, sustulī, sublātum, v. tr. *raise, carry, carry away*

torrens, -entis, m. *torrent*

torus, -ī, m. *couch*

tot, num. adj. indecl. *so many*

totiēns, adv. *so many times*

tōtus, -a, -um, adj. *whole*

trabs, trabis, f. *beam, plank; wood panel,* 481

trahō, -ere, traxī, tractum, v. tr. *drag, draw along, drag on;* **trahit ruīnam,** see **ruīna**

trāiciō, -ere, -iēcī, -iectum, v. tr. *throw through, pierce*

tranquillus, -a, -um, adj. *calm*

transferō, -ferre, -tulī, -lātum, v. tr. *carry across, remove to*

tremefaciō, -ere, -fēcī, -factum, v. tr. *make to tremble,* **tremefactus,** *trembling*

tremendus, -a, -um, *terrible,* gerundive of **tremō**

tremō, -ere, -uī, v. intr. *tremble, quiver*

tremor, -ōris, m, *trembling*

trepidō, -āre, -āvī, -ātum, v. intr. *tremble much; hurry,* 685

trepidus, -a, -um, adj, *alarmed*

tridens, -entis, m. *trident*

tristis, -e, adj. *sad; stern, baneful, fatal*

trisulcus, -a, -um, adj. *with three furrows; forked,* 475, of serpent's tongue

Trītōnis, -idos, f. 226; **Trītōnia, -ae,** f. 171, 615, a name of Pallas, said to have been born at Lake Triton in Libya

triumphus, -ī, m. *triumphal procession, triumph*

Trōes, -um, m. pl. *Trojans,* 325

Trōia, -ae, f. *Troy,* the famous city, the Greek siege of which is the subject of the *Iliad,* 11, 34, etc.

Trōiānus, -a, -um, adj. *Trojan,* 4, 63

Trōius, -a, -um, adj. *Trojan,* 763

trucīdō, -āre, -āvī, -ātum, v. tr. *kill, butcher*

truncus, -ī, m. *trunk, body without limbs*

tū, tuī, pers. pron. *you*

tuba, -ae, f. *trumpet*

tueor, -ērī, tuitus (or tūtus) sum, v. dep. tr. *see; defend, protect*

tum, adv. *at that time, then*

tumeō, -ēre, -uī, v. intr. *swell, puff out,* 381

tumidus, -a, -um, adj. *swelling, swollen,* 472

tumultus, -ūs, m. *uprising, tumult, disorder.* **magnō t.** 122, *amid mighty uproar*

tumulus, -ī, m, *mound, tomb*

tunc, adv. *at that time, then*

turba, -ae, f. *crowd*
turbō, -āre, -āvī, -ātum, v. tr. *throw into confusion, disturb.* turbātus, 67, *distraught, confused*
turbō, -inis, m. *whirlwind, hurricane*
turpis, -e, adj. *foul, dishonorable*
turris, -is, f. *tower*
tūtor, -ārī, -ātus sum, v. dep. tr. *make safe, protect*
tūtus, -a, -um, adj. *safe*
tuus, -a, -um, possess. adj. *your.* tuī, *your men, your people,* etc. 283, 661
Tȳdīdēs, -ae, m. *son of Tydeus,* viz. Diomede, 164, 197
Tyndaris, -idis, f. *daughter of Tyndarus,* viz. Helen, 569, 601

U

ubi, adv. *where, when; in what position or condition,* 596
ubīque, adv. *everywhere*
V̄calegōn, -ontis, m. a Trojan, 312
ulciscor, -ī, ultus sum, v. dep. tr. *avenge*
Vlixēs, -is, -ī, or eī, m. king of Ithaca, noted among the Greeks for his cleverness, 7, 44, etc.
ullus, -a, -um, adj. *any*
ulterior, -ius, comp. adj. *further;* superl. ultimus, -a, -um, *furthest, last;* neut. pl. ultima, 446, *the end;* lūx ultima, 668, *the day of death*
ultor, -ōris, m. *avenger*
ultrix, -īcis, f. adj. *avenging, vengeful*
ultrō, adv. *beyond* what is needed or asked, 145; *willingly, unasked, unprovoked; unaccosted by us,* 372; *first,* i.e. without waiting for him to begin, 279
ululō, -āre, -āvī, -ātum, v. intr. *howl, shriek*
ulva, -ae, f. *sedge, marsh-grass*

umbō, -ōnis, m. *boss* of a shield; *shield*
umbra, -ae, f. *shade, gloom; spirit, ghost*
umerus, -ī, m. *shoulder*
ūmidus, -a, -um, adj. *wet, damp, dank*
umquam, adv. *at any time, ever*
ūnā, adv. *at one time, together*
unda, -ae, f. *wave*
unde, adv. *whence, from which*
undique, adv. *on all sides, everywhere, from every side*
undō, -āre, -āvī, -ātum, v. intr. *rise in waves; swell; roll in billows,* 609
ūnus, -a, -um, adj. *one; one only, alone,* 567; iustissimus ūnus, 426, *the most just of all men*
urbs, -is, f. *city*
urgeō, -ēre, ursī, v. tr. *press hard;* fātō urgentī, 653, *fate pressing down on*
ūrō, -ere, ussī, ustum, v. tr. *burn*
usquam, adv. *anywhere*
usque, adv. *continually*
ūsus, -ūs, m. *use, employment;* pervius usus, 453, *passage*
ut, adv. and conj. *as, when, how; so that, in order that*
uterque, utraque, utrumque, pronom. adj. *each of two*
uterus, -ī, n., *womb*
utī = ut, *when, as,* etc.
utinam, adv. *If only...!*

V

vacuus, -a, -um, adj. *empty*
vādō, -ere, v. intr. *go, advance*
vagor, -ārī, -ātus sum, v. dep. intr. *wander; am spread abroad,* 17
valeō, -ēre, -uī, -ītum, v. intr. *am strong;* with inf. *can;* valē, *farewell,* 789
validus, -a, -um, adj. *strong*
vallis, -is, f. *valley*

vānus, -a, -um, adj. *empty, vain, false;* n. pl. *idle things,* 287

varius, -a, -um, adj. *different, changing; many different kinds of,* 284

vastus, -a, -um, adj. *huge, immense*

vātēs, -is, m. and f. *prophet, bard*

-ve, enclitic conj, *or*

vel, conj, *or*

vellō, -ere, vulsī, vulsum, v. tr. *pluck, tear away, rend*

vēlō, -āre, -āvī, -ātum, v. tr. *cover, veil*

vēlum, -ī, n. *sail, covering*

velutī, adv. *just as*

venēnum, -ī, n. *poison*

veniō, -īre, vēnī, ventum, v. intr. *come.* **ventūra,** 125, *the future*

venter, -tris, m. *belly*

ventus, -ī, m. *wind, blast*

Venus, -eris, f. *Venus,* goddess of love, mother of Aeneas, 787

verbum, -ī, n. *word*

vērō, adv, *in truth, indeed*

versō, -āre, -āvī, -ātum, v. tr. *keep turning, ponder*

vertex, -icis, m. *top, head*

vertō, -ere, vertī, versum, v. tr. *turn, overturn, overthrow;* pass. 250, *revolve*

vērum, adv. *truly; but indeed, but yet*

vērus, -a, -um, adj. *true;* n. **verum,** 141, *the truth*

Vesta, -ae, f. goddess of the hearth, 296, 567

vester, -tra, -trum, possess. adj. *your*

vestibulum, -ī, n. *porch, entrance*

vestīgium, -ī, n. *footstep*

vestis, -is, f. *raiment, robe, dress*

vetō, -āre, vetuī, vetitum, v. tr. *forbid*

vetus, -eris, adj. *old;* superl. **veterrimus**

vetustus, -a, -um, adj. *ancient*

via, -ae, f. *road, path, street*

vibrō, -āre, -āvī, -ātum, v. intr. *quiver, flicker*

vicis (gen.), **vicem, vice,** f. defective *change of fortune, vicissitude*

victor, -ōris, m. *conqueror,* as adj. *conquering*

victōria, -ae, f. *victory*

videō, -ēre, vīdī, vīsum, v. tr. *see:* pass. *seem.* **dīs aliter vīsum,** 428, *the gods willed it otherwise*

vigeō, -ēre, viguī, v. intr. *flourish; am powerful,* 88

vigil, -ilis, adj. *watchful;* as subst. *watchman*

vinculum or **vinclum, -ī,** n. *chain, band, bond*

vincō, -ere, vīcī, victum, v. tr. *conquer*

vīnum, -ī, n. *wine*

violābilis, -e, adj. *that may be violated, violable*

violō, -āre, -āvī, -ātum, v. tr. *do violence to, violate*

vir, virī, m. *man; hero; husband*

virgineus, -a, -um, adj. *belonging to a maiden*

virgō, -inis, f. *virgin, maiden*

virtūs, -ūtis, f. *manliness, courage, virtue*

vīs, vis, f. *violence, force;* pl. **vīrēs, ium,** *strength*

vīsō, -ere, vīsī, *go to see, visit, see*

vīsus, -ūs, m. *sight, vision*

vīta, -ae, f. *life*

vītō, -āre, -āvī, -ātum, v. tr. *shun, avoid*

vitta, -ae, f. *fillet, garland*

vīvus, -a, -um, adj. *living; running* stream, 719

vix, adv. *scarcely*

vōciferor, ārī, -ātus sum, v. dep. tr. *cry aloud*

vocō, -āre, -āvī, -ātum, v. tr. *call, summon*

volō, -āre, -āvī, -ātum, v. intr. *fly*
volō, velle, voluī, v. irreg. intr. *wish,*
    will
volucer, -cris, -cre, adj. *swift*
volūmen, -inis, n. *fold, coil*
volvō, -ere, volvī, volūtum, v. tr. *roll*
vōs, pl. *you*, see tū
vōtum, -ī, n. *vow; votive offering*, 17
vox, vōcis, f. *voice, utterance*; pl. *words;*
    cries, 768; rumpit vōcem, 129,
    breaks silence

Vulcānus, -ī, m. the God of fire; *fire*,
    311
vulgus, -ī, n. but m. 99, *common*
    people, public, crowd, rabble
vulnus, -eris, n. *wound*
vultus, -ūs, m. *face, expression,*
    appearance

Z

Zephyrus, -ī, m. *West wind* 417

Index

This index lists grammatical, metrical, and stylistic items mentioned in the commentary; numbers refer to lines in the Latin text and the corresponding commentary notes.

Ablative
Absolute: 40, 52, 100, 108, 181, 209, 304, 351, 416, 473, 496, 637, 657, 743, 804
Cause: 12, 82, 84, 90, 109, 145, 379, 412, 690, 715
Degree of difference: 199
Description: 186
Manner: 225
Means: 16, 25, 72, 84, 127, 140, 196, 215, 249, 291-2, 352, 421, 514, 516, 530, 565
Place where: 245, 421, 528, 761, 771
Price: 104
Quality: 333, 482
Separation: 44, 85, 109, 134, 153, 165, 224, 260, 608
Source: 74, 289, 331, 727
Specification: 88, 174
Time: 268
Time when: 516
Accusative
Cognate: 494, 693
Duration: 126
Place to which: 326, 742, 756
Retained: 273
Specification: 57, 221
Greek form: 213
Adjectives
Translated adverbially: 1, 32, 125, 307, 374

Used as substantives: 91, 123, 427
Alliteration: Appendix B; 9, 87, 199, 207, 209, 245, 273, 303, 313, 418-9, 498
Anaphora: Appendix B; 108-10, 154-5, 218, 501
Anastrophe: Appendix B; 515, 564
Aposiopesis: Appendix B; 100
Apostrophe: Appendix B; 56, 160, 431, 432
Archaism: 139 (*fors*), 164 (*sed enim*), 176 (*extemplo*), 242 (*Dardanidum*), 467 (*ast*), 507 (*uti*), 515 (*nequiquam*)
Arsis, lengthening in: 369, 411, 563
Assonance: Appendix B; 313
Asyndeton: Appendix B; 27-8, 85, 183-4, 602 (adversative), 663
Attributive noun: 86
Caesura: Appendix A
Chiasmus: Appendix B; 13, 167, 281, 636, 728
Comparison clause: 438
Compound adjectives: 477
Conative sense of verbs: 111, 382, 686
Conditionals
Mixed: 56, 291-2
Future more vivid: 94-5, 161, 189
Past contrafactual: 54, 55, 291-2
Present contrafactual: 56, 291-2, 521-2, 599-600